About the author

Alejandro Nadal is an economist working in the Centre for Economic Studies, El Colegio de México. He has a law degree from the National Autonomous University and earned a doctor's degree in economics from the University of Paris. He has published articles and books in the field of general equilibrium theory, macroeconomics, the economics of technical change and natural resource management. He is co-chair of the Theme on the Environment, Macroeconomics, Trade and Investment (TEMTI) of CEESP in IUCN. He writes a weekly column for *La Jornada*, one of Mexico's leading national newspapers.

Rethinking macroeconomics for sustainability

Alejandro Nadal

Zed Books
LONDON | NEW YORK

Rethinking macroeconomics for sustainability was first published in 2011 by Zed Books Ltd, 7 Cynthia Street, London N1 9JF, UK and Room 400, 175 Fifth Avenue, New York, NY 10010, USA

www.zedbooks.co.uk

Copyright © Alejandro Nadal 2011

The right of Alejandro Nadal to be identified as the author of this work has been asserted by him in accordance with the Copyright, Designs and Patents Act, 1988

Set in OurType Arnhem and Futura Bold by Ewan Smith, London
Index: ed.emery@thefreeuniversity.net
Cover designed by Rogue Four Design
Printed and bound in Great Britain by the MPG Books Group, Bodmin and Kings Lynn

Distributed in the USA exclusively by Palgrave Macmillan, a division of St Martin's Press, LLC, 175 Fifth Avenue, New York, NY 10010, USA

All rights reserved. No part of this publication may be reproduced, stored in a retrieval system or transmitted in any form or by any means, electronic, mechanical, photocopying or otherwise, without the prior permission of Zed Books Ltd.

A catalogue record for this book is available from the British Library
Library of Congress Cataloging in Publication Data available

ISBN 978 1 84813 505 5 hb
ISBN 978 1 84813 506 2 pb
ISBN 978 1 84813 507 9 eb

Contents

Box, figures and tables | vi
Acronyms | vii   Acknowledgements | ix

   Introduction 1
1 Macroeconomics and the environment 9
2 The macroeconomic policy connection 33
3 Macroeconomic policies and climate change 65
4 The Green Economy Initiative 86
5 Latin American focus 104
6 Guidelines for macroeconomic policy and sustainability . . 140
7 International macroeconomic reform for sustainability . . . 163
   Conclusion 192

Notes | 195   Bibliography | 214
Index | 227

Box, figures and tables

Box

1.1 The invisible hand: metaphor or scientific result? 24

Figures

2.1 The IS–LM model 62
2.2 Macroeconomic policy in the IS–LM model 63
2.3 Environmental equilibrium in the IS–LM model 64
5.1 Reprimarization: Argentine sectoral GDP 1935–2004 114
5.2 GDP and GDP per capita growth rates, 1990–2007 118
5.3 Costa Rica: evolution of GDP, 1992–2008 123
5.4 Costa Rica: evolution of inflation rates, 1984–2008. 124
5.5 Ecuador: trade balance in monetary and physical terms 128
5.6 Mexico: monetary policy and money supply 134
5.7 Mexico: fiscal policy and Financial Requirements of the Public Sector. 136
5.8 Mexico: GDP and environmental costs. 137

Tables

1.1 Annual GDP rate of growth, 1950–98. 10
3.1 UNFCCC estimates of adaptation costs 68
3.2 UNFCCC estimates of mitigation costs, 2030 71
5.1 Growth rates in GDP per capita: selected countries in Latin America 106
5.2 Fiscal policy priorities in Argentina, 1993–2001 112
5.3 Brazil: cattle by region, 1995–2005. 121

Acronyms

AR4	Fourth Assessment Report of the IPCC
BW	Bretton Woods
CEESP	IUCN Commission on Environmental, Economic and Social Policy
CFTC	Commodity Futures Trading Commission
CTDL	Currency Transaction Development Levy
DSGE	Dynamic Stochastic General Equilibrium
ECLAC	Economic Commission for Latin America and the Caribbean
EKC	environmental Kuznets curve
FAO	Food and Agriculture Organization
FDI	foreign direct investment
FRPS	Financial Requirements of the Public Sector
GATS	General Agreement on Trade in Services
GATT	General Agreement on Tariffs and Trade
GDP	gross domestic product
GEF	Global Environment Facility
GEI	UNEP's Green Economy Initiative
GGND	Global Green New Deal
GHG	greenhouse gases
GPS	Global Positioning System
HIPC	Heavily Indebted Poor Countries
IAASTD	International Assessment of Agricultural Knowledge, Science and Technology for Development
ICA	international commodity agreement
ILO	International Labour Organization
IMF	International Monetary Fund
IPCC	Intergovernmental Panel on Climate Change
ISI	import substitution industrialization
ITT	Ishpingo-Tambococha-Tiputini oilfields in Ecuador (also called Yasuní)
IUCN	International Union for Conservation of Nature
LG	limits to growth
MDG	Millennium Development Goals
MNC	multinational corporation

MP	Mesarovic and Pestel
NAFTA	North American Free Trade Agreement
ODA	official development assistance
OECD	Organisation for Economic Co-operation and Development
PES	payment for environmental services
PPES	Programme for Payment of Environmental Services (Costa Rica)
R&D	research and development
SAP	structural adjustment programme
SDT	special and differential treatment
SEE	school of ecological economics
TEEB	*The Economics of Ecosystems and Biodiversity*
TEMTI	Theme on the Environment, Macroeconomics, Trade and Investment
TINA	there is no alternative
TRIMs	Trade-Related Investment Measures (WTO agreement)
UNCTAD	United Nations Conference on Trade and Development
UNDP	United Nations Development Programme
UNEP	UN Environment Programme
UNESCO	UN Educational, Scientific and Cultural Organization
UNFCCC	UN Framework Convention on Climate Change
URAA	Uruguay Round Agreement on Agriculture
WHO	World Health Organization
WTO	World Trade Organization

Acknowledgements

Natural wealth belongs to the realm of *res communis*, but its stewardship is being transferred to the world of commodity relations and private management. This is one reason why inequality and environmental degradation march together. Macroeconomic policies are not the sole culprit, but they are a critical driving force behind this process. Redefining the priorities of macroeconomic policies is indispensable to offset this course of events. There is not much time left. While long-term sustainability is the ultimate goal, in the short run survival is the name of the game.

In 2007 I was invited to be a member of the jury in the first Independent Peoples' Tribunal on the World Bank Group in India. During the proceedings at the Jawaharlal Nehru University in New Delhi, people from all walks of life came and delivered their testimony: from displaced *avidasis* and *dalits*, to farmers and peasants, trade union members, small entrepreneurs, even survivors of the 2004 tsunami. The policies related to World Bank intervention were examined and their adverse effects exposed in hydropower and the extractive industries, electricity, health, education, banking, the privatization of water and judiciary reform. The depositions revealed how macroeconomic policies directly affect livelihoods and shape the economic forces that destroy the environment. Discussions with Rohan D'Souza, Amit Bhaduri, Aseem Shrivastava, Devinder Sharma, Awala Longkummer, and many others during and after the proceedings were the crucible and inspiration for the research behind this book.

Later, in conceiving and writing this book in Mexico City I benefited from exchanges with my younger colleagues at El Colegio de México: Francisco Aguayo, Hugo García, Marcos Chávez, Tania Hernandez and Juan Pablo Pardo-Guerra. They offered severe criticism to old ideas and refreshing views on novel perspectives. Our debates provided a rich laboratory for the main ideas in this book.

In 2005, as chair of the Theme on the Environment, Macroeconomics, Trade and Investment (TEMTI) I launched a flagship project on macroeconomic policies and the environment in five

Latin American countries. TEMTI is part of the Commission on Environmental, Economic and Social Policy (CEESP) of the International Union for Conservation of Nature (IUCN). The project received a grant from the IUCN special 3IC Fund. Throughout the life of that project, the support of John Bishop, IUCN's chief economist, was critical in many respects.

My colleagues in the project, Alan Cibils, Sergio Schlesinger, Pablo Samaniego, Carlos Murillo and Marcos Chávez, worked hard to complete a demanding time schedule and a challenging research framework. The workshop held in Quito, Ecuador, in 2008 gave the project on macroeconomic policies in Latin America new energy.

Several years ago, in the midst of discussions on Keynesian thought with Carlo Benetti of the University of Paris, I started to think about the relationship between endogenous crises in capitalist economies and environmental sustainability. I am indebted for his thoughtful insights on Keynes and macroeconomics: they have been an unending source of inspiration in my research.

Ken Barlow's thoughtful advice and encouragement during the writing of the book proved essential for the successful completion of this enterprise.

Finally, and above all, my gratitude goes to Lorena and my daughter Lucía: more than they know, their love and patience mark every page of this book.

Coyoacán, Mexico City, 27 August 2010

Introduction

International conferences on poverty and the environment come and go. They are concerned with themes crucial for the survival of humankind and even for the future of the biosphere. Achieving their objectives implies major transformations in economic structures. Sometimes their recommendations involve sweeping changes that would require deep economy-wide reforms. And yet, macroeconomic policy has been conspicuously absent from their deliberations. Even as the worst financial crisis in seven decades unfolded, the routine of these conferences has not changed. It's as if a big elephant with the words 'Macroeconomic Policies' stamped on its forehead had been standing in these conference rooms and nobody wanted to see it.

Consider the following. The Millennium Development Goals approved by the UN General Assembly were debated in myriad conferences, but nobody spoke about the macroeconomic policy framework needed to achieve them. As if reducing hunger and extreme poverty, generating employment and providing health services and education had nothing to do with public expenditures, monetary policy, capital flows and financial deregulation. Aside from some pious words about financing and official development assistance (ODA), the implicit message was that the world could carry on with the same macroeconomic policies. That was some faith in the trickle-down potential of neoliberal globalization.[1]

At the conferences of the UN Framework Convention on Climate Change (UNFCCC) everyone recognizes that emission reductions and adaptation to climate change require massive amounts of resources. Generating these funds involves redefining the aims of macroeconomic policies, but everyone avoids talking about the way in which macroeconomic priorities need to be rearranged in order to meet the challenges of climate change. Also, although there is a consensus that vulnerability and poverty go hand in hand, the link between neoliberal macroeconomic policies and deprivation is shunted aside as if these two had no connection. Even the Stern Report safely skirts around the thorny issues of macroeconomic policies in developing countries.

The eruption of the global economic and financial crisis in 2008 led the UN Environment Programme (UNEP) to launch its Green Economy

Initiative and the Global Green New Deal (GGND). The objective is to revive the global economy, boost employment and accelerate the fight against climate change, environmental degradation and poverty. According to UNEP, the multiple crises unfolding today demand the same kind of initiative as shown by Roosevelt's New Deal of the 1930s. The difference is that this has to be done 'at the global scale and embracing a wider vision'. The punchline is that 'rebooting the world economic system' is simply not enough to get us on the road to sustainability.

One would think that macroeconomic policy would be a relevant issue in this context, especially after the reference to FDR's 'New Deal'. But the sponsors of this initiative think differently: the Global Green New Deal is unconcerned with macroeconomic policies. This doesn't make much sense. The world crisis that exploded in 2007/08 is still under way and is entering a very dangerous phase. Its effects will drag on for years to come: it has already put millions of people below the poverty line and every year that goes by with high unemployment rates makes it harder for the unemployed to find a job, increasing the probability of falling into the poverty trap. The specific environmental implications of this are not easy to discern, but things do not bode well. In some cases, more poverty may mean greater pressure on forests and other habitats. It will certainly cause greater stress on the social fabric of communities that could play a role in environmental stewardship. In many instances it will also bring about cuts in public resources to invest in education and health, or in environmental stewardship.

The origins of this global crisis are not confined to the financial sector and may also be found in the real economy, where stagnant wages over a prolonged period had to be compensated by the expansion of private debt. This was accompanied by unsustainable waves of speculation-led growth. Clearly, redesigning macroeconomic policies and reforming the international economy, including the world's monetary system, should be an essential part of a 'green economy initiative'. More efficient automobiles, greater reliance on renewable resources and intelligent buildings will not, by themselves, give us a 'green global economy' at the end of the day. Yes, pressing the reboot button will not work, but this means that we need to take a hard look at the macroeconomic relations and policies that brought about this phenomenal crisis.[2]

Macroeconomic policies affect the rate of economic activity, can bring about deep structural economy-wide transformations, determine the patterns of distribution of income and equality in a society, and condition the dynamics of investment, and thus of the introduction of new technologies and employment in any economy. There should be no disagreement: macroeconomic policies must play a prominent role in discussions concerning sustainable development. Unfortunately, most of the debate on sustainable development has taken place in the context of sector-level analyses related to agriculture, industrial activities, energy, construction, transportation and the like. But sustainable development cannot be a notion restricted to individual economic sectors. It blends with the *aggregate* relations of modern economies expressed in the dynamics of income, savings, investment and employment. Even the original definition of sustainable development accords with this view.[3] Sustainability is not restricted to sector-level problems. It is not limited either to the rates of extraction of natural resources, or the technological features of the machines, buildings and gadgets that surround our lives. The fundamental issues of fairness in access to opportunities, the preservation of livelihoods and equitable income distribution are core components of sustainable development. And if we don't bring macroeconomics to the discussion of sustainability, we will have failed in the endeavour to make this a better world.

During the past thirty years, the world has become dominated by a particular style of macroeconomic policy. It was based on the premise that markets are well behaved and converge to equilibrium. In this view, any problem that arises is caused by frictions that impede this adjustment, or by external shocks. The resulting policy package was organized around financial liberalization, balanced fiscal accounts, extensive deregulation and privatization and free trade. The framework of this was the belief that stability engenders investment and growth. In reality, this policy framework subordinated macroeconomic policies to the needs of financial capital, imposing financial deregulation and the overarching priority of price stability. In fiscal policy, it gave precedence to generating a primary surplus over anything else. This meant cutting expenditures on such things as healthcare, education and the environment in order to generate resources to cover debt service.[4] Actually, this policy package brought about inferior growth rates, increased inequality and poverty and, in the end, its performance was crowned by a formidable crisis of historic proportions.

During this time the environment continued to deteriorate. The most important assessments of the global environment confirm that the world's ecosystems are losing their capacity to provide services (MEA 2005), that drylands, forests and aquifers have been continuously degraded (UNEP 2007) and that the accumulation of greenhouse gases in the atmosphere is accelerating (IPCC 2007). Of course, the impact of a significant increase in population (from 5 billion in 1987 to 6.8 billion in 2010) is an important factor in this process. Certainly, the additional burden that this level of population poses to soils, aquifers, forests and oceans is significant. But this negative effect is compounded by several other problems. The disparities in rates of consumption of the world's natural resources are just as important when it comes to discussing environmental deterioration. Also, poverty has increased at the global level, and more people will fall below the poverty line as the global crisis unfolds. According to the World Bank, approximately 50 per cent of humankind lives on a daily income of US$2.50 or less: that's 3.4 billion people living on or below this particular poverty line.[5] Also, the social fabric of communities and small-scale agricultural producers that play a key role in environmental stewardship has been seriously degraded during these years by economic forces. At the same time, macroeconomic policy contributed to the containment of wages: according to the International Labour Organization (ILO 2008) real wages increased at a slower rate than productivity, and this situation will worsen with the current global crisis. Finally, investment in items that are crucial for sustainability, such as healthcare, education, sanitation and environmental stewardship, has been severely hampered.

The time has come to redefine the priorities of macroeconomic policies. There can never be sustainable development in a world where half of the total population lives in poverty and where economic crises send millions into destitution. A healthy environment will not be attained under a system that centralizes decision-making on economic strategies unconcerned by impact on the livelihoods of billions of people. This implies putting macroeconomic policies directly at the centre of any discussion on sustainable development. This book is a contribution to this debate.

Today there is very little dialogue between, on the one hand, academics and policy-makers in the field of macroeconomics and, on the other, the community of environmentalists and social activists. The first group perceives environmental issues through a very narrow lens: it is concerned with macro aggregates and the environment is hardly a matter of concern here because markets and relative prices take care of it. On the other hand, environmentalists are distrustful of macroeconomics, their complicated models and the lack of a clear-cut consensus in this 'young and hesitant' science (Blanchard and Fischer 1989). The end result is that the analysis of the framework that shapes the economic forces behind social inequality and environmental degradation is ignored. It is as if monetary and fiscal policies, financial regulation, exchange and interest rates, capital flows and incomes policies had nothing to do with social responsibility and environmental sustainability.

It is clear that environmentalists and all those concerned with social justice should not leave macroeconomics to a handful of 'specialists' in government and mainstream academia. And yet this is something that has been taking place in many instances. Even in conferences of the World Social Forum, for example, there has never been any space for discussions on the entire set of macroeconomic policies. On the other hand, the establishment does not accept that macroeconomic policies should be reoriented, let alone radically modified, in order to make them work for sustainability.[6] This book is an effort to bring together macroeconomics and current debates on environmental sustainability. It is based on the premise that the world will never reach anything resembling sustainable development if we don't redefine macroeconomic policies, their priorities as well as their instruments.

Macroeconomics as a field in academic research and policy-making has much to gain by entering this realm of analysis and controversy. By engaging in a constructive dialogue with environmentalists searching for urgent solutions to the problems of runaway environmental destruction, macroeconomic theory and policy will have to abandon their safe haven of nice but irrelevant models.[7] The scientific credibility of macroeconomic theory has been seriously tarnished. It is fair to say that by and large it was asleep at the helm when the global economic and financial crisis erupted in 2008. For more than ten years, the discipline embraced the idea that at long last the fluctuations of the business cycle had been domesticated and its volatility subdued. In the 1990s, with the ideological triumph of neoliberalism, the phrase 'the Great Moderation' proclaimed the end of the business cycle.[8] But with a full-blown crisis hitting advanced capitalist economies in 2008, anyone could see that as a discipline, mainstream macroeconomics had failed to get its act together. According to its theoretical models, this crisis shouldn't be happening.

It is a good time to seize the opportunity to go back to basics and redefine the object and the role of macroeconomics. It is time to rethink macroeconomics for sustainability. Progressive movements need to seize the initiative in defining new avenues for macroeconomic policy. They have done this in debates on agricultural policies, as well as with social and environmental policies. But there's still a long way to go in redesigning macroeconomic policy priorities to make them compatible with sustainability. The purpose of this book is to contribute to the construction of a bridge between themes that somehow have remained mysteriously disconnected. It aims to improve communications between two communities – macroeconomists on the one hand, and environmentalists and activists on the other – that have been living in indifference to and ignorance of each other for too long.

The plan of the book is as follows. The first chapter provides a panoramic view of growth in the world economy over the past sixty years and examines how economic theory has treated the relation between growth and the environment. It discusses how, although efforts were made to link macro considerations to environmental concerns, these attempts ignored the all-important linkages between the financial and the real sectors of the economy.

The second chapter examines how macroeconomic policies are related to environmental sustainability. It provides an overview of the evolution of macroeconomic theory over the last sixty years, a precondition for understanding the scope and limitations of recent efforts to incorporate sustainability into macroeconomic policy models. This chapter also examines in some detail the most important efforts to integrate macroeconomic policy with environmental issues. Its final paragraph analyses several key issues that need to be addressed in order to amalgamate macroeconomic policy and sustainability.

The third chapter looks at the relation between climate change and macroeconomic policies. It considers the magnitude of the resources that are needed to attain the objectives of mitigation (greenhouse gas reductions) and adaptation under the most widely accepted scenarios for climate change. It analyses the references to macroeconomic policies in the Intergovernmental Panel on Climate Change (IPCC)'s Fourth Assessment Report (AR4). Finally it discusses the need to redefine macroeconomic policy priorities in order to meet the challenge of climate change. The central message here is that more neoliberalism will not bring about sustainable reductions in emissions.

The fourth chapter examines the Green Economy Initiative and its main component, the Global Green New Deal. We focus on its sector-level analysis and examine the macroeconomic implications and constraints. Emphasis is placed on several critical issues, such as poverty, climate, small-scale agriculture and the study of the economy of ecosystems and biodiversity.

The fifth chapter centres on the results of a research project in five Latin American countries (Argentina, Brazil, Costa Rica, Ecuador and Mexico). It describes the development strategy followed in the region in the period 1945–80. The results from the five-country study show environmental problems directly related to macroeconomic policies in the context of the open economy model applied in the region after 1985.

The sixth and seventh chapters adopt a more normative approach, contributing criteria and guidelines that are considered indispensable for the redefinition of macroeconomic policy priorities. Chapter 6 concentrates on reforms at the national level, while Chapter 7 starts with the premise that sustainability has to be global and requires important reforms in international macroeconomic relations. It centres on the reforms to the system of international payments and the international trade regime required to advance the cause of global sustainability.

1 · Macroeconomics and the environment

Introduction

Environmental degradation at the macro level entered the realm of political debate in a grand manner in 1972. That year the first world summit on Development and the Environment took place in Stockholm under the auspices of the United Nations. For the first time, global issues related to environmental stewardship were raised. The need to safeguard the global environment for future generations appeared in the conclusions of the conference in a prominent position. More importantly, the first debates about the possible trade-offs between economic growth and environmental degradation started to appear, if timidly, on the horizon.

But 1972 also witnessed the publication of *The Limits to Growth*, the first report to the Club of Rome. This study was based on the first simulation model of the interaction between demographic growth, food supply, non-renewable natural resources and economic growth at the global scale. The main contribution of this analysis was to transfer the debate on the environment from local pollution problems (à la Rachel Carson or Barry Commoner) towards a more systemic investigation of usage rates and the over-exploitation of the natural resource base. The debates on 'zero growth', de-growth and steady-state economies are part of this discussion on the long-term survival of humankind, as we shall see in the next section.

The world is simultaneously experiencing an economic and an environmental crisis. The analysis of recent economic history is important for an understanding of how we got here and how we can move out of this quagmire. The way we think about the interactions between an economic system as a whole and the environment is a matter of great importance. It may help us identify the road to a sustainable future, one in which humankind may live in harmony and prosperity. If we fail to understand how macroeconomic policies and dynamics affect the environment, we may never find the way to attain this bright future. This chapter begins the journey.

Growth after the Second World War

Redefining macroeconomic policy priorities to serve the objective of sustainability requires examining how real-world economic processes have been operating and how economists and others have been thinking about growth. Our journey starts with the 1944 Bretton Woods conference that established the norms regulating international trade and finance after the Second World War. The international monetary system created there was based on a gold-exchange standard fixing the value of the US dollar at $35 an ounce, while all other currencies were fixed to the dollar. Fluctuations were allowed on a narrow band and convertibility of dollars into gold was guaranteed on demand. In the case of temporary balance-of-payments difficulties, governments were allowed to intervene through revaluations or devaluations. The International Monetary Fund, the International Bank for Reconstruction and Development and the General Agreements on Tariffs and Trade were created there. The stability that came with the Bretton Woods system has been given much of the credit for the rapid growth experienced by the world's economy after the Second World War. Other factors contributed to this period of rapid expansion. The Marshall Plan was critical in ensuring the reconstruction of the European economies ravaged by the war. It is clear that, after the turbulent interwar years and the destruction brought about by conflict, there were many opportunities for profitable investments. Perhaps the most important contribution of the Bretton Woods framework was that it set the conditions of stability needed for investment and trade after the turbulence of the previous twenty years.

In the quarter-century after 1945 the world economy experienced average annual GDP growth rates of 5 per cent, while several regions attained even higher rates. In contrast with the performance of the

TABLE 1.1 Annual GDP rate of growth, 1950–98

Regions	1950–73 (a)	1973–98 (b)	% rate of change (b − a) / (a)
Western Europe	4.81	2.11	−56.1
Japan	9.29	2.97	−69.0
Asia (excl. Japan)	5.18	5.46	5.4
Latin America	5.33	3.02	−43.3
Africa	4.45	2.74	−38.4
World	4.91	3.01	−38.7

Source: Maddison 2001 (Table 3-1a)

1930s, this was close to a miracle. The extent of that miracle can be seen in the evolution of the macroeconomic aggregates in West Germany, France, Italy and Great Britain. By the end of the Second World War, per capita GDP in these countries had regressed to the levels of 1905 (Italy), 1919 (France) and 1890 (Germany). But by the early 1950s, the evolution of per capita GDP in all of these countries was exceeding the best performance of the interwar period. By 1960, not only was the economic performance of all countries better than the best interwar performance, it was well above levels that would have been predicted by extrapolating pre-1939 or pre-1914 trends into the indefinite future.

The outstanding issue here is that these high expansion rates were sustained for more than a quarter-century. This was in very marked contrast with the experience of the interwar period, and especially the 1930s, when the Great Depression had ravaged the world economy. During that decade, the world's richest economies had suffered chronic deficiencies of aggregate demand, output had dropped below normal, and financial chaos had left an ugly scar. Because market forces alone had been unable to restore aggregate demand to normal levels, public policy intervention became almost a matter of routine.

As economist David Felix (2006) has explained, the *historic lesson* appeared to be that guidance and public policy intervention were required to achieve these *sustained* rapid growth rates. After the experience of the Great Depression and the global financial chaos of the period between the two world wars, the message that emerged from macroeconomic thought was that capital controls, financial regulation and state intervention were needed to prevent instability and misallocation of resources. If there was a risk of 'policy failure', it was better than 'market failure'.

Two important elements helped sustain these growth rates. One was the Marshall Plan, while the second was the US market, which remained open to European exports. Together they helped reconstruct the ravaged European economies and to prevent shortfalls in aggregate demand. In the aftermath of the Great Depression, the policy-making atmosphere favoured intervention and regulation. By 1950 everybody appeared to be preoccupied with growth: reconstruction was a key objective in the war-ravaged economies; for underdeveloped countries that had recently attained independence, growth was an imperative; finally, the centrally planned economies were determined to overtake their capitalist rivals by rapid economic expansion.

Thinking about growth Against this setting, it is no surprise that economic growth occupied a prominent place in the agenda of economic theorists immediately before and after the Second World War. For example, the Harrod–Domar model was concerned with the possibility of steady growth and employment (Harrod 1939; Domar 1946). In this very abstract model, both the savings ratio and the capital–output ratio (the proportion by which new capital stock was needed to increase output) were fixed and played a very prominent role. The key outcome of this model was that expected demand and actual output would be equal if, and only if, the growth rate equalled the relation between the savings and the capital–output ratios. Whenever this was not the case, a highly unstable process would emerge, with no adjustment mechanisms returning the economy to the steady growth path. The result would be either unemployment or inflation. In reality, the model provided the disagreeable result that growth in capitalist economies was closer to instability and periodic crises than to equilibrium, a highly relevant finding considering the economic history of the second half of the twentieth century.

In view of this unpleasant result, Solow (1956) and Swan (1960) offered a reply. In their model the growth path was endowed with stability thanks to the flexibility of factor prices: as the economy tries to break through the full employment barrier, labour becomes more expensive and this induces labour-saving technical change. Thus, with price flexibility and substitutability between capital and labour, the stability of neoclassical growth equilibrium would be established and macroeconomic crises averted.

The main question addressed by these models was how steady-state and optimum growth rates could be attained. In this sense, they did look into some of the macroeconomic problems that had haunted capitalist economies in the previous decades: unemployment and the relation between investment and savings. But the treatment of these issues in the Solow–Swan tradition had been cleansed of most of the problems identified by the Keynesian insights about uncertainty and deficiency of aggregate demand.[1] Not only that, these models assumed that stability of optimal growth paths depended on the substitutability between capital and labour, and on the flow of induced technical innovations. This assumption is quite problematic and is not supported by any theoretical model.[2] The substitution between capital and labour in such a manner that stability of the growth path is attained requires that the market gets the prices of these factors right. If the right prices are adopted by the market, then the allocation of production factors is the correct one and the optimal growth path is attained. But what happens if these prices are not adopted by the market? Or what guarantees that the 'right' prices will be adopted by the market? These are unsettling questions because there is no reason to assume that these outcomes will result.

From the point of view of environmental issues, most of these models were not concerned with the question of finite resources. For example, Joan Robinson's famous model of capital accumulation (Robinson 1956) identified six determinants of equilibrium growth: technology, investment policy, savings, competition, the wage bargain and financial conditions. The environment was just the landscape against which the drama of balanced or unstable growth would unfold.

In spite of the attention given to the environment after 1972, this dimension continued to be absent from mainstream economic modelling. And when the natural resource base was taken into account, it was mainly to show that there was no reason to worry about the question of finite resources. In a famous paper published in 1974, Joseph Stiglitz examined a model of economic growth in an economy in which exhaustible natural resources, limited in supply, were essential for production (Stiglitz 1974). Once again, the model described the optimal growth path for the economy and the conditions under which a sustainable level of per capita consumption was feasible. Although the critical issue of limits to growth was explicitly addressed in this article, the problem of exhaustible resources was thrown out of the window owing to the model's assumptions. These included the notion that capital, labour and natural resources are all substitutes: whenever natural resources became depleted, their relative scarcity could be offset by technical change. In this model, 'a sufficient condition for sustaining a constant per capita income with a general production function is that there be *resource augmenting technical change* at any positive rate (no matter how small)' (ibid.: 38, emphasis in the original). Technology would always break the limits to growth imposed by exhaustible natural resources.

Critique: parables and fables of growth models In a story by Borges, a Chinese emperor commissions his head cartographer to draw a map of the Celestial Empire on a one-to-one scale. This is, of course, senseless. A good map is a simplifying description of geography, not an exhaustive list of all of its components. In this, a map is like a theoretical model. Every theoretical model needs to make some simplifying assumptions and omit many particular phenomena judged to be irrelevant to the problem at hand. Thus, although the aggregate growth models mentioned here have been criticized for being highly abstract, that accusation may be dismissed as irrelevant: all models are abstract constructs of the real world. And once we accept that, the big test lies in their logical consistency or coherence: does the model perform in a rigorous manner?

Applying this question to the aggregate growth models mentioned above, we identify four serious problems. Failure to take these problems into consideration leads to flawed thinking about economics and the environment, and this can hardly be beneficial for good counsel in policy-making. As we shall see, this is something that is affecting the schools of environmental economics and of ecological economics in their efforts to provide guidance in the field of macroeconomics and the environment.[3]

The first critical problem in these growth models is related to an implicit assumption concerning the role of markets. These models presume that if the market adopts the right prices, then stable growth paths can be attained. Can we expect the market to adopt the right set of prices? The answer: economic theory has not been able to show that in a world of a decentralized economy, the free play of market forces leads to equilibrium (i.e. a set of prices that leaves everybody satisfied). This has significant negative implications for the models examined here.[4] For example, if technical change responds to factor prices, and the new technologies are able to guarantee balanced growth trajectories, it would be nice if the factor prices that induce this equilibrating technical change were the 'correct' factor prices. However, nothing guarantees that this will be the case.

The second problem with these growth models is that they use an aggregate measure of capital. This is part of the foundations of the neoclassical economic theory of distribution, according to which factors of production, capital and labour are rewarded in conformity with their contribution to social output (or, in technical terms, their marginal productivity). If capital is thought of as a collection of heterogeneous machines and intermediate inputs, the only element that they have in common is their price. Neoclassical economists think it is all right to add these prices and get to the money sum of 'capital'. Thus, capital as a sum of money and capital as the set of machines used in production are presented as equivalent, with the money prices of machinery used in production accurately representing the amount of machinery involved in productive processes. The reward to capital is thought of as a rate on the value terms of the collection of machines used in the production of goods.

This is incorrect. After the work of the Italian economist Piero Sraffa, in a world in which commodities are produced by means of other commodities (i.e. in which capital goods are commodities), the structure of relative prices changes as distribution (profits and wages) is modified. And this leads to the conclusion that rather than the rate of profit depending on the amount of capital, the measure of capital depends on the rate of profit. In a nutshell, the problem leads to a fatal circularity: if the rate of profit depends on the quantity of capital, the quantity of capital (measured in value terms) depends on the rate of profit. In simpler terms, the circularity can be presented in the following terms: the price of machines depends on the expected profit, but the rate of profits is a ratio of profits to the price of machines. One of the results of the above analysis is that a technique chosen at a given rate of profit (being the most profitable one), but discarded at a higher rate of profit, may once again become the most efficient one at even higher rates of profit. The possibility of a 'reswitching' of techniques destroys the notion that capital is a homogeneous substance that can be measured by prices independently of distribution.

The controversies over the concept of capital in the 1970s concluded with the neoclassical school accepting this fact whenever an aggregate measure of capital is used, as in all the growth models we examine here (see Samuelson 1966).[5] In a recent analysis Petri (2004) shows the relevance of the capital controversies for macroeconomic theory and policy.

The third problem concerns the postulates on technical change embedded in these models: they are not justified, either in theoretical terms or by empirical studies on the history of technology. An underlying assumption of these growth models (especially those in which choice of technique is important) is that there exists a smooth succession of production techniques that goes from the more labour intensive to the more capital intensive, and that movements along this curve respond to changes in relative factor prices. However, it is impossible to ascertain that there is a continuous sequence of techniques of production, from less to more capital intensity as factor prices change.

Another problem is that technical change is understood in these models as variations in the combination or proportions of the 'factors' of production. Capital, labour and natural resources or energy (as in the Stiglitz model) are considered to be perfect substitutes and technical progress takes place along the frontier of possibilities that are known to society. Thus, technology (i.e. the set of possible combinations of capital and labour) is exogenously and uniformly determined. This contradicts the history of technology, which abounds in examples of discontinuous technical change. Innovations come more in swarms or batches of innovations. Furthermore, technical change does not necessarily respond to relative factor prices (see Fellner 1962; David 1974).

The fourth problem is related to the absence of money in these models. As Hahn (1984) recognizes, that does not mean they are barter models because no attention is paid to transactions (the mediating role of money is performed costlessly by some external agency).[6] But it does pose a problem in relation to the role of money and finance in any economy. Not surprisingly, in this context there is no significant role for macroeconomic policies, such as those embodied in fiscal and monetary policy.

The growth models mentioned here were analytical constructs designed to respond to one line of inquiry: is there a golden path of balanced, optimal growth for a capitalist economy? A closely related query is the following: under which conditions is it possible to attain this trajectory? Thus, the models revolve around an existence question ('does the golden path exist?'), with no attempt to unravel the thorny question of the process through which a capitalist economy can attain this growth trajectory. This explains why there is no attention given to price formation processes, transactions or money. To be sure, growth models are macroeconomic models without financial institutions, banks or hedge funds, etc. They have very little room for macroeconomic policy.

'Limits to growth': a new perspective As the rapid growth rates of the 'Golden Age of Capitalism' continued through the sixties, a new preoccupation arose: what happens when the supply of non-renewable natural resources becomes depleted? In April 1968, a small group of people from industry, diplomacy and science met in the Accademia dei Lincei in Rome at the invitation of Aurelio Peccei, an Italian industrial entrepreneur, and Alexander King, a Scottish scientist. The Club of Rome was born with the objective of raising worldwide awareness regarding the complex web of relations between unrestrained growth in material consumption in a world with finite resources and an ever more fragile environment. Its first task was to commission a report from a group of systems analysts at the Massachusetts Institute of Technology.

The study that emerged from this project had a short title, *The Limits to Growth* (Meadows et al. 1972), and unleashed a heated debate. It was based on a mathematical model formed by blocks of equations for the systems of food production, manufacturing, demographics and non-renewable natural resources, as well as a system for pollution. The main conclusion of the report was that if the trends observed in 1972 were continued, limits to growth (LG) would be encountered at some point during the following 100 years. As these physical constraints were reached, there would be a collapse in the absolute numbers of world population and industrial output. In the majority of the scenarios of the model, the collapse would be caused by the depletion and exhaustion of the natural resource base.[7]

In the ensuing debate, there were severe criticisms directed at the LG model. Of course, one of the most important was that it worked at an extremely aggregate level. For example, world population was an undifferentiated unit, where only average features of the planet's inhabitants were taken into consideration. Also, there was only one class of pollutants, namely the family of persistent pollutants whose dynamics were just beginning to be understood in the early seventies.

But perhaps the critique that generated the fiercest debate was related to the assumptions concerning technological change. The LG model allowed for exponential growth of population and output, but did not introduce any similar assumption on technical progress. However, one of the scenarios explored by the model introduced the hypothesis that environmental pollution would decrease by a factor of four after 1975, that average per hectare yields worldwide would double and that nuclear energy would be able to satisfy global needs. But even in this scenario, the collapse of the global industrial system and the decline in population would occur before 2100. In other words, technical progress was capable of prolonging the time span of growth but would not be able to eliminate the physical limits that will eventually bring it to an end.[8]

The 1972 LG model inaugurated a race to obtain more accurate projections on the evolution of the world economy (Mesarovic and Pestel 1974; Leontief 1977; Herrera 1977). These models established the foundations for a more rigorous representation of the interdependencies between economic processes, natural resource usage rates and environmental deterioration. They also allowed for greater accuracy in the analysis of global trends and in the construction of future evolution scenarios that permitted a less coarse analysis of the world system.

The Mesarovic and Pestel (MP) model disaggregated the world into ten regions examined through five levels of analysis. This allowed a move away from the simplistic vision of the LG model in which the entire planet reached the limits to growth at the same time. Now each component (or region) would reach its limits at different moments and the experience of a total collapse in the model depended on its structure and on its interdependencies. But in some scenarios, a global collapse or regional catastrophes could still take place, in some cases even before the mid-twenty-first century. The critical result was that, sooner or later, the entire world system would suffer the consequences of these regional catastrophes.

The MP model also entailed a series of policy recommendations. The most important was that the only course of action was 'organic growth', defined as a process in which a master plan would provide enough general coordination for all of the system's components. For humanity, the choice was between undifferentiated growth (and collapse) and organic growth (with something akin to what we now call sustainable development). But the common thread of the model's sections was related to the conflicts that would arise from intense socio-economic inequality and the struggle for access to the natural resource base. This is why its first set of scenarios was related to the severe per capita income disparities, and the main question was whether these disparities would vanish over time or whether, on the contrary, they would intensify in the future. In spite of several benign assumptions (population growth would stabilize in less than thirty-five years), the model's conclusion was that inequality in per capita income levels would intensify. The only way to reverse this negative trend would be through a spectacular increase in official development assistance (ODA) to developing countries. The contrast with real-world trends could not have been starker. As we shall see, in the years that followed the publication of the LG and MP models, ODA flows were to suffer their worst drop ever.

The so-called Latin American model prepared by researchers at the Fundación Bariloche in Argentina took a different starting point. The team in Bariloche saw the LG model as a neo-Malthusian discourse that emphasized the need to avoid a catastrophe that would come about through the exhaustion of natural resources: that catastrophe was already happening in 1970 because two-thirds of humanity was submerged in poverty and exclusion.[9]

The Bariloche model adopted a normative approach with its core concept being the eradication of poverty at a global level and the satisfaction of people's basic needs. Population growth would be stabilized when life standards improved in the poor countries of the world. With these premises the model then went on to examine whether the world's endowment of natural resources was a real constraint. The Bariloche model differed from the LG and MP models because, instead of examining trends and forecasts, it examined the physical or material viability of a desirable society (one in which all basic needs were covered). The mathematical component of the model was simply the support for this feasibility study.

The Bariloche model used a novel definition of resource scarcity in which all natural resource reserves are the expression of investments in exploration, and they do not portray with absolute accuracy the total available stock of resources. From this perspective, total endowment of resources depends on technology and on material production conditions, and the signals concerning the relative scarcity of natural resources depend on specific historical conditions.[10] This was supported by findings of the study by Barnett and Morse (1963) on the evolution of production costs in the US mining industry between 1870 and 1960.[11] The data show that after 1890 production costs measured in both labour and capital inputs have persistently declined.

The Bariloche model concluded that the *physical* feasibility of the desired society was not a problem. The difficulty was in the field of socio-political relations, where unfair economic structures threatened the future of civilization. Although official development assistance could ameliorate things, a big difference with the MP model was that even increments to meet the UN recommendations could not have a decisive impact. In order to bring about the desired changes at the global level (satisfaction of the basic needs of the entire population), changes in the international economic structure were required, especially in relation to the terms of trade of the commodities exported by developing countries in order to eliminate their balance-of-payments constraints.

Ironically, the LG debate was inaugurated precisely when the world economy was about to start a period of slower growth rates. In this sense, the period 1971–73 represents a crucial turning point in the history of the world's capitalist economies. In those years the institutional framework that had regulated the fast growth performance of the post-war era was ripped down and replaced by a new regulatory regime.

Back to the real world The world of models in which economists live and thrive does not exist in a void. The context in which the first debates on the limits to growth and the importance of the environment took place was itself shaped by several important events that would shape the world economy for ever.

In 1973 the Bretton Woods system of fixed exchange rates was abandoned. The reasons for the demise of the BW system are multiple, but one deserves to be highlighted. The exchange rates determined after the war were based on the fact that the US economy was running sizeable balance-of-trade surpluses. But once the European economies recovered, those surpluses vanished and in the late 1960s the US economy was already experiencing a current account deficit. For a short period of time, this was tolerated without problem by other governments, but later these persistent deficits led directly to a manifestation of the so-called 'Triffin dilemma': if a nation's currency is also the world's reserve currency, that country needs to keep a current account deficit in order to provide liquidity for the global economy, but this leads to loss of credibility in that currency. It soon became clear that the dollar had to be devalued. The gold window was closed by the United States in 1971 and the system of fixed exchange rates disintegrated soon afterwards.

In the words of Eatwell and Taylor (2000), this led to the privatization of risk. In a system of fixed exchange rates, the private sector was shielded from the risk of fluctuating currencies. Once the Bretton Woods regime was gone, the risks of foreign currency variations fell squarely on private sector agents of all types, and it became urgent to reduce these risks. Because the system of stable exchange rates was accompanied by controls on transboundary capital flows, in the new world of flexible rates traders operating in international markets needed to be able to diversify their portfolios at will, changing the mix of currencies and financial assets in line with perceptions of foreign exchange risks. The deregulation of capital flows became an imperative in order to hedge against the costs that fluctuating exchange rates entailed for the private sector.

The new system of fluctuating exchange rates offered a novel horizon for arbitraging operations. And this is why the volume of international capital flows increased exponentially. Annual turnover in the world's currency markets expanded from US$4 trillion in 1973 to US$450 trillion in 2007 (Hillman et al. 2006). Most of these operations are strictly speculative in nature. This generates greater volatility in exchange and interest rates and less capital formation, and reduces growth rates.

An important element that disturbed the world economy during the seventies was of course the oil crisis of 1973. In October of that year, the Arab members of the Organization of the Petroleum Exporting Countries (OPEC) declared an oil embargo against the United States in reprisal for its decision to resupply the Israeli military during the Yom Kippur war. Although the actual embargo lasted only for a period of six months, its impact on oil prices was long lasting. Prices returned to something comparable to pre-1973 levels in 1986. In addition, the embargo also increased awareness that Middle East supplies of crude could be easily disrupted, generating more uncertainty. Investment dropped, inflationary pressures were amplified and growth rates stagnated. The US economy set forth on a trajectory of recessions and inflation, experiencing the 'stagflation' period of the seventies. As we shall see in the next chapter, this had a profound impact on macroeconomic theory and policy-making.

In 1980, in order to stop inflation, the Federal Reserve increased the federal fund target interest rate from 10 to 20 per cent. While this succeeded in bringing inflation under control, it achieved this at the cost of provoking the deepest recession of the post-war era (with 11 per cent unemployment in the USA). In addition, it caused havoc in the international economy as interest rates increased dramatically just as the recession caused significant reductions in the price of critical raw materials.

Developing countries were caught in a trap of high debt service payments (due to the interest rate hikes) and of dropping prices of raw materials (due to the recession), and this brought about the international debt crisis of the 1980s. For many developing economies, getting their external accounts back in shape meant subordinating macroeconomic policy and even development strategy to the demands of the International Monetary Fund (IMF) and the World Bank. Together, these institutions imposed 'structural adjustment programmes' (SAPs) that ensured debt repayment through cuts in social spending, massive lay-offs, selling of state-owned firms, and large-scale privatization at fire-sale prices. The containment of aggregate debt in order to curtail inflationary pressures was another flagship initiative of SAPs. This was achieved through wage freezes and the dismantling of labour organizations. The end result of this adjustment was an increase in unemployment, inequality and poverty. The environmental impact was felt through greater pressure on natural resources, the reduction of expenditure on environmental stewardship and the degradation of monitoring and environmental law-enforcement capabilities.

By the end of the 1980s, many countries had succumbed to the pressure applied by the IMF, the World Bank and foreign investors. Many adopted the policy package that later came to be known as the 'Washington Consensus'. This policy package was not an emergency programme, but a policy mix that would control the destiny of these nations for years to come. It consisted of tight monetary policies (to curb inflation), fiscal policies dominated by debt service, incomes policies to reduce aggregate demand, financial deregulation, trade liberalization, the abandonment of state-directed policies and large-scale privatization. Slow growth and the implementation of pro-cyclical macroeconomic policies centred on austerity measures earned the eighties the name of the 'lost decade'. The Washington Consensus would rule macroeconomic policy and development strategies as the nineties and neoliberal globalization got under way.

In 1992 the UN Conference on the Environment and Development was held in Rio de Janeiro. This was an important event, coming twenty years after the Stockholm conference. The main results of the Rio conference included the United Nations Framework Convention on Climate

Change (UNFCCC), the Convention on Biological Diversity (CBD) and the Agenda 21 declaration. This last item was an ambitious plan of action to be implemented in every area in which human actions have impacts on the environment. It included such things as science and technology transfer, environmental education and some references to official development assistance. But it simply left the entire edifice of macroeconomic policies unattended. This was the heyday of the Washington Consensus, with multilateral free-trade negotiations getting ready to culminate in the creation of the World Trade Organization in Marrakesh in 1994.

Although the policies of the Washington Consensus were supposed to bring about stability, a long string of financial crises in the nineties (starting with Mexico in 1994, followed by South-East Asia, Brazil, Russia and Argentina) revealed some of the flaws of the neoliberal economic model. By the end of the nineties, many developing countries had suffered another 'lost decade'. Development was being affected, the environment continued to deteriorate, but macroeconomic policy remained largely outside the scope of debates concerning sustainability.

One example of how macroeconomic policies could have devastating effects on the environment was provided by the plight of Indonesia's forests and the communities trying to preserve them. This country suffered a financial crisis after large-scale speculative attacks on its currency following the Thai crisis in 1997. The demise of the Indonesian rupiah spelled disaster for many corporations that had borrowed heavily in dollars. The rupiah's devaluation brought about a drop in GDP surpassing 13 per cent in 1998. The intervention of the IMF led to a draconian adjustment programme that increased the exploitation of natural resources in an attempt to raise revenue and redress the country's external accounts. Under pressure from the IMF the Indonesian government lifted a ten-year ban on exports of raw, unprocessed logs. At the same time, public spending cuts and widespread deregulation opened Indonesia's forests to illegal logging and to the swift expansion of oil palm plantations on deforested land. Because of the policy package imposed on Indonesia (high interest rates, fiscal austerity), more than half of Indonesia's population today lives below the two-dollars-per day poverty line (Jubilee Australia 2007). The toll is also visible in deforestation rates: between 2000 and 2005 Indonesia lost a yearly average of 1.9 million hectares (Butler 2007). Most of this deforestation took place in Kalimantan, where traditional land tenure rights are being overridden and unique Dypterocarp forests are being destroyed (Wertz-Kanounnikoff and Kongphan-Apirak 2008; Butler 2005).

From limits to growth to ecological economics In 1971, the Romanian economist Nicholai Georgescu Roegen published his book *The Entropy Law and the Economic Process*. In it, he forcefully insisted that economists had failed to pay attention to the critically important second law of thermodynamics or entropy law. The key message was that failure to recognize the second law of thermodynamics implied ignoring the fact that productive processes were carried out against a backdrop of finite resources. Because this law expresses a time asymmetry (entropy cannot be reversed), this was a reformulation of the limits to growth idea. For Georgescu Roegen, 'the entropic nature of the economic process, which degrades natural resources and pollutes the environment, constitutes the present danger. The earth is entropically winding down naturally, and economic advance is accelerating that process. Man must learn to ration the meager resources he has so profligately squandered if he is to survive in the long run' (Georgescu Roegen 1967: 97).

This idea was picked up by several economists who became the founding fathers of the school of ecological economics (SEE). The basic underlying principle of the SEE is that economic thinking has to take into account the laws of thermodynamics. According to SEE, economic systems are embedded in a physical system, and failure to acknowledge this leads to serious misconceptions about economic processes. Because ecology is defined as a discipline that deals with the components of the physical world that are relevant to economics, it is a logical imperative that these two dimensions (ecology and economics) be fused into one discipline. For the followers of ecological economics, the main problem with neoclassical (mainstream) economics is that it concentrates on resource allocation and assumes an infinite resource base, infinite waste sinks and no limits to growth.[12]

The school of ecological economics has made important contributions to academia and policy-oriented research. The work of Herman Daly and Robert Costanza, for example, has been a significant input in the debate on economics and the environment. However, the basic premises of this school entail unsolved problems that seriously limit its scope and hamper its future development. As we will see in Chapter 2, these problems are highly relevant to our analysis of macroeconomic policies and the environment.

For Daly, determining the optimal scale of an economy is the main issue of our time. The market solves the quandary of allocating resources, and it does that 'very well', but what it does not do is 'solve the problem of optimal scale and of optimal distribution' (Daly 2002: 66). According to his analysis, the primary attention of mainstream

> **Box 1.1 The invisible hand: metaphor or scientific result?**
>
> Economic theory never produced a scientific demonstration that market forces (the invisible hand) lead to equilibrium positions. The most advanced theoretical construct built for this purpose (general equilibrium theory, GET) failed to deliver the goods. Although this has been the main objective of economic theory since Adam Smith launched his famous 'invisible hand' metaphor, it has been unable to prove the case. In the 1950s stability theory produced some results for very special economies and with the aid of very restrictive assumptions (for example, gross substitutability). Arrow et al. (1959) advanced the conjecture that the results could be generalized. With a counter-example Scarf (1960) poured cold water on that belief. Later the work of Mantel (1976), Debreu (1974) and Sonnenschein (1973) confirmed the bad news: the structural features of GET allow the price adjustment process to be essentially arbitrary (additional conditions need to be imposed on excess demand functions to obtain convergence to equilibrium prices). In addition, GET suffers from other problems. One is its reliance on the figure of a centralizing entity (the auctioneer) charged with the task of adjusting prices. The auctioneer is closer to a central planning agency than to the workings of a decentralized capitalist economy. GET has not been able to rid itself of this entity (Fisher 1983). In addition, GET is a model for a non-monetary economy, something that belittles its explanatory power (for an excellent analysis of this problem, see Benetti 2004). To summarize, the 'invisible hand' metaphor remains just that, an ingenious metaphor.

macroeconomics is 'full employment without inflation via an ever-growing GNP'.

And here we encounter the first difficulties with ecological economics. The critique addressed by Georgescu Roegen and Herman Daly to mainstream economics is that it ignores the problem of scale. In other words, it correctly solves the problem of allocation (i.e. the question of equilibrium prices), but is unable to deal with the problem of growth in a world of finite resources. In fact, there are two serious problems with these assertions. The first is that mainstream neoclassical economics has failed to provide a demonstration of how the competitive forces of decentralized markets lead to the formation of equilibrium prices (Box 1.1). Thus, we simply do not have a theory showing that markets 'solve the allocation problem'. Ignoring this casts a dark shadow over Daly's analysis and ultimately undermines the capacity of ecological economics to contribute to our understanding of the economic forces that drive environmental degradation.

The second problem with Daly's assertion is that since the debates of the seventies (concerning stagflation and the Phillips curve), macroeconomics ceased to be obsessed by full employment and decidedly put the control of inflation in the forefront of the policy agenda. Failure to understand this has serious implications for ecological economics. The lack of a thoughtful discussion of Keynes, of how his insights were co-opted and ultimately betrayed, and how the monetarist and rational expectations critiques led to the rebirth of classical macroeconomics (to mention the most salient events in sixty years of academic and policy debates), ultimately undermines Daly's call for a more relevant macroeconomic theory. We return in the following chapter to this part of Daly's contribution as we examine the evolution of macroeconomic theory.

The final part of Daly's paper focuses on policy implications, the main objective being defined in terms of how to limit scale to a sustainable level. Daly mentions four policy implications: a) the main principle is to limit the human scale to a level that is within carrying capacity; b) technological progress needs to be efficiency-increasing rather than throughput-increasing; c) in the case of renewable resources, harvesting rates should not exceed regeneration rates and waste emissions should not exceed the renewable assimilative capacity of ecosystems; d) non-renewable resources should be exploited at a rate not exceeding the creation of renewable resources.

It is unfortunate that Daly's call for an 'environmental macroeconomics' has this very weak policy component. None of his recommendations belongs to macroeconomic policy-making. The first is part of demographics; the second belongs to technology policy. The third and last pertain to management practices. The fourth principle resembles something called 'weak sustainability', a notion that has many problems.

The inability to carry out a deeper and comprehensive critique of mainstream economics makes it difficult for ecological economics to transcend the narrow boundaries of neoclassical theory. One good example is England (2000). This author presents a growth model in which the production function includes N, the value of natural capital, together with capital (K) and labour (L).[13] The main conclusion of this model is that growth may continue if there are enough nature-saving innovations and preservation of the remaining natural capital becomes a social priority.

But the interesting question here is what does the introduction of 'natural capital' mean? When you slap the notion of capital on nature, you impose a metric that has nothing to do with nature and which has nothing natural about it. This can be a dangerous approach as it leads down the road of stamping the categories of 'assets' on things such as forests and aquifers, and putting prices on all components of nature, an approach that takes us closer to the transformation of nature into a commodity. Although England does not make the mistake of considering that 'natural assets' can be substituted by human-made technological innovations, he nevertheless erases history as the capitalist mode of production becomes natural: 'the conception and measurement of capital should be broadened to include these natural assets' (ibid.: 428). This is confirmed by the following passage: 'During the past 10,000 years, humanity has invented both agriculture and industry. These developments have been linked historically to growth of human population, accumulation of produced capital goods and labour saving innovations' (ibid.). Of course, the problem with this statement is that capitalism had not yet been born when agriculture was 'invented'. This shows how ecological economics assesses the problem: there are no distributional issues, no classes, objects and commodities are the same thing, there is no private appropriation (and the notion of 'environmental services for humankind' is meaningless). The model proposed by England ignores markets, transactions, money and distribution.

This discussion about macroeconomics and the environment is completely centred on the macro scale of economies. This is in reality another way of looking at the limits-to-growth question. Although scale and finite resources remain legitimate issues, focusing exclusively on them does not provide a good vantage point for the analysis of the economic forces that are behind environmental deterioration and natural resource depletion. In fact, it contributes very little to the analysis of the macroeconomic *policy* setting that is required to attain sustainability.

Growth: friend or foe?

In the fifties and sixties Nobel laureate Simon Kuznets analysed the experience of several countries in the post-war era and concluded that in the first stages of development inequality in income distribution could intensify, but as income per capita increased, it would subside. The idea that a similar process could apply to environmental deterioration was born through several studies in the nineties (Selden and Song 1994;

Shafik and Bandyopadhyay 1992, Grossman and Krueger 1995). Today, studies abound trying to prove the existence of an inverted U-shaped curve depicting how environmental degradation increases as per capita income increases until a threshold is attained, after which higher per capita incomes are associated with less environmental destruction. This construct received the name of the inverted environmental Kuznets curve (EKC). And the corollary of this was that insofar as globalization, trade liberalization and financial liberalization provided a healthy framework for growth, they too became environmentally friendly.[14]

The EKC changed the terms of the debate on the physical constraints to growth. Not only are there no limits to growth, but in fact growth is the road to environmental stewardship. The key assumption here was that the environment is a normal good, i.e. its demand rises as income increases. In addition, structural changes in an economy as development proceeded (for example, the demise of polluting activities and the rise of cleaner industries) would bring about this change. Soon the EKC hypothesis became an industry in itself, and studies proliferated checking for the curve in relation to individual contaminants.[15]

There are three fundamental problems with the EKC mindset. The first is that the environment is multidimensional and it is not possible to treat it as if it were made up of just one item. Thus, even if the evolution of one pollutant respects the EKC pattern, it may coexist with other pollutants that don't. Or it may coexist with deforestation and depletion of aquifers.

The second is that the EKC assumes that environmental decline is non-cumulative and is not irreversible.[16] It ignores the fact that gradual environmental degradation can accumulate until critical thresholds are crossed. Repair can take extremely long periods of time (as in soil restoration). Frequently, as when extinctions take place, there is no going back, no matter how many resources a society is willing to spend. Ironically, the same process that generates a demand for an improved environment prevents ecosystems from satisfying that demand for a better environment. In fact, pollutants or destructive forces continue to accumulate even when per capita income passes the threshold point and environmental 'improvement' begins.

A third issue is that the EKC treats countries as environmental units. This is problematic insofar as trade flows can allow one national economy to displace its environmental costs. Thus, although one country may exhibit an EKC from some critical pollutants, a closer look at the composition of its international trade could reveal that its economic growth was leaving a negative footprint elsewhere. Muradian et al.

(2001) estimated the environmental load displacement of eighteen industrialized countries. The study reveals evidence of the displacement of environmental costs from rich to developing countries. The net effect is very difficult to establish. This clearly shows that the EKC construct is insufficient to capture the complex relation between growth and the environment.

Even if we ignore these problems, the vast majority of developing countries have experienced very low growth rates in GDP per capita. This means that they have been approaching the tipping point at which environmental deterioration begins to diminish at a very slow pace. The global financial and economic crisis that exploded in 2008 will slow their advance further. Many countries will remain in the vicinity of the vertex of the EKC, the zone where environmental damage is more intense.

Summing up, the EKC was an appealing idea for some, but it contained little substance. In 2008, when the worst financial and economic crisis in seven decades exploded, pushing back development levels in many economies and throwing millions back into poverty, the notion of an EKC went on to the back burner, if not into the trash can.

India: the case of 'predatory growth' Growth can be anti-poor and anti-environment with the help of perverse macroeconomic policies. The best example can be found in India, a country that has been promenaded as a success story of neoliberal sector and macroeconomic policies. Its average annual growth rates (7–8 per cent in the last decade) have been touted as spectacular by the international business press. But this rosy picture is only a small part of the story. In fact, India has been immersed in a process of 'predatory growth', a term coined by Amit Bhaduri (2009) to denote the type of perverse dynamics surrounding the Indian neoliberal experience. In a nutshell, predatory growth is sustained by a mutually reinforcing mechanism between higher growth rates and rising income inequality. Environmental degradation is a key by-product of the process.

According to Bhaduri, three factors help explain how this predatory growth came about. First, India's growth rates are indeed high, but there has been very little formal employment creation. In the last decade, formal employment increased by only 1 per cent. This means that productivity has risen dramatically, but wages have remained stagnant and inequality has intensified. (India always had a dismal record in this field, but things have worsened.)

Second, fiscal and monetary policies have been conditioned by financial liberalization (opening of the capital account). Monetary policy remains obsessed with the struggle to control inflation in order to maintain capital flows (Debabrata Patra and Ray 2010). India's exports have increased, but not as much as its imports. Its trade deficit has been financed by incoming capital flows. This explains why its international reserves have increased (more than US$260 billion in 2009). But there's a big difference compared with China, a country that has been running a trade surplus for two decades now and whose reserves are owned by the country's central bank: India's 'reserves' are made up of foreign capital inflows and could evaporate in weeks or even days if foreign investors start having doubts regarding the capacity (or willingness) of India's economic authorities to sustain the exchange rate. In order to placate any fears or doubts, authorities in New Delhi have been maintaining a fiscal policy organized around the principle of a balanced budget. This is achieved through cuts in healthcare, housing, education, rural development and environmental stewardship (sanitation, water management). Cutting expenditures is done to prevent debt from growing, to reduce the size of state intervention in the economy, and to maintain firm control over inflation in order to send the 'right signals' to the financial markets. Thus, fiscal policy is dominated by considerations more related to capital inflows than anything else.

Another key element of predatory growth has been the policy of land acquisition for corporate-led 'development'. In addition to the infamous special economic zones, this also includes land for mining, industry, infrastructure projects and tourism. Examples of this can be found in the mineral-rich and densely forested areas of Orissa or Assam. These land concessions typically displace the country's poorest, the *adivasis* (literally the original dwellers) or tribespeople, who constitute 8 per cent of the population but account for nearly 40 per cent of those displaced in the name of development (Bhaduri 2009: 37).

In the state of Arunachal Pradesh, for example, projects to build 103 dams will submerge the lands of thousands of indigenous peoples. Powerful transmission lines will carry the electricity produced by these dams to urban centres thousands of miles away from the fertile but submerged lands of the *adivasis* in that state.[17] The coal-mining operations in Meghalaya (Assam) and the bauxite mining complex and refineries in Lanjigarh (Orissa) provide more examples of human rights violations and loss of livelihoods for local *adivasis*. Other abuses associated with predatory growth include child labour and violations of the right to water and health (Shrivastava 2007). This process leads to mass displacement as thousands are forced to migrate to already overpopulated cities.

Third, more than 75 per cent of India's population has no access as consumers to the goods produced by the large corporations responsible for the production of consumer goods. Catering to the needs of the high-income brackets in that society has brought about an output mix with the same bias that exists in developed countries: intensive energy consumption, high materials usage rates and waste of non-renewable natural resources. As Bhaduri (2009: 75) points out, the production structure resulting from this growth is heavily biased against the poor: not only is there little growth in the purchasing power of the poor, but the reduction in welfare expenditures dictated by the need to maintain capital flows stunts growth in demand for basic necessities. This output mix in favour of the rich crystallizes into a rigid structure that will be very difficult to change.

The process of predatory growth is fuelled by inequality and environmental destruction. But its frame of reference is built around India's macroeconomic policy priorities. Monetary and exchange rate priorities combine with fiscal policy objectives, and together they work in a perverse feedback loop that translates into greater inequality and an output mix that carries a terrible burden of environmental destruction.

De-growth and steady-state economics The limits-to-growth debate and the notion of sustainable development have opened the door for a discussion on de-growth. This notion focuses on the alternative to an economy that is obsessed with growth and which seems oblivious to everything else. De-growth is defined as 'a reduction of production and consumption in physical terms through down-scaling (and not only through efficiency improvements)' (Kallis 2010). From this perspective, current consumption patterns of high-income groups are leading to the excessive appropriation of natural resources, with accompanying social and environmental damages. Downscaling would appear to be an appropriate answer to the challenges posed by the unbridled expansion of the economy.

It is clear that the notion of de-growth has its own challenges as it must reconcile downscaling with social justice and equity, a formidable problem as it would have to be carried out at the global level. Thus, there is not only a technological dimension to this process, but a political and social aspect that requires careful consideration. In this context, a recent conference in Barcelona presented several policy measures that would be aimed at bringing de-growth to fruition. Some of these are related to macroeconomic policies, but their effectiveness remains unclear. For example, monetary reform with the elimination of fiat money may or may not lead to de-growth or stable steady-state economies.[18]

But there is a fundamental problem with de-growth (or zero growth) theories: they perceive growth as stemming from cultural or psychological roots (a review can be found in Martínez Alier et al. 2010). The problem with this perspective is that the cause of growth becomes psychological, a question of mentalities and even fashion. The idea that growth could originate from endogenous forces in capitalist economies is ignored.

Growth is not only a cultural phenomenon or a feature of a maniac mentality. It is the direct consequence of how capitalist economies operate. This is true of capitalism as it operated in Genoa in the sixteenth century, and it is true today with the mega-corporations that rule global markets. The purpose of capital is not to produce useful things or useless stuff; its object is to produce profits without end and more capital. This is the engine of accumulation, and it is fuelled by inter-capitalist competition.

In the words of Marx (1973: 220): 'Conceptually, competition is nothing other than the inner nature of capital, its essential character; appearing in and realized as the reciprocal interaction of many capitals with one another, the inner tendency [presents itself] as external necessity. Capital exists and can only exist as many capitals, and its self-determination therefore appears as their reciprocal interaction with one another.' By the forces of competition, 'capital is continuously harassed: March! March!' Thus, Marx's analysis shows quite convincingly that capital can exist only as private centres of capital accumulation that are driven by (inter-capitalist) competition. This is why, in its quest to expand and survive (as an independent centre of accumulation), capital is continuously opening new spaces for profitability: new products, new markets. The corollary of this is that the only way in which we can get rid of 'growth mania' is by getting rid of capitalism. It is not possible to have capitalism without growth.

Is there a technological fix out of this? In other words, can we have such an efficient technological infrastructure (in buildings, energy and transport systems, manufacturing, etc.) that even with growth the ecological footprint could be reduced? This remains to be seen, but one phenomenon seems to conspire against this: the rebound effect. As technologies become more efficient and unit costs become smaller, consumption increases. Either existing consumers deepen their consumption, or more people have access to the objects or services being put into the marketplace. The end result is that the positive effects of greater efficiency are cancelled by deepening consumption rates. And let's not forget what happens when consumption stops or slows down: those centres of accumulation cannot sell their commodities, inventories grow, unemployment soars and we have recessions, depressions and crises.

From the point of view of production, for those individual centres of accumulation every gadget, every nook and cranny in the world, or any vast expanse of geographical space is a space waiting to be occupied for profit. From pep pills to tranquillizers, food and water, healthcare and even genetic resources or nano-materials, to the anxious eyes of capital all of these dimensions are but spaces for profitability. Talk about investing in 'natural capital' as a way out of the dilemma is devoid of any sense. It could very well be that, in the words of Smith (2010), we either save capitalism or save ourselves; we cannot do both.

Concluding remarks

Although the world economy continued to grow between 1975 and 2005, it did so at a slower rate than in the period 1945–75. The environment has continued to deteriorate as more pressure is put on forests, aquifers, biodiversity, atmosphere and oceans. There are many references attesting to this: UNEP's *Global Environmental Outlook*, the Millennium Ecosystem Assessment, the World Resources Institute databases, various publications of the International Union for Conservation of Nature (IUCN), etc. In this chapter we explored how macroeconomic models started to address the relations between economics and the environment.

In the first growth models the environment was ignored and instability was a feature of capitalist development. A second generation of models took care of the instability question by assuming that flexible factor prices would ensure balanced growth trajectories. When the limits-to-growth debate took place, technology was assumed to solve the problem of finite resources. Later, ecological economics attempted to bring the environment into the models in a more meaningful way. Unfortunately this school failed to put enough distance between its own research objectives and mainstream theory. In all cases, macroeconomic *policies* are omitted from the analysis. In the next chapter we examine the implications of this.

2 · The macroeconomic policy connection

Introduction

The way policy-makers think about macroeconomic relations is a crucial determinant of the policies they implement. Suppose for a minute somebody adopts the view that markets are self-regulating and that macroeconomic equilibrium is a natural result of the workings of capitalist economies. The policy corollary will be to leave markets to do their job with as little outside intervention as possible. Or imagine that an adviser to the president embraces a variant of this view, i.e. that markets do operate correctly but that there are frictions and rigidities that impede their operations. In that case, the recommended course of action would be to eliminate the source of those frictions. The point is that in both cases, the policies would be a logical consequence of the analytical vision you adopted.

What policies would you recommend if you had a different vision of how capitalist economies work? Suppose you develop a model in which capitalist economies lack the adjustment mechanisms to attain macroeconomic equilibrium and that they are inherently unstable, generating crises and slumps. Furthermore, suppose your analysis allowed you to conclude that these repeated crises intensify inequality, destroy people's livelihoods and have negative repercussions on the environment. Clearly, your policy advice would have to be consistent with this vision, proposing preventive action or at least steps to mitigate the repercussions.

Thus, how we think of capitalist economies is crucial for our ability to design and implement macroeconomic policies for sustainability. The approach we follow depends largely on how we conceive of the operations and dynamics of capitalist economies. From this perspective, it is necessary to examine how macroeconomic theory has evolved and its current status. It is essential if we want to identify the limitations and contradictions of the models currently being used. This is an urgent task if we want to move on and design socially responsible policies that can strengthen environmental stewardship.

In addition, using macroeconomic policies for sustainability will require tackling several important issues that have not received sufficient attention. For example, macroeconomics implies working with aggregates and in economics this can be problematic. For example, a capitalist firm would like to pay very low wages to its workers, but if every capitalist firm behaves in the same manner, there will simply be no purchasing power to soak up the supply of merchandise, unsold stuff would accumulate in inventories and there would be a great slump. When going from the micro level to a macroeconomic perspective, many things change.

Examining the evolution of macroeconomic theory is useful if we want to identify and solve the crucial problems lying at the crossroads of macroeconomics and sustainability. It is also vital if we don't want to repeat mistakes. This is an important chapter that poses several challenges for readers. In recounting the evolution of macroeconomic theory over the past seven decades, we will try to avoid technical jargon and unnecessary complications. Nevertheless, macroeconomic theory and policy-making remain complex areas, a fact used by the establishment to make political decisions and disguise them as technical necessities. The reader's patience may perhaps be put to the test in this chapter, but hopefully rewarded. Awareness about the assumptions made will take us a long way in reclaiming the way we think and act when seeking alternatives to today's policies. We cannot leave macroeconomic policy-making to a small group of specialists who rely on simplistic and inconsistent theoretical models.

The discussion that follows is not far removed from current events. During the past sixty years macroeconomic theory and policy-making have suffered fundamental changes. In a first stage (roughly 1950–75) the main message was that markets do not always attain balanced growth with full employment, and that government intervention was needed to ensure that macroeconomic result. In the second stage (from 1978 to 2008) the lesson was different: the private sector was always right and government intervention was useless, if not evil. In the summer of 2008, when the signs of trouble in the banking system became clear and a full-blown crisis erupted, government intervention became fashionable once again. Now, as the crisis continues to unfold, macroeconomics lacks a clearly defined storybook with some robust consensus behind it. As austerity measures are implemented in Europe (and to a lesser degree in the USA), resources for environmental stewardship will be cut. The world will move away from environmental sustainability and social equity.

Macroeconomics: evolutionary paths

Twenty years ago Herman Daly made a plea for an environmental macroeconomics. He claimed that macroeconomics had a role to play in ecological economics and that this had not been adequately recognized. The main problem that he saw for macroeconomics was the question of an optimum scale for the aggregate economy. His call was heeded by economists who concentrated on a macroeconomic model that has probably been the most successful construct in the history of the discipline. But it has been under fire from all quarters for more than thirty years. In order to appraise the scope, range and validity of this contribution from ecological economics, we need to understand the genesis of this model, as well as its limitations. This will in turn require a brief tour of the evolution of macroeconomic theory over the past sixty years.

What follows should not be seen as a simple literature review. As we have pointed out, in macroeconomics theory and policy are one and the same thing. In addition, current debates on how to face the challenges of the global crisis show that macroeconomic theory needs to be revised. In fact, substantial parts of mainstream theory have been shown to be intellectually bankrupt. If we want to move in the direction of using macroeconomic policy for sustainability, and if we want to move away from the platitudes of mainstreamers, we had better start looking at the big picture of the evolution of macroeconomic thinking. This is not an academic exercise, but an expedition into territory that has been abandoned to the whimsical and ideological thinking of the establishment in academia and policy-making.

Keynes Macroeconomic theory was born in 1936 as Keynes published his *General Theory of Employment, Interest and Money*. This book opened an era of revolution in economic theory. Before this work, macroeconomic analysis was really an extrapolation of the core neoclassical microeconomic doctrine with its faith in the notion that free markets always clear (i.e. prices are such that demand equals supply) and resources are fully utilized. There was no role for economic policy. To get things started, Keynes slapped the label of 'classical economists' on all of his predecessors.[1]

Before Keynes, classical economics asserted that the economy always tended towards full utilization of resources (thus full employment) and the best social policy was laissez-faire. They relied on a model of a barter economy that was supposed to determine equilibrium prices. A monetary theory of the price level was attached to this model almost as an afterthought, and there was no role for monetary policy. From the macroeconomic perspective, supply created its own demand owing to the fact that the sale of goods in a market is the source of income from which purchases are financed. This is called Say's Law, and it implies that there can never be a slump due to an overall deficiency in aggregate demand. If a community saved some of its income, this did not detract from total demand because savings were also spent as investment: flexibility in the interest rate maintained equilibrium between the supply and the demand for loanable funds. Finally, any slack in employment could be reabsorbed through flexibility in wages. Whatever problems emerged they had to be caused by rigidities in prices and wages that impeded the smooth operation of markets.[2] The removal of these rigidities and obstacles would ensure the automatic functioning of the system at full employment.

The Great Depression questioned this faith in the all-equilibrating virtues of markets. Keynes's contribution was at the theoretical, as well as the policy, level. He was concerned with the ugly problem of unemployment, inequality and uncertainty, and the problems posed by the stubborn presence of slumps and sharp fluctuations in aggregate activity and prices in capitalist economies. He concluded that laissez-faire led to fluctuations in employment. In addition, he emphasized the importance of aggregate demand as the key economic driver. His conclusion was that during a recession aggregate demand had to be stimulated through fiscal and monetary policies.

Keynes's work entailed a revolutionary transition towards a comprehensive monetary approach to output and employment. According to Keynes, capitalist economies are afflicted by deficient aggregate demand and involuntary unemployment exists. This deficit cannot be corrected through automatic adjustment mechanisms in the system, so government intervention is required. Monetary policy may have a role to play, but under certain circumstances government spending is required.

There are many elements in Keynes's works that are crucial to understanding the range of his revolutionary insights. For the purposes of our analysis, we need to underline three fundamental perceptions. First, uncertainty plays a central role in investment and money-holding decisions. Investment is undertaken on the basis of expectations about the future, which remains uncertain. Fundamental uncertainty is not amenable to probability calculations, and this is its essential difference compared with the notion of risk.

Second, the economy is determined by effective aggregate demand. Employment depends on demand, and, conversely, unemployment results from a deficiency of total demand. Effective demand is expressed through the spending of income. As the real income of a community increases, consumption will also increase, but by less than the increment in income. Therefore, if demand is to sustain increased employment, there needs to be an increment in investment. Employment cannot increase without the expansion of investment, which in turn depends on the interest rate and expected profitability.

The third element is that the demand for money is determined by liquidity preference: agents prefer to hold money instead of other interest-bearing assets because of the liquidity it offers. This is important in times of greater uncertainty, and thus interest is the reward for parting with liquidity. This desire of individual agents to hold liquid monetary assets can lead to situations in which effective demand is insufficient to employ all the resources in the economy.

According to Keynes, liquidity preference determines the interest rate. In periods of greater uncertainty about the future, increases in the interest rate are necessary in order to reward sacrificing unprofitable but safe cash for potentially profitable but volatile assets. This was truly a revolutionary insight that clashed with the classic view in which the interest rate is the variable that equates the demand and supply of loanable funds. The interest rate for Keynes became an exogenous variable that was determined not by 'economic forces' but by expectations and confidence or distrust in the future.

A corollary of this is that flexibility in prices (the capacity of prices to vary in accordance with demand changes) did not necessarily lead to equilibrium. In fact price flexibility could generate runaway processes of instability and could worsen a recession. For example, lower wages can generate greater unemployment because a reduction in wages means less purchasing power, greater inventories and, through the pessimistic expectations of capitalists, less investment. For Keynes wage and price stickiness is the 'classical' explanation for unemployment, to be contrasted with his explanation, in terms of the principle of effective demand, where the flexibility of wages and prices cannot automatically shift long-period equilibrium to full employment. To mainstream theorists of his day, Keynes's ideas appeared to be not only radical but dangerous.

Putting all of this together, we have the following sequence. The interest rate affects investment, the main driver of output and of the level of activity (and thus of employment). The interest rate is affected by expectations and uncertainty. Thus, nothing can guarantee that it will adjust so that the point of effective demand coincides with full employment even if wages and prices are perfectly flexible. This is an essential problem of capitalist economies, not a question of rigidities and cycles. The core message from Keynes was both simple and enormous: even with complete flexibility in prices and wages, capitalist economies could live for a long time with unemployment. State intervention was required to redress this situation. These Keynesian insights carried a message that was considered too critical for an academic establishment accustomed to the idea of well-behaved markets.

The establishment responds Very rapidly the academic establishment started to absorb the shock of the subversive side of Keynes's message by reinterpreting his theory. Working from Keynes's *General Theory*, John Hicks (1937), Franco Modigliani (1944) and Alvin Hansen (1963 [1949]) built essentially static models that translated the Keynesian vision into more palatable constructs. The resulting model was to become a commanding and simple manner of synthesizing what Hicks thought was what Keynes meant. While this view of Keynes was very successful in many circles, and soon became the new orthodoxy, it was at the price of betraying the most important perceptions in Keynes's contribution. In the famous words of Professor Joan Robinson, this was the age of 'bastard Keynesianism'.

Soon after the appearance of Keynes's general theory, John Hicks developed a new model, trying to synthesize and re-explain what Keynes really meant. The new model was very successful and was to become the mainstay of pedagogy in macroeconomics for decades. Hicks redefined Keynes's theory in several very important ways. Parts of the model maintained a resemblance with Keynes's work, but major differences were introduced surreptitiously. The main element in this model is that it shows that the goods market (i.e. where aggregate demand meets total supply of all goods and services) may be in equilibrium, and the money market (where the demand for money encounters the supply) may also be in equilibrium, but this does not need to coincide with a level of activity that is needed for full employment. Thus, a capitalist economy may exhibit the strange phenomenon whereby macroeconomic equilibrium in the goods and money sectors does not necessarily bring about full employment.

Appendix I at the end of the chapter provides a more detailed explanation of the model's structure. Readers unwilling to undertake the task of examining the model in more detail may proceed with the analysis in this chapter without any loss of generality in our argument. When the model was completed by Modigliani (1944) the picture became clearer: the level of activity associated with macroeconomic equilibrium did not necessarily coincide with the level of activity needed to bring about full employment. And because there were no mechanisms in the model that led to an adjustment process, external intervention was required to change the level of output (and employment). As pointed out, this looks rather similar to Keynes's theory, but essential modifications had surreptitiously been introduced.

This model of the aggregate economy involved separating the goods market from the money market. In the goods market, aggregate demand was explained by consumption and investment; the former depended on income and the latter on the interest rate. In equilibrium, the level of aggregate demand (the sum of consumption and investment) is sufficient to purchase the existing level of output. The interest rate was not determined within the goods market (investment was determined for a given interest rate). The goods sector in the model determined the total level of output.

As for the money market, supply of money was determined exogenously by the central bank, while demand was determined by the need for transactions and by liquidity preference. The transactions motive for demanding money was determined for a given level of income. Thus, for a given level of output, the money sector in the model determined the interest rate.[3]

With reference to the model as presented in Appendix I, in equilibrium, investment was equal to savings, thus the first component of the model was labelled IS. This can be represented in a graph where the vertical axis corresponds to the interest rate and the horizontal axis to levels of output. On the IS line every point is an equilibrium between total demand and total supply (output), and it is downward sloping because, as the interest rate increases, the level of investment decreases and output is reduced.

On the other hand, in equilibrium liquidity preference was such that the demand for money was equal to money supply, and this part of the model was branded LM. A line representing equilibrium between supply and demand of money can also be represented by a line in the same graph, and this line will be upward sloping because as the level of output increases, the demand for money will rise.

The reader may refer to Appendix I for a more technical explanation. But only two crucial points need to be retained. The first is that the level of economic activity that corresponds to the equilibrium in the goods market and the money market does not need to coincide with full employment. The second point is that macroeconomic policies can have an effect on the level of activity, and thus on the level of employment.

The IS–LM model was to be the most successful machine of economic pedagogy, in part because it allowed in a very schematic presentation an examination of how changes in monetary and fiscal policy could affect the level of activity (and employment) in the economy. But it also showed how in some cases monetary policy would not be an effective tool to affect the level of activity. For example, a drop in the interest rate may fail to induce greater investment because entrepreneurs harbour very negative expectations about the future and, no matter how low the interest rate may be, new investments will not be forthcoming.[4]

Because this model is a way of approaching the question of scale of the economy, this aspect of the IS–LM model attracted the attention of researchers concerned with Professor Daly's plea. The IS–LM model was to become a tool for the introduction of environmental concerns in macroeconomics.

The neoclassical synthesis Once the IS–LM framework had crystallized in a system of simultaneous (equilibrium) equations, the stage was set to conclude that Keynes's system was compatible with the results of general equilibrium macroeconomics. Keynes's subversive side had been eviscerated.

Samuelson helped consolidate what became known as the neoclassical synthesis, a model of simultaneous equations in which Keynesian insights and neoclassical theory would blend in a 'harmonic' way.[5] In this synthesis authors like Hicks, Samuelson and Modigliani reformulated Keynesian ideas and concluded that only assumptions concerning flexibility of prices and wages differed. Thus, both the classic and the Keynesian results were valid, but were related to different time horizons. Classic results were obtained in the long run, when markets were supposed to converge to equilibrium. The Keynesian scheme was valid in the short run, when rigidities and inertias play a role and unemployment is not reabsorbed. Economic policy had a role to play only in the short run.[6]

In the complete 'Keynesian model' the intersections of the IS and LM schedules do not necessarily coincide with a position of full employment. However, because the labour market in this model remained broadly similar to the classical labour market, as long as money wages and prices were assumed to be flexible it could be shown that the complete model would, over time, tend towards a single position of equilibrium and full employment. Because the IS–LM model tended to yield results that were closer to (classical) full employment, neo-Keynesians appealed to the notion of rigid monetary wages in order to generate 'unemployment equilibrium'. In the 1950s 'Keynesian' macroeconomists believed that unemployment equilibrium could only be interpreted as a case of rigid money wages. But justifying rigid money wages was not easy, although there were many who relied on market imperfections and monetary illusion. These 'imperfections' of the system were obstacles to the natural tendency of the system to self-equilibrate and were the justification for macroeconomic policy.

Summing up, the neoclassical synthesis implied that in the long run the IS–LM model would yield 'classical' results, while in the short run 'Keynesian' results would ensue and macroeconomic policies would be justified. In other words, in the short run the economy could very well reach a Keynesian equilibrium (i.e. equilibrium with involuntary unemployment). In those cases, intervention through stabilizing economic policies was desirable. In the long run, economies converge to equilibrium positions through the price adjustment mechanisms that were supposed to be perfectly flexible.

From the Phillips curve to rational expectations The Keynesian analysts following in the tradition of Hicks, Modigliani and Samuelson had to assume rigid wages in order to prevent their model from yielding classical results (i.e. the labour market would reabsorb unemployment). The problem for these authors was how to justify the assumption about holding wages rigid. After all, this was contrary to what Keynes had attempted to do. The work of Alban Phillips provided an answer.

The Phillips curve had established an empirical inverse relation between inflation and unemployment: increments in the price level coexisted with a fall in unemployment. This permitted the establishment of a relation between money wages and unemployment, which is what 'Keynesian' authors had been seeking to establish.

The Phillips curve became a central component of modelling and macroeconomic policy. Macroeconomic models were now endowed with wage and price sectors that indicated major trade-offs between the rate of inflation and the level of activity (and employment). Typically models would show that the effect of reducing the long-run rate of inflation would be an increase in the unemployment rate. The nature of the trade-off between inflation and unemployment became central to macroeconomic policy and modelling. The Phillips trade-off appeared to hold remarkably well.

During the seventies, however, the old classical views concerning the impossibility of 'Keynesian solutions' regained importance. One reason was that stagnation and inflation coexisted for several years, bringing down the edifice built around the Phillips curve trade-off between unemployment and inflation. This had been the culmination of the 'Keynesian' neoclassical synthesis and had led to the conclusion that government policy could accommodate itself around the objectives of less unemployment but higher inflation, or vice versa. This meant there was plenty of room for macroeconomic policy. But the contradiction between the Phillips curve and empirical reality opened the door to a more fundamental critique of 'Keynesian' macroeconomics. The academic establishment that had always distrusted the Keynesian insights about unstable capitalist economies was ready to launch a counter-revolution.

At first, monetarism appeared to threaten the neoclassical synthesis because it criticized the basic aspects of the synthesis, especially the notion that fiscal policy was effective, as well as the structural stability of the Phillips curve. It also insisted on the stability in the behaviour of private sector agents. But monetarism shared some important aspects of the synthesis, in particular that the source of instability (or the business cycle) was price stickiness. The Lucas critique of macroeconomic policy and the introduction of rational expectations into macroeconomics led to a broader questioning of the synthesis.

Rational expectations In the 1970s Robert Lucas and Thomas Sargent developed a model based on their 'rational expectations' hypothesis and introduced a new critique of Keynesian economics as expressed in the neoclassical synthesis. Under the premises of their work, economic agents develop expectations in a 'rational' way about the evolution of the economic variables that affect their behaviour. By this they meant that agents have access to all the available information, as well as to the relations that the theoretical model itself established for these variables. In other words, these agents would never get it wrong and would always act as if they knew what the model would predict because their expectations were formed along the same lines. The consequence of this rational-expectations assumption is that economic policy measures, perfectly anticipated by agents, have no effect and are useless. Thus, even in the short run there was no room for macroeconomic stabilizing policies.

Once price expectations were incorporated into the analysis, Lucas and Sargent reached the conclusion that the trade-off existed in the short run only. In the long run there was a unique unemployment rate, the natural rate of unemployment (NRU), compatible with any inflation rate. The NRU corresponds to the level of unemployment that exists when markets are in equilibrium: it is a frictional and structural sort of unemployment. According to Friedman (1968), 'the natural rate of unemployment is the level that would be ground out by the Walrasian system of general equilibrium equations'. In this context, stabilization policies would be unable to have any effect on activity rates. Later, in the seventies, the application of the rational-expectations hypothesis extended this conclusion to the short term: unemployment would differ from its natural rate only in the case of unanticipated circumstances and, thus, stabilization policies systematically implemented would be perfectly anticipated and understood by agents, making them ineffective. This is why this assumption is called the policy ineffectiveness proposition: if governments wanted to manipulate output (for example, if they thought the environment was being damaged beyond the limits of sustainability), agents would foresee the effects of the policies being implemented (for example, monetary expansion) and would revise their wage and price expectations accordingly. Real wages and prices would remain constant and there would be no effects on the real economy. Output would remain constant.[7]

In the eighties and nineties several publications contested this view and questioned the idea that fluctuations were due only to errors and imperfectly anticipated events. Market failures were singled out as the driver of fluctuations. Gregory Mankiw, Olivier Blanchard and Joseph Stiglitz were among the most well-known contributors to what came to be known as the 'New Keynesian' macroeconomics. The importance of market failures would provide the microeconomic foundations for the behavioural functions at the aggregate level. Special attention was focused on the processes that determine wages and prices, because the main premise here was that their rigidity led to the large-scale fluctuations in the level of activity.[8]

Mainstream macroeconomics today Mainstream macroeconomics was caught sleeping at the helm when the global financial crisis struck in 2008. And even as the crisis unfolded, it revealed that the academic establishment had little to show in terms of policy recipes. Over the previous two decades, macroeconomic theory had seen a revival of the position championed by pre-Keynesian classical authors. Serious problems, such as aggregation or the micro-foundations of macroeconomics, had been an opportunity to go back to the most simplistic (and erroneous) of solutions. The notion that there existed a 'representative agent' that behaves like a textbook agent, optimizing with perfect foresight, is an absurd construct, but one that has been used widely in mainstream macroeconomic models seeking to provide micro-foundations to macro theory.[9]

In the 1990s a 'new neoclassical synthesis' was born with a new strand of research in macroeconomics. The central question behind this research programme is a typical question of decentralized markets and corresponds to the framework of general equilibrium theory. In the new models (called Dynamic Stochastic General Equilibrium or DSGE models), the macroeconomic problem is simplified and becomes the optimization problem of representative households and firms. These representative agents optimize inter-temporal utility and profit functions. The models are capable of determining a solution using rational-expectations hypotheses. But they need the introduction of several heavyweight assumptions in order to avoid disruptive events that prevent the model from yielding well-behaved trajectories.

In this new consensus, the New Keynesians adopted the DSGE model, while the new classics embraced the set of frictions and stickiness of markets that characterizes the old synthesis of half a century ago. Thus, in the DSGE the economy behaves like a stable general equilibrium system whose self-regulating properties are hampered by frictions and imperfections. As in the first synthesis, the capitalist system is assumed to be a set of stable and self-equilibrating markets in spite of the fact that there is simply no scientific or rational foundation for this 'intuitively appealing' belief (see Box 1.1 in the previous chapter). As a result, all sources of instability are left aside. Macroeconomics is now squarely based on perfect foresight, infinite time optimization and universal perfect competition. Thus although macroeconomics began with the study of large-scale pathologies, in these new models there is simply no room for them: pathologies became unthinkable (Hahn and Solow 1997).

From a policy perspective, agents in a DSGE model are not passive and they respond by adjusting their actions to take expected policy into account. The most important policy prescription that emerges from this is inflation targeting, whereby a central bank announces an inflation target and adjusts interest rates to achieve its goal. In DSGE models, this allows agents to base their dynamic optimization on firmer ground, as inflation targeting helps coordinate individual decisions.

During the nineties, the real world of macroeconomic policy-making remained exclusively committed to controlling inflation. The mantra from macroeconomic theory was that use of a central bank's power and resources to affect real variables such as output and employment would have, at best, transitory effects, and at worst undesirable consequences. As for fiscal policy, this had already been pronounced useless by previous debates. So macroeconomic policy was seen as a passive set of priorities and tools, largely determined by the assumptions of self-equilibrating markets. Mainstream macroeconomic theory has largely erred in the direction of assuming that markets do possess this ability to stabilize and converge to equilibrium positions. And macroeconomic theory became dominated by the idea that when this does not occur, it is because of rigidities and lack of price flexibility.

The nineties were a (false) placid era in which neoliberal economists chanted hymns to the 'Great Moderation' and the passing away of the brutal shocks of severe business cycles. Even the long string of financial crises in that decade was not enough to alert them to the eruption brewing inside the volcano of financial liberalization. This shouldn't be a surprise: for mainstream theory this crisis shouldn't even be happening.

Post-Keynesians As the academic establishment was trying to domesticate what were considered to be the more subversive Keynesian insights, a group of macroeconomists insisted that what was being presented as 'Keynesianism' was in fact a misrepresentation of Keynes's work and of the revolutionary contents of his analysis. According to these economists, this distortion marks the neoclassical synthesis, as well as the 'Keynesian' and New Keynesian schools that have dominated mainstream economic thought.[10]

There has been considerable debate as to what really qualifies to be classified as 'post-Keynesian' analysis. Some key features of post-Keynesian analysis are the following (Lavoie 2006; Tily 2007). First, aggregate demand is not always sufficient to ensure full employment. The principle of effective demand is critical in the short and long run, so that economic policy may be required to increase aggregate demand.

Second, post-Keynesians emphasize the difference between historical and logical time. Historical time is irreversible. One implication here is that equilibrium positions are path-dependent. This leads to the need to develop dynamic models capable of dealing with the evolution through time of stocks of physical assets, financial wealth and the productive structure of the economy.

Third, flexible prices do not necessarily lead to equilibrium. The most important feature of post-Keynesian authors is their vision that a competitive market economy does not possess self-equilibrating mechanisms leading to full employment. Disequilibrium and unemployment are not mere consequences of pathologies, but the result of the essential dynamics of capitalist economies.

In some cases, price flexibility may bring about runaway processes that guide the economy away from (hypothetical) equilibrium. The best example of this is the classical idea that flexibility in wages is part of an equilibrating mechanism that brings about full employment. For post-Keynesians, a reduction in wages does not necessarily induce greater demand for labour because this causes a reduction in effective demand, burdening firms with greater debt and bigger inventories.

Fourth, the role of uncertainty is critical. Uncertainty means that it is impossible to calculate the probability of an event taking place or the possible outcomes of a particular situation. This means that the future is not amenable to probabilistic calculations of risk, but is rather unpredictable. The world is non-ergodic (i.e. one cannot use ensemble statistics to make inferences about particular situations). This has profound implications for Keynesian theory in terms of liquidity preference, expectations (or Keynes's 'animal spirits'), investment and rationality.

Fifth, post-Keynesian analysis takes into account income distribution as an important element of macroeconomics. It also admits that income distribution is socially determined. In other words, post-Keynesian macroeconomics does not take wages and profits to be determined by the marginal contribution to output of labour and capital.

One of the most important examples of post-Keynesian analysis is that provided by Hyman Minsky (1992). His work has now been rediscovered because in many ways he was one of those who had analysed how financial crises develop in capitalist economies. For him, the financial system is essentially unstable. It operates while giving the impression that it is stable, but it is continuously generating the conditions for crisis. For Minsky, instability is an essential trait of capitalist economies. This is of course a far cry from the well-behaved markets of mainstream macroeconomics.

There are several important lessons that we can derive from looking into the evolution of macroeconomic theory. The first is that we need to fully grasp the complexities of a monetary economy (or what Keynes called the 'monetary theory of production'), and in particular how money is created in modern economies with a fully developed banking system. The second is that this will help us understand how monetary factors affect both the short term and the long term. The third is that unless we have a clear understanding of the rate of interest (its nature and how it is determined) we will not be able to fully grasp its impact on economic activity and the environment. Finally, we need to be aware of the fact that capitalist economies do not possess mechanisms that lead to either balanced growth or equilibrium positions. Capitalist economies are not endowed with self-regulating capabilities that lead to a long-run equilibrium. The corollary is that there is a need for state intervention in order to stabilize the economy.

Macroeconomic policy and the environment

In 1991 Herman Daly published an article pleading for an environmental macroeconomics (Daly 2002). The response within the school of ecological economics has been limited to the use of the conventional IS–LM model examined above, the argument being that this is the workhorse model in macroeconomics (Daly and Farley 2004: 278; Lawn 2003: 119). It is more accurate to say it was the Trojan horse from which the effort to distort and recover Keynesian theory was launched by the establishment. Perhaps the choice is guided because the IS–LM model allows for a very schematic presentation of how fiscal and monetary policies affect the level of activity of an economy. Because the main concern of ecological economics is the scale of activity of an entire economy, it was natural to think of the IS–LM construct to see how policies can maintain the level of activity near the level of environmental sustainability.

While it is certainly true that the IS–LM model was very successful in the past, it is less used today, in part because it has attracted severe criticism from all quarters. Clearly the IS–LM model is plagued by serious problems that do not make it the best choice to start integrating the environment with macroeconomics.

Thampapillai (1995) was the first author to try to assimilate the environment into a macroeconomic model by defining an environmental cost function and projecting it on to a conventional IS–LM model. The model is used to try to identify how policies might be used to alter the IS–LM equilibrium in order to attain a position that maintains 'the assimilative capacity of the environment' (ibid.: 49). The issue is how macroeconomic policies can be used to attain a position of environmental equilibrium.

The analysis begins by presenting the case of an economy in which the equilibrium of the goods and money markets corresponds to a level of economic activity exceeding the limit determined by the environmental cost function. At this equilibrium point, the level of activity does not have to coincide with a level of activity needed to maintain full employment, but Thampapillai is making another point: that equilibrium is associated with a level of activity that surpasses the point of assimilative capacity for the environment. In this case, the level of activity has to be cut back through restrictive fiscal or monetary policies, or both. In the first case, taxes can be raised and expenditures cut back. In fact, taxes could be imposed on polluters and other agents that negatively affect the integrity of ecosystems, forcing them to internalize the environmental costs. A restrictive monetary policy could also be implemented. Because of higher taxes and a tight monetary policy, the level of activity would be reduced, returning the economy to the level of environmental sustainability. If the economy is operating at a level that is below the limit determined by the environmental cost function, expansionary policies can be used because the economy would be operating at a scale that is not optimizing the use of resources to full capacity.

Heyes (2000) and Lawn (2003) use a modified IS–LM model to examine how monetary and fiscal policies affect the environment. The philosophical approach is the same (returning to the limits to growth), but their method differs from Thampapillai's because they introduce the environmental restriction directly as a curve of environmental equilibrium, EE, as in Figure 2.3 of Appendix I. Each point of this EE curve corresponds to a situation in which the wear-and-tear effect on the environment is being restored. In the EE curve the rate at which the economy is using the natural resource base or the environment is equal to its resilience. A key assumption is that new capital-intensive technologies are better suited to achieving this result. Thus, in this model this means that at lower interest rates the scale of activities in the economy can be increased because cleaner technologies are being used. (This is compatible with the IS–LM approach in which lower interest rates bring forth more investment.)

In a nutshell, the EE curve is introduced into the IS–LM model to show how monetary and fiscal policies can return the economy to a position of environmental equilibrium. Here the scale of the economy depends not only on the absolute size of the population and its consumption rate, but also on the technology being used. Traditional fiscal and monetary policies can set the economy on a scale that is compatible with environmental equilibrium.

The model assumes that when interest rates decrease, capital becomes cheaper and new, more capital-intensive technologies that are more efficient in their use of natural resources will be introduced. But this is not enough to ensure that the economy continues to operate at environmental equilibrium. Other policy instruments are required to force firms to internalize the environmental costs associated with their activities. Lawn (2003: 126) suggests tradable resource permits and pollution taxes.

Daly and Farley (2004: 302) adopt a different approach to the use of an IS–LM model. First they assume it is possible to calculate the throughput intensity per unit of output. Second, they also assume it is possible to estimate the *maximum ecologically sustainable level of output*. This can then be imposed as an external (physical) constraint.

The new physical restriction is introduced into the model through a vertical line, EC (for 'ecological capacity'). Each point on the vertical line EC is a 'biophysical equilibrium': given the technology used in the economy, the line EC denotes the balance between usage and extraction rates, and the capacity of the environment to replace used materials and restore the health of ecosystems. The points on the EC line are ignored by the actors whose behaviour 'is captured in the IS–LM curves' (ibid.: 302).

Three possibilities are examined. First, equilibrium in the goods and money markets coincides with the biophysical equilibrium. As Daly and Farley state, this would be a great coincidence, for there is no adjustment mechanism operating in the economy that would lead to this result. Second, if the goods and money markets' equilibrium is associated with a level of activity that is below the level of biophysical equilibrium, the economy can grow without damaging the environment. Finally, if the equilibrium of goods and the money markets is linked to a level of activity that is bigger than the level associated with biophysical equilibrium, then the real sector is eating away the natural resource base and 'natural capital' consumption is being counted as income (ibid.: 303). This is another view of the problem of national accounts that consider the destruction of the environment as something that contributes to 'growth'.

Efforts to integrate the environment with macroeconomic theory and policy are a step in the right direction. However, grafting ad hoc assumptions about scale and throughput into existing models that are well known for their deficiencies is not the right way to proceed. The use of the IS–LM model by the authors we have commented on above is a good example. Already the IS–LM model entails serious problems given its analytical mission. These problems are compounded by the incorporation of a notion of environmental equilibrium and sustainability. Their analysis is important if we are to make any progress in blending social and environmental sustainability with macroeconomic policies.

The first difficulty in using the IS–LM model is that it was built to show that equilibrium in the goods and money sectors of a capitalist economy coexists with unemployment. This is not corrected by self-adjustment mechanisms. Thus macroeconomic policy interventions are required to set the economy at a level of activity compatible with full employment. If this point of equilibrium unemployment coincides with a position in which the level of activity is greater than the point of assimilative capacity or of biophysical equilibrium, macroeconomic policies would be used to return the economy to a level of activity compatible with environmental equilibrium. But what would happen to the level of unemployment that existed in the economy? It could worsen, and in that case any benefits from the environmental standpoint would have been achieved at the expense of greater inequality and poverty. Clearly, this would not take an economy any closer to sustainability.[11]

The second problem with the IS–LM model relates to several specific traits of its dynamics. This is essentially an equilibrium model: it serves to show how equilibrium in the goods and money markets coexists with unemployment. The model cannot say anything about the adjustment processes that lead to equilibrium in these sectors. In fact, it may even be possible to argue that the substratum of this model is a neoclassical general equilibrium model.[12] Lawn (2003: 125) states that 'natural forces already exist to ensure that the macroeconomy adjusts towards the IS and LM curves'. This is an unjustified leap of faith. The implications are important: the model may provide a set of snapshots of a hypothetical economy, one for every combination of levels of output and for a given interest rate. But it does not explain how the economy actually moves from one point to another. This may not be irrelevant for the analysis of sustainability.

Not knowing anything about the adjustment process can be a convenient expedient, depending on the questions the model is supposed to clarify. But if we want to relate macroeconomic policy to environmental sustainability, the adjustment process may be of critical importance. Among other things it would be interesting to know whether fiscal and monetary policies would be effective. Situations in which monetary policy is ineffective do exist and are more than a theoretical curiosity. If the interest rate is already very low (or zero) the central bank may increase money in circulation but this will have no impact on output or prices.[13] On the other hand, fiscal policy may have important distributional effects, causing greater inequality or promoting a better income distribution pattern. Assuming that income distribution remains unaltered can be very misleading, as the analysis of structural adjustment programmes reveals.

The third problem is related to the obsession with the limits-to-growth approach to sustainability. This not only eliminates crucial aspects of macroeconomic policy, it also entails a very naive way of dealing with the environment. In this approach, the words 'environmental sustainability' are used as a synonym of 'scale of production'. Notions like aggregate biophysical equilibrium constitute a very crude assumption. The environment is multidimensional and it is not possible to assess all of its components by a homogeneous unit of measure.

But more important than the question of a unit of measure, the difficulty is that the different dimensions of the environment can move in opposite directions. At the aggregate level, the notion of 'more environmentally benign technologies' is devoid of any sense. For example, soil erosion, suspended particulates, species extinction and depletion of aquifers may all be moving in different directions and at quite different rates. Also, movement in one direction for some of these components may also vary as we move from one region to another in the same economy. Can the improvement in the health and resilience of one ecosystem in one region compensate for the weakening or even the destruction in another region? Here we encounter the same criticism addressed in Chapter 1 to the environmental Kuznets curve.

The assumption that more capital-intensive technologies are more environmentally friendly is absurd. Although it matches the nature of the model, it contradicts almost everything we know about the exploitation of natural resources. The disaster involving British Petroleum's Deepwater Horizon rig in the Gulf of Mexico was caused by a highly capital-intensive technology. The assumption is tantamount to claiming that the huge trawlers and factory ships that are depleting the world's fisheries are better suited for environmental conservation. Are the purse-seiners that operate in the tuna fisheries of the world, guided by GPS and using powerful sonars to locate their prey, better adapted to maintaining the sustainability of those living marine resources? Or, to provide yet another example, it's as if mountaintop removal and strip mining, which are capital-intensive methods in the mining industry, were considered ecologically benign in spite of the damage they inflict on people's livelihoods and the environment. Clearly, if we want to move in the right direction, we have to get away from the assumption that the nature of the model we want to use is more important than the facts.[14]

New Keynesian macroeconomics and the environment Mäler and Munasinghe (1996) recognize that economy-wide policies have much more powerful environmental effects than mere project-level investments. However, the impacts of broad macroeconomic reforms on natural resource and pollution management are far more difficult to trace, therefore hampering efforts to design better sustainable development strategies. Their analytical framework to trace the environmental impacts of macroeconomic policies assumes that markets allocate resources efficiently, except when there are rigidities. The key example is the labour market, where price stickiness prevents 'automatic equilibration and there may be unemployment or excess demand for labour with ensuing inflationary pressures'. The adjustment process needs the help of monetary policies: 'with unemployment, an increase in money supply would tend to increase all monetary prices of goods services outside the labour market, while nominal wages would remain unchanged'. The result would be a fall in the real price of labour and this would lead to full employment (ibid.). The environment is introduced through another distortion in the economy, namely in the market for environmental resources. The distortion here takes the form of an externality due to ill-defined property rights. This leads to an over-exploitation of natural resources that calls for macroeconomic policies.

The model used by Mäler and Munasinghe (ibid.) is a general equilibrium model with a representative consumer and a representative producer. In this model agents value real balances for several reasons (especially transaction costs) and the demand for such balances is determined by prices, wealth and initial balance. Finally, the representative producer emits pollutants that are taxed by the government in order to force firms to internalize the environmental cost. The analysis shows that 'if it is not possible to optimize the allocation rule regarding the environment, it is not optimal to try to achieve first-best macroeconomic policies' (ibid.: 163). In this context, if it is not possible to determine the optimal environmental policy, then it is not optimal to try to attain full employment.

Mäler and Munasinghe pose an interesting question, but their theoretical approach leaves much to be desired because there is no true macroeconomic problem in a general equilibrium setting unless one assumes some kind of distortion in one or more sectors (which is what Mäler and Munasinghe do). Apart from this case, there is no room for maladjustments or crises. Also, the use of a representative agent is most unfortunate as it boils down to having an economy with a single agent. Although this abstraction may allow people to hide the ugly problems surrounding aggregation, it reduces the scope of the model to a very particular case. Finally, in this model all environmental problems arise from ill-defined property rights and market failures. This is an erroneous view of how environmental problems arise and shows the commitment of these authors to neoclassical general equilibrium theory (see Box 1.1).

An additional issue pertains to the role of money in these models. Hahn (1965) and Arrow and Hahn (1971) have shown that this is an important problem in general equilibrium theory because fiat money is devoid of any use value. General equilibrium models are condemned to be non-monetary models, unless deep theoretical difficulties are swept under the rug. Relying on a 'macroeconomic' model that rests on Walrasian assumptions of instantaneous price adjustments that clear all markets[15] and in which money is present is an awkward procedure.[16]

There have been other attempts to study the relation between macroeconomic policies and the environment. For example, Abaza (1995) concludes that structural adjustment programmes (SAPs) may have significant negative implications for the environment because substitution effects may bring about important export-oriented biases with negative environmental effects. Deforestation may expand livestock production but at a very high environmental cost. Export crops may be more profitable, but may tend to rely more on mono-crops, damaging soils and agro-biodiversity. In addition, changes in public expenditure and in relative prices may also have adverse distribution effects, hurting the poor and leading them to put more pressure on the scant land resources that they own. But other case studies conclude that, in general, some of the main features of SAPs (such as the removal of price distortions or the promotion of market incentives) lead 'generally' to favourable environmental effects (Munasinghe and Cruz 1994).

One crucial problem when focusing on SAPs is that the analysis is limited to a particular phase of macroeconomic policy-making. This is the moment of reforms when getting out of a crisis. It's as if the relation between the casino being operated in your neighbourhood and the environment was limited to the day it was ablaze and the fire department came along. Extinguishing the conflagration would certainly have important effects for the environment, but we must also ask whether before and after the inferno there are other long-term, deep negative environmental consequences. If so, we need to establish the causality relations, the lines of transmission and the way in which we can remedy the situation.

Key issues for environmental macroeconomics

Developing a macroeconomic policy framework for sustainability will not be an easy task. Several key issues need to be tackled and a solid theoretical foundation needs to be worked out. Concentrating on a 'limits to growth' perspective or on frictions and rigidities ignores critical issues and constrains the analysis to a very narrow field. These narrow approaches will not help us understand how we can design and implement a better macroeconomic policy setting for sustainability. From this perspective, the most relevant frame of reference is provided by post-Keynesian macroeconomics. The following paragraphs contain a checklist of lessons we need to consider as a first approximation in an attempt to develop an environmental macroeconomics.

Capitalism: socially determined and unstable Capitalist economies are historically determined social systems. They are not natural in any sense of the word, certainly not in the sense that they are the culmination of an evolutionary social process. Economic theory claims that capitalism is the natural way of organizing production and consumption. But this 'denies its specificity and the long and painful processes that brought it into being, limiting our understanding of the past' (Meiksins Wood 2002). It also hampers our efforts to recognize opportunities for change through macroeconomic policies.

Market economies are not the same as capitalism. In fact, capitalist relations help undermine markets and eventually destroy people's livelihoods, which are intimately related to local and regional markets. Both markets and capitalism are social systems lacking any inherent tendency towards equilibrium. Their evolution is marked by instability and crises. Any exercise in macroeconomic policy for sustainability has to recognize these facts right from the starting point, abandoning the obsession with 'equilibrium' and the fallacy of efficient allocation of resources by market forces.

Growth is an essential feature of capitalist economies. It is not the result of some manic inclination or an addiction. Growth is driven by endogenous forces that are the essence of capitalism. Marx (1973) shows that capital cannot exist except as separated spheres that act as private centres of capital accumulation. From the perspective of production, inter-capitalist competition is a fratricidal struggle that forces each individual accumulation centre of capital to grow or perish. From the standpoint of consumption, spending and using stuff being produced is critical to prevent the system from collapsing. This is why low growth rates are a problem and receive the names of recessions and crises. Anyone thinking about the macroeconomics of no-growth, de-growth or steady-state economies needs to understand this important fact. Capital understands no limits to its quest for accumulation. It is better to start thinking, as Smith (2010) points out, about a true macroeconomic alternative to the fantasy of no-growth capitalism.

Income distribution and classes are important Markets may determine prices, but they do not ensure that income distribution is equitable. And in macroeconomics there is no automatic adjustment that leads to just and fair income distribution patterns. Under capitalism, active intervention is required to achieve this.

Rethinking macroeconomics for sustainability has to avoid using the same abstractions about the economy as a whole. After all, in a capitalist society there are classes, inequality and poverty. At the very least, there is a distributional conflict in capitalist societies, and any attempt to think about macroeconomic policies for sustainability has to recognize this. Energy and materials consumption patterns of high-income brackets put greater pressure on the environment than the poorest groups. On the other hand, when the social fabric of poor communities is destroyed (by forced migration, for example), they may have to abandon labour-intensive practices that are more environmentally friendly and resort to putting greater pressure on their resources (soils, biodiversity). Distinguishing between social groups is critical in the use of macroeconomic policies.

Income distribution is not determined by the contribution of each person or group to social product. This is an old and discredited view: productivity does not determine wages and the 'labour market' is not like any other market, as mainstream economics claims. Indeed, as Galbraith (2000: 265–6) points out, there's no such thing as a labour market, 'an entity that no one has ever seen, where no one has ever been, an entity that lacks the mechanisms of price adjustment that would be required for the marginal productivity theory to work'. Of course, this has vast implications for macroeconomics: incomes' policy is not determined by a technical constraint, but by power relations.[17] This is indeed the lesson of the compression of wages that started in the seventies.

Money matters The economic forces driving environmental destruction are determined by social relations with a monetary expression. Understanding the role of money in production and investment is essential to understanding the way in which macroeconomic policies might be used for sustainability. The expansion of the financial sector over the past three decades is one of the most important features of the world economy. Capital flows dwarf economies and multilateral financial institutions like the IMF. They have a decisive impact on economic structures and income distribution. It is urgent to incorporate them into the analysis of environmental macroeconomics.

Georgescu Roegen's admonitions about the Second Law of Thermodynamics led the school of ecological economics to conclude that the main problem with neoclassical or mainstream economics is its inability to deal with materials flows. This is not true. Neoclassical economics abounds with examples in which physical flows of materials are at the centre of the analysis (see Kandelaars 1999; Ibenholt 2002). In fact, it is the other way around. Conventional economic theory starts by abstracting from money and then constructing a value theory to restore a unit of measure. It then develops a theory of markets and relative prices. Only then does it attempt to integrate money back into the analysis without much success. The terms of this problem are well defined and to this day remain without a satisfactory solution (see Benetti 2004; Hahn 1965). An environmental macroeconomics should not repeat the same mistake.

Ignoring endogenous finance and monetary flows is perhaps the most serious flaw of macroeconomic models (those belonging to the school of ecological economics are no exception). As Lance Taylor (2004: 258) says, 'the trouble with most macroeconomic models of finance is that they don't let anything interesting happen'. They have no room for financial innovation, and they have no important feedbacks between the financial and the real sectors of the economy.

Materials flows may provide measurements of pressure on an ecosystem, but they will never explain the economic forces behind this pressure. This does not mean that material flows analysis is not useful. In examining how international trade helps displace environmental costs, this type of analysis is particularly useful (Muradian et al. 2001; Muradian and Martínez Alier 2001). But in macroeconomic analysis, money plays a key role in transmission mechanisms and in adjustment processes.

Aggregation This is a problem intimately connected with the issue of scale of an economy. Although it may be tempting to assume that macro variables can be determined starting from many utility-maximizing individuals, it is well known that simple aggregation is not acceptable. The proposition according to which the properties of an aggregate function will reflect those of the individual functions has no theoretical foundations. The implication from this is that it is not possible to say anything about scale if you believe that *macroeconomic* actions are the result of optimizing decisions by agents. This is not only a theoretical question, it is also an empirical issue: aggregating heterogeneous agents is inappropriate. Ignoring this will generate spurious statements on scale (Delli Gatti et al. 2000). Through the notion of a 'representative agent' mainstream macroeconomic theory assumes away the problems of aggregation (Hartley 1997). An environmental macroeconomics cannot make the same mistake.

Macroeconomic theory and policy work with homogeneous aggregates. This is their strength and their weakness. The strength stems from the fact that economy-wide variables (for example, the exchange rate) can have a very decisive impact on all agents in the economy and cause an adjustment to take place. But it also becomes a weakness when only the final result of an aggregate account is taken into consideration (for example, the fiscal balance). Clearly, the structure of aggregate accounts is an important item that demands careful consideration. This may have many environmental implications: for example, if a fiscal surplus is attained through cuts in social and environmental spending. Finally, the macroeconomics of sustainability requires disaggregating and restoring some heterogeneity to macroeconomic variables. This can be done through regulatory interventions.

Uncertainty Uncertainty plays a major role in the dynamics of capitalist economies. Uncertainty is not the same as risk. Uncertainty is not amenable to any kind of probabilistic risk assessment because there simply aren't enough elements to carry out this exercise. It is a critically important dimension of capitalist economies. It affects liquidity preference and investment decisions and has important implications for aggregate demand and employment.

Uncertainty generates instability in investment portfolios and financial relations. This in turn brings about deep variations and cycles in the evolution of important aggregates such as investment. From the viewpoint of expectations formation, uncertainty is closely related to processes in which history and irreversibility are important. When a process is path dependent, choices made on the basis of transitory conditions can persist long after those conditions change. Under these conditions expectations formation can become a highly unstable process with negative effects on investment decisions.

In evolution and social processes 'history matters'. Environmental irreversibility is a frequent phenomenon that can be found at the scale of a single species, or in entire ecosystems. A macroeconomics for sustainability needs to take this into account instead of pretending that 'natural capital' can be replaced by 'man-made capital'.

Realistic 'microeconomics' A relevant macroeconomic approach to sustainability requires a new and more realistic view of how individual agents operate. Not only do we need to reconsider the fact that there is no such thing as perfect competition (in which no firm has control over prices), but we need to understand how prices are formed when we are confronted with oligopolistic markets. The role of multinational corporations, whether in the extractive industries, manufacturing or finance, is something we cannot sweep under the rug in order to build a well-behaved model. These corporations are at the centre of economic life, and their economic power often translates into investment projects that destroy people's livelihoods and damage the environment. Today, it is no exaggeration to say that macroeconomic policy is geared to the needs of the interest groups behind these mega-corps. Many of these corporations go around doing more or less what they feel is needed in their self-aggrandizing projects without any monitoring or supervision. The case of British Petroleum in its operations in the Gulf of Mexico or Alaska could be an example among many others. Macroeconomics needs an approach to 'microeconomics' that recognizes the role of these agents. We return to this point in our final chapter.

Time horizons Macroeconomic policy appears to be almost entirely focused on a short-run time horizon. The issues it addresses are more related to stabilization problems and they require rapid action. In many instances, the effects of macroeconomic policies are very short lived; in some cases these effects last one or two years (for example, a fiscal stimulus). The importance of the financial sector in today's capitalist economies accentuates this as short-term considerations come to predominate in decision-making. For example, frequently the performance of fund managers is judged exclusively on the basis of short-term returns of fund assets.

The problems that are of relevance to environmental stewardship are usually (very) long-term problems. An environmental macroeconomics needs to look at this difference in time horizons and integrate it in a meaningful way into the analysis. The relation between green national accounts and standard national accounts needs to be examined in light of these discrepancies in time horizons.

Concluding remarks

Developing a macroeconomic policy framework compatible with social and environmental sustainability remains an important task. Much remains to be done, not only at the theoretical level, but also in analysing the actual workings of the policy framework currently implemented in the developed and developing countries. Macroeconomic policy for open economies under neoliberal globalization was supposed to bring about greater stability, growth and efficiency gains. Under the Kuznets curve hypothesis, this would lead to a significant improvement in environmental health. However, the neoliberal policy mix failed to deliver these results. Greater volatility in financial markets has dominated the economic landscape as international financial crises followed one another in rapid succession. By the end of the nineties, it became clear that greater volatility had not bought improved economic performance in terms of growth.[18]

Can the dominant model of macroeconomic policy work in the future and contribute to sustainable development? The answer is no. From the purely economic standpoint, the neoliberal policy model as implemented in many developing countries has several important built-in contradictions between policy objectives and instruments.[19] For example, although flexible exchange rates are considered a key element in balancing external economic relations, there are built-in rigidities that prevent timely exchange rate adjustments (capital flows and anti-inflationary objectives lead typically to exchange rate overvaluations). Another example is provided by the need to sterilize some of the incoming capital so that money supply remains stable; while this maintains money supply constant, it destroys the adjustment process and capital flows continue. These and other contradictions affect the economic performance of the entire policy package. Not much should be expected in terms of economic good health from this model of open economy. It is difficult to expect sustainable development to emerge from an economic model based on bankrupt theories.

Appendix I: The IS–LM model and the environment

In this appendix we explain the basic structure of the IS–LM model and how it has been used in recent efforts to blend environmental concerns with macroeconomic policies. This construct was aimed at developing Keynes's theory by explaining three critical aspects of a capitalist economy. First, it reveals how the goods sector and the money sector are related. Second, it shows that a capitalist economy can operate with equilibrium in the goods market and in the money market, but this equilibrium does not necessarily coincide with a level of output in which there is full employment.[20] The model also shows that there is no inherent mechanism driving the economy towards a full employment position. Third, the model illustrates how macroeconomic policies can be used to affect the level of activity so that full employment may be attained.

The goods market The goods market is what economists call the real sector of the economy. Equilibrium in this sector is obtained when total demand (given by consumption plus investment) is equal to total output. In this case, investment (I) equals savings (S). Consumption is a function of income, while investment is a function of the rate of interest. From the real sector we can determine the level of output, but not the rate of interest.

We define aggregate demand Y^d in terms of total expenditures:

$$Y^d = C + I \qquad (1)$$

where C is consumption, I stands for investment. In an equilibrium position, total demand Y^d is equal to total supply (Y):

$$Y^d = Y$$

And because total income is either consumed or saved, there is another way of looking at total (aggregate) income:

$$Y = C + S$$

If we assume the equilibrium condition ($Y^d = Y$) holds, the above relations give:

$$C + S = C + I \qquad (2)$$

From this we can simply write the equilibrium condition as I = S (this will be used for the IS curve in the diagram).

In the spirit of Keynes, the level of output that corresponds to these equilibrium conditions is determined by aggregate demand (which is the key driver of the model). The model is telling us that for any given level of demand, producers will try to meet that demand, and this means that aggregate output will increase or decrease to meet that aggregate demand.

The money market Equilibrium in the money market occurs when the supply of money equals the demand for money. Simplifying, the demand for money is determined by two factors: the transactions motive, which depends on the level of income t(Y), and the liquidity motive, which is a function of the rate of interest L(r). Agents normally prefer to hold money instead of interest-bearing bonds because it offers liquidity. This is especially true in times of uncertainty. In order to get agents to part with liquidity, bonds offer interest payments. As r increases the demand for bonds rises and the demand for money falls. The desire of individual agents to hold on to their monetary assets can lead to a reduction in effective demand, and thus in the level of activity and in employment. Thus liquidity preference L(r) is closely related to uncertainty.

The theory of liquidity preference is used by Keynes to determine the interest rate. For a given level of income, the money sector determines the interest rate. In contrast with neoclassical theory, the rate of interest is not the price that equilibrates the demand for resources to invest with loanable funds. It is rather the reward for parting with liquidity. Or, in other terms, it is the price that balances the desire to hold wealth in the form of liquid resources (cash) and the available quantity of money.

The demand M^d for money can be expressed as follows:

$$M^d = t(Y) + L(r) \qquad (3)$$

where $t(Y)$ is the demand for money for transactions and $L(r)$ is the demand for money determined by liquidity preference. The first component increases proportionately with income (agents need more cash to carry out their transactions as their income increases) while the liquidity term is a negative function of the interest rate. For simplicity, the model assumes that there are only two assets: interest-bearing bonds and money. The advantage of holding money is that it provides a cushion of liquidity against uncertainty. Interest is the reward for parting with this liquidity (thus, when interest rates increase, agents in the model demand less money).

The supply of money M^s is determined exogenously (by monetary authorities). Equilibrium is defined as follows:

$$M^s = tY + L(r) \qquad (4)$$

The money market determines the rate of interest through the liquidity preference theory.

The IS–LM diagram The IS–LM model studies the interaction between the output market and the financial markets. Clearing on the bond market implies clearing on the money market and vice versa. 'Clearing' on these 'two markets' means that the nominal interest rate has adjusted such that the existing stocks of bonds and money are willingly held. So it is enough to consider only one of these stocks explicitly. Usually the money stock and the 'money market' are considered.

The standard IS–LM model assumes clearing at both the output and the money market:

IS $\quad Y = C(Y) + I(r) \qquad (5)$
LM $\quad M^s = t(Y) + L(r) \qquad (6)$

These two equations constitute the traditional IS–LM model. The two sectors are interdependent: from the goods market we obtain the level of income (or of economic activity), and from the money market we obtain the rate of interest. These two variables affect elements in the other market: income affects demand for money (transactions motive) and the rate of interest affects investment. There appears to be a circular reasoning here: in order to determine Y, we need to determine r, and vice versa. The way out of this conundrum is through the simultaneous solution of the two equations.

It is now possible to draw a diagram in which we relate what happens in the goods and money markets simultaneously. In this diagram we have Y, the level of income (output) on the horizontal axis, and r, the rate of interest, on the vertical axis. Every point in that space is a combination of points (Y, r).

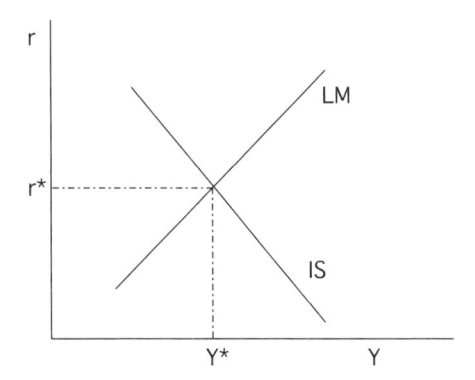

Figure 2.1 The IS–LM model

In this space we can draw the sets of points that correspond to equilibrium positions in the goods market for combinations of different levels of income (or output) and of the rate of interest. This schedule is labelled IS and will have a downward slope because investment decreases as r grows (I is a negative function of r), aggregate demand is reduced, and thus the equilibrium level of income. The degree of steepness of the IS schedule depends on how sensitive investment is to changes in r. The important thing to remember here is that every point on the IS schedule represents a point of equilibrium in the goods market for that particular combination of values of Y and r.

It is possible to draw another line for the equilibrium positions of the money market. This line is called LM. Its slope is positive: the demand for money increases as output grows because agents need more money to carry out more transactions. At the same time, the demand for money is a negative function of the interest rate: when r increases, agents are more willing to part with money and the term L(r) becomes smaller. The reader can easily verify this in equation (6): maintain the money supply (M^s fixed) and imagine Y increases, inducing an increment in the demand for money for transactions. In that case, because the left-hand side of the equation is constant, as t(Y) increases, L(r) must be brought down, and this is achieved when the interest rate rises (agents need a bigger reward to part with cash).

The diagram does not show how the Y* position of equilibrium is arrived at. In addition, the diagram does not explicitly show why this equilibrium might coexist with unemployment. To analyse this we need an additional quadrant that would explicitly show the relation between equilibrium output Y* and employment – this was the contribution of Modigliani (1944). The key point here is that for Y* we have equilibrium in the goods and money markets, but this level of economic activity does not necessarily coincide with full employment. Thus, in stark contrast with neoclassical theory, the model tells us that a capitalist economy can function at a level of equilibrium with unemployment.

Macroeconomic policy Fiscal policy may increase expenditures and this will affect the position of the IS curve because one of the components of aggregate demand corresponds to government outlays. In this case, the IS curve shifts to the right (to IS'), as shown in Figure 2.2. On the other hand, if government spending is curtailed, aggregate demand will contract and the IS curve will move back to its original position. Monetary policy can also be introduced in similar terms. If, for example, the money supply is increased, then the entire LM curve shifts to the right and the interest rate is lowered. The opposite happens when there is a tighter monetary policy (the LM schedule moves leftward and the level of activity is reduced).

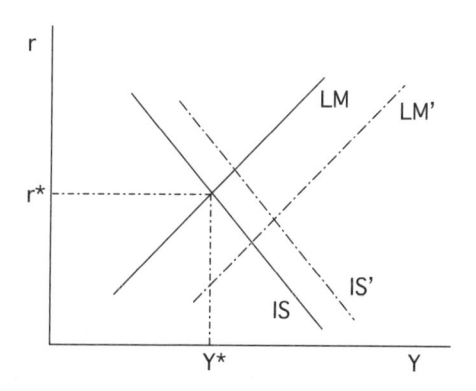

Figure 2.2 Macroeconomic policy in the IS–LM model

This is the type of public intervention analysed in the works of

Thampapillai, Heyes, Lawn and Daly–Farley. In the case of Heyes (2000) and Lawn (2003), an 'environmental equilibrium' curve EE is added to the IS–LM model (Figure 2.3). Each point in this curve corresponds to a level of activity and to the interest rate for which the assimilative capacity of the environment leads to biophysical equilibrium. The EE curve has a negative slope because it is assumed that lower interest rates bring more capital-intensive techniques that are more environmentally friendly.

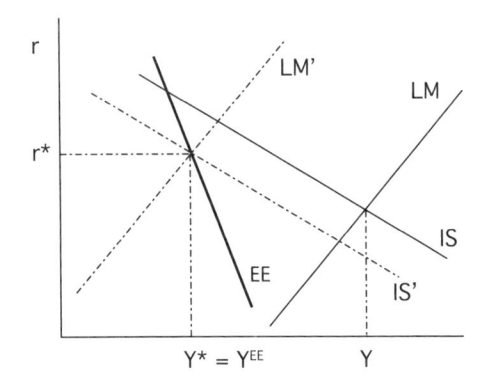

Figure 2.3 Environmental equilibrium in the IS–LM model

If, for example, Y is a level of activity that involves putting a degree of pressure on the environment higher than its capacity to restore its integrity, then fiscal and/or monetary policies can be used to reduce that level of activity and bring the economy back to the point $r^* = Y^* = Y^{EE}$. In this case, the structure of the economy has remained the same; only its scale has been modified to bring it back to biophysical sustainability.

In the case of Thampapillai (1995) and Daly and Farley (2004) there is no need to project an EE curve on to the diagram. Their assumption is that a biophysical equilibrium level of activity can be directly identified as a point on the Y axis.

3 · Macroeconomic policies and climate change

Introduction

Climate change is now recognized as the most important challenge for humanity. The scientific evidence is overwhelming: climate is changing and human activity is the main cause. The risk of a runaway process of global warming with potential catastrophic consequences cannot be denied (Solomon et al. 2007). In fact, the debate has ceased to be a dispute about the robustness of scientific data and has become more focused on the economics of climate change (Ackerman 2009).

A considerable amount of attention has been devoted to the question of how to estimate the magnitude of the damage that climate change will cause. In this context the discussion has revolved around the discount rate being used. With a high discount rate the present value of damage in the far future is insignificant, and in terms of cost–benefit analysis very little climate protection can be justified. A low discount rate will increase the value of today's investments required to prevent damage in the future. The *Stern Review* (Stern 2006) was criticized for using a very low discount rate (Nordhaus 2007; Dasgupta 2007).[1] But although choosing the right discount rate is a well-known issue in cost–benefit analysis, the problem is not restricted to this question. A deeper and more serious difficulty arises from the possibility of reswitching in discount rates. Baumol (1997) has demonstrated that a high and a low discount rate may yield the same present value figure for a given project. This justifies adopting a more cautious attitude towards cost–benefit analyses using discount rates.

Today, things have changed and the debate goes beyond the levels of discount rates used to estimate damage and preventive investments. The disagreements that led the latest Conference of the Parties (COP15) of the UN Framework Convention on Climate Change (UNFCCC) to a resounding failure in December 2009 were more about who will bear the costs than about the validity of scientific evidence. Of course, one of the main foci of debate concerns the financial needs of developing countries.

This and other aspects of the international negotiations are intimately related to macroeconomic policy. Yet macroeconomic policy priorities have not been discussed in any of these negotiations.[2] Even the *Stern Review* (Stern 2006), the foremost analysis of the economics of climate change, carefully skirted around the tough macroeconomic policy questions that need to be addressed in this context.

The central objective of the UNFCCC is to achieve the stabilization of greenhouse gas (GHG) concentrations in the atmosphere at levels that prevent dangerous anthropogenic interference with the planet's climate. Article 2 of the UNFCCC specifies that this objective should be achieved within a time frame that allows ecosystems to adapt naturally to climate change, to ensure that food production is not threatened and to enable economic development to proceed in a sustainable manner. Reducing emissions is not only a question of scale. Because these objectives are closely linked to major structural changes in an economy, it is clear that macroeconomic policies should be at the centre of this debate. Besides, the magnitude and the economy-wide nature of the challenges posed by climate change lead to this conclusion.

The main point in this chapter is that macroeconomic policies need to be taken into account in the international debate on climate change. Redefining the priorities and posture of monetary and fiscal policies, as well as the operation of the financial system, is crucial to meet the challenges of adaptation and mitigation. Macroeconomic policies will not only affect how costs are covered. They will also be critical in the transition from today's economic structure to a platform with the emission levels required to avoid disaster.

Climate-change costs: how big a problem?

The total cost of climate change is difficult to calculate because of the uncertainties in the precise magnitude and speed of its effects and their specific geographical manifestation. The conventional view today is that the climate-change burden is composed of three items: adaptation (trying to reduce the impact of damage from climate change), mitigation (reducing GHG emissions) and residual (unavoidable) costs.[3] But the total cost remains a hazy notion that depends on variables such as the level of temperature rise, the emissions reduction trajectory and its concomitant effects. It is also critically dependent on regional and local conditions, as well as the level of development and income per capita. These two components are closely related to each other. For example, adaptation costs in the future may be lower if mitigation expenditures (to reduce GHG emissions) are significant today.

Adaptation costs A critical issue frequently ignored is that vulnerability to anthropogenic climate change (as in natural disasters) depends on the level of development. It is a well-known fact that poor people and poor countries are more vulnerable to the damage associated with climate change. In this sense, per capita income, literacy and health indicators are related to vulnerability indicators. Thus, poor countries encounter an 'adaptation deficit' (Fankhauser 2009: 21) that affects the poorest countries and the poorest people in the world. This adaptation deficit is the investment required to reduce vulnerability to thresholds similar to those of developed countries. Adaptation deficits are even more alarming considering that poor countries will be hit first and harder by climate change.

Here we encounter a first relation with macroeconomic policies as they represent one of the main components of development strategies. Vulnerability and the capacity to implement a successful strategy for emissions reductions depend on the development strategy that is being followed by a given country, and this is intimately related to its macroeconomic policy package. Development is the best adaptation strategy because it means building a system that is resilient to the damage of climate change.

Clearly, it is difficult to identify a clear-cut line dividing socioeconomic development from adaptation and mitigation capabilities. The complexity of calculating estimates is obvious. Most estimates rely on an incremental investment over and above current investment trends in areas or sectors considered to be sensitive to climate change. The World Bank (2006) developed this methodology by first considering current investments in sensitive areas and then adding the cost of 'climate proofing' them. This implies a downward bias in cost estimates. The UNFCCC study does not escape from this bias: its estimates set total *annual* funding requirements for *adaptation* by 2030 between US$49 and 171 billions, of which US$27–66 billion would correspond to developing countries.

These estimates are based on studies commissioned by UNFCCC covering six sectors: agriculture (forestry and fisheries), water supply, human health, coastal zones, infrastructure and ecosystems. The salient features of these studies are described in Parry et al. (2009). It is important to note that the largest cost item is infrastructure, and that all costs are over and above what would have to be invested in the baseline to renew capital stock and accommodate income and population growth. The estimates do not include ecosystems adaptation.

The UNFCCC figures for developing countries are broadly in agreement with other estimates: World Bank (2006), US$9–41 billion; Stern

TABLE 3.1 UNFCCC estimates of adaptation costs (US$ billions)

Sector	Total	Developed	Developing
Agriculture	14	7	7
Water	11	2	9
Health	5	n.e.	5
Coastal zones	11	7	4
Infrastructure	8–130	6–88	2–41
TOTAL	49–171	22–105	27–66
			86–109 (UNDP 2007)

Notes: Estimates for per annum adaptation costs by 2030 in present-value US$; n.e. = not estimated.
Source: Parry et al. (2009)

(2006), US$4–37 billion; Oxfam (2007), > US$50 billion; UNDP (2007), US$86–109 billion. Of course, the estimates depend crucially on the amount of global warming that is being considered. The UNFCCC estimates are based on a scenario (called A1B) in which temperature rises are in the range of 2.8 degrees Celsius (best estimate) and on a sea-level rise of between 0.21 and 0.48 metres in 2090 (IPCC 2007).[4]

Parry et al. (2009) conclude that these figures underestimate the importance of funding requirements for several reasons.[5] First, there is incomplete information for many of the sectors included in the UNFCCC studies. Second, the methodology employed is based on a 'mark-up' on current investments, but for most developing countries these 'climate mark-up' estimates are based *not* on the investments that *would be required* to attain adequate policy objectives in adaptation, but on current investment trends. This leads to estimates that are substantially lower than if one assumed a development pathway that focused on adaptation and reducing vulnerability to climate change. Third, there are sectors that have been left out of these estimates (industry, tourism, energy, damage to ecosystems).

In fact, the current deficit in investments (caused by fiscal priorities obsessed with balanced budgets) is one of the important reasons why vulnerability in developing countries is higher. Clearly, there appears to be a strong relation between high adaptation costs and the vulnerability of developing countries. Parry et al. (ibid.) conclude that removing the housing and infrastructure deficit in low- and middle-income countries would cost around US$315 billion per year over the next twenty years, while adapting this infrastructure to meet the challenge of climate change would cost an additional US$16–63 billion per year (this is the mark-up). According to Parry et al. (ibid.), the UNFCCC studies underestimate the investments needed to prevent catastrophic damage from climate change by a factor of between 2 and 3 for most of the included sectors. For infrastructure that factor could be higher, and if ecosystems are included, the total cost could skyrocket by an additional US$300 billion.[6] Of course, if higher estimates for MDG-related requirements are used the climate mark-up leads to higher requirements for climate-change policy. For example, estimates in the UN Millennium Project (2005) are considerably higher for MDG financing from ODA. According to this report ODA would have to increase gradually from US$121 billion in 2006 to US$189 billion in 2015. The shortfall in current ODA flows would be significant (US$416 billion in 2015, according to UNCTAD 2008), and the new estimates for adaptation funds would increase significantly.

Some of these figures are relevant to our discussion of fiscal policy insofar as they pertain to public expenditures. For example, the UNFCCC estimates of adaptation investments in agriculture are based on a 'climate mark-up' of only 10 per cent of R&D and 2 per cent of infrastructure expenditures in this sector. The estimate of adaptation costs is therefore very low, at US$11.3–12.6 billion per year for 2030. This low figure contrasts with the non-climate annual investment required for the Millennium Development Goals of US$40–60 billion and estimates for 2015 of US$200 billion per year (Sachs and MacArthur 2005, quoted in Parry et al. 2009). The global financial and economic crisis has exacerbated matters, and it is now thought that the investments required to meet the 2015 targets will have to be even greater. Parry et al. conclude that without this non-climate investment the estimates for adaptation will come out very low.

In fact, it would be more accurate to say that developing countries' spending on agriculture has been very low in the past three or four decades owing to fiscal priorities. And this can be extended to cover other categories of public spending: social expenditures, education, infrastructure and R&D. The reason is that fiscal policy in developing countries has been dominated by the paramount objective of generating a primary surplus, and because this goal coexists with the objective of maintaining a 'competitive' tax structure (i.e. low taxes on capital and on high income brackets), cutting expenditures on healthcare, education, housing, R&D and infrastructure has become the pathway to attaining systematic primary surplus.

This fiscal policy posture is part of a broader macroeconomic stance that also involves monetary and exchange rate policies. This combination of macroeconomic policies corresponds to the reforms undertaken in the aftermath of the international debt crisis of the eighties and implemented with great rigour in the nineties. The policy package included trade liberalization, deregulation of the capital account and financial reform. These reforms constitute the neoliberal policy package, and they did not bring about growth or macroeconomic stability, as recognized even by research undertaken by the World Bank (Montiel and Servén 2004). Clearly, fiscal expenditures in developing countries during the last decade should not be the basis for estimates of investment requirements.

In some critical cases, the calculations ignore the very important dimension of relocation and livelihoods. For example, the study on coastal zones (Nicholls 2007) refers basically to infrastructure expenditures, not to costs of relocating populations. In the case of agriculture, adaptation estimates ignore the cost of adapting peasant production systems to climate change in the most vulnerable areas of the world. Loss of livelihoods is not considered in these estimates. This is especially relevant for Africa, where it is expected that the IPCC scenarios will bring about major devastation in agricultural systems.

It is interesting to note the differences between developed and developing countries in Table 3.1. Population in the latter is far greater than in the former, but the estimates are greater for developed countries. The difference comes essentially from infrastructure, where developing countries are seriously lagging behind. In the case of agriculture, it is surprising that both groups have the same estimate of US$7 billion. The fact that developed countries invest more than developing countries in agriculture (subsidies in OECD countries are about US$350 billion per year) could explain this result in the UNFCCC estimates. For adaptation costs, this evidently is a significant underestimate given population and land surface in developing countries, as well as the fact that tropical regions are particularly vulnerable to environmental changes. With better data, greater coverage of sectors and health factors, as well as a more rigorous approach to calculating costs in agriculture and industry, considering population and the existing development deficit, a new and more credible estimate would be substantially increased.[7]

Mitigation costs What about the costs associated with emissions reductions? Mitigation implies economy-wide structural transformations due to a shift in the energy profile (decarbonization and greater emphasis on renewables). This is associated with significant changes in investment patterns as industry, transportation, construction, manufacturing and the energy sector transform their base of capital goods and equipment. The best estimates of the type of investments that will be required are from UNFCCC (2008) and they cover eight major sectors of GHG emissions: power supply, fossil fuel supply, waste, building, transport, industry, forestry and agriculture. Table 3.2 contains a summary of the data.

TABLE 3.2 UNFCCC estimates of mitigation costs, 2030 (US$ billions)

Sector	Total	Developed countries	Developing countries
Energy supply infrastructure	695	312.7	382.2
CCS for power plants (a)	75	n.a.	n.a.
Industry (b)	35.7	16.5	19.2
Transport	88	49.3	38.7
Buildings	51	36.8	14.2
Waste (c)	1	0.4	0.6
Agriculture (d)	35	12.3	22.7
Forestry	21	2	18
TOTAL	1,001.7	430	495.6

Notes: (a) CCS = carbon capture and storage. There is a lot of uncertainty concerning this technology. (b) Industry: pulp and paper; cement, lime and non-metallic minerals; non-ferrous metal smelting and iron and steel; metal and non-metal mining; chemical products; other manufacturing. (c) Landfills and waste water treatment. (d) Non-CO_2 GHG and energy-related CO_2 emissions.
Source: UNFCCC (2008)

The higher level of investment requirements for developing countries stems from the fact that these economies will have the fastest-growing rates for GHG emissions. Reducing emissions here is urgent, and this entails high investment costs. As with adaptation, some mitigation costs are to be covered by the public sector, while others will have to be met by the private sector. Mitigation costs in sectors where important state-owned enterprises operate (for example, utilities and oil extraction) will have to be covered through public spending. This will not be forthcoming if fiscal policy continues to be dominated by the mantra of a balanced budget and by debt management considerations (i.e. the need to generate a primary surplus).

On the other hand, a significant proportion of the investment required for this structural transformation to take place will have to come from private sector agents. Mitigation will call for large-scale private investments as technological trajectories change. Adoption of new technologies in the energy sector, as well as in large-scale industries that are energy and capital intensive (cement, glass, pulp and paper, petrochemicals, aluminium, steel), will require adequate incentives for adoption and diffusion. These incentives may come from market signals, subsidies (for example, for R&D and through preferential interest rates on investments), or from regulatory norms.

The neoliberal macroeconomic policy package does not appear to be an adequate framework to meet the challenge of this structural transformation. In the past three decades, gross capital formation in developing countries has slowed down, owing partly to the distortion in investment patterns brought about by new opportunities for speculation, partly to the high cost of credit that accompanies restrictive monetary policies.[8] In addition, exchange-rate volatility and instability of financial markets have increased. The unrestricted freedom of capital flows has not brought about a reduction in interest rates. This has not only slowed down productive investment, but has intensified inequality as resources are transferred to owners of financial assets, further reducing the size of domestic markets and increasing the deficit in aggregate demand, all of this feeding into a vicious cycle in which speculative investments become more attractive over time. On top of this, one consequence of neoliberal fundamentalism has been the complete dismantling of industrial policy in most developing countries.

Total adaptation and mitigation costs in the UNFCCC estimates could surpass the figure of US$600 billion in 2030 (with adaptation costs grossly underestimated). This means that annual flows should start with at least US$50 billion by 2012 in order to keep a uniform rate of growth in accordance with absorption capacity in developing countries. The various policies mentioned by the IPCC and the UNFCCC (2008) to meet this challenge are the following: regulations and standards, taxes and charges (but curiously, not subsidies), carbon market and tradable permits and financial incentives. There are also calls to blend the instrument mix with other broader development policy instruments. Typically, measures fall short of mentioning the need to retool macroeconomic policies.

It is interesting to compare this with total ODA flows in recent years. Total ODA from OECD countries increased in 2005–08 in comparison with the average of the 1990s. In 2008, total ODA flows (in constant 2007 US$) reached US$115 billion, an amount significantly higher than the US$76 billion of 2001. Approximately 10 per cent of this amount goes to debt relief. Because aid flows dropped during the previous decade, average per capita ODA remains today at levels comparable to those of the sixties (ibid.: 137). It has been recommended that ODA should reach the level of 0.7 per cent of GDP of the OECD countries, but this level has not been attained. And with the current financial and economic crisis, it is highly unlikely that these flows will increase significantly.

Data show that OECD countries provided US$3.8 billion in bilateral ODA in 2007 to help developing countries reduce GHG emissions. This is 4 per cent of total bilateral ODA that year, with Japan (US$1.3 billion), Germany (US$0.8 billion) and France (US$0.5 billion) being the largest donors. The sectors that have been targeted here are energy, transport, water and forestry. To this figure we need to add contributions to the Global Environment Facility (GEF) and the United Nations Environment Programme. Clearly, existing flows are extremely low and well below estimated needs.

Flows earmarked for climate policy may find competition from other items on the ODA agenda. The lessons from the special MDG commitments are relevant here. Since the adoption of the Millennium Declaration, securing sufficient financing to enable developing countries to meet the MDGs has not been an easy task. The 2001 Report of the High-Level Panel on Financing for Development estimated that an additional US$50 billion had to be added to existing ODA flows. Although ODA increased significantly (see previous paragraph), a large part of the increment went to debt relief. Until 2007 total ODA disbursements net of debt relief remained *below* the level estimated as being needed by the United Nations report for the MDG, and only a fraction of the increase in ODA went directly on MDG-related uses (ibid.).

The so-called Copenhaguen Accord (18 December 2009) states that

> scaled up, new and additional, predictable and adequate funding as well as improved access shall be provided to developing countries [...] to enable and support enhanced action on mitigation, including substantial finance to reduce emissions from deforestation and forest degradation, adaptation, technology development and transfer and capacity-building, for enhanced implementation of the Convention. The collective commitment by developed countries is to provide new and additional resources, including forestry and investments through international institutions, approaching USD 30 billion for the period 2010–2012 with balanced allocation between adaptation and mitigation. [...] In the context of meaningful mitigation actions and transparency on implementation, developed countries commit to a goal of mobilizing jointly USD 100 billion dollars a year by 2020 to address the needs of developing countries. This funding will come from a wide variety of sources, public and private, bilateral and multilateral, including alternative sources of finance.

Although this doesn't sound too bad, it is important to note that this is not ODA and it includes private foreign direct investment. This means it's part of a promise that may or may not crystallize. In the recent past OECD countries have been slow to meet their ODA targets, and it is clear that the global financial and economic crisis is already making these commitments even more fragile.

The magnitude of costs and the nature of the problem clearly point to a serious reconsideration of the macroeconomic policy package needed to meet the challenges of climate-change policy. Stabilization of GHG concentrations in the atmosphere will require systemic technical change that can best be understood as an economy-wide phenomenon. This is not only a problem of high cost estimates; it is also a question of the long-run conditions that will enable countries to meet their emissions reduction obligations. 'Properly designed climate change policies can be part and parcel of sustainable development, and the two can be mutually reinforcing,' say Rogner et al. (2007: 97), but this requires taking a fresh, hard look at macroeconomic policies and how they will affect climate-change policy implementation.

Macroeconomic policies in the IPCC's AR4

One of the most important instruments in estimating GHG emissions is the so-called Kaya identity. This is a decomposition that expresses the level of energy-related CO_2 emissions as the product of four indicators: carbon intensity (CO_2 emissions per unit of total primary energy supply or TPES), energy intensity (TPES per unit of output), gross domestic product per capita (GDP/cap), and population. The decomposition analysis shows that the global average growth rate of emissions between 1970 and 2004 of 1.9 per cent per year is the result of the following annual growth rates: population 1.6 per cent, GDP/cap 1.8 per cent, energy intensity −1.2 per cent and carbon intensity −0.2 per cent. Thus, the main drivers of net emission change during the past three decades are GDP per capita (GDP/cap) and population growth (ibid.: 107).

This means that the declining carbon and energy intensities of global output have been unable to offset the income effects, and population growth and emissions have continued to grow. Under the reference scenario of the International Energy Agency (cited in ibid.: 107), these trends are expected to remain valid until 2030; in particular, energy is not expected to be further decarbonized under this baseline scenario. What this confirms is that bringing down energy and carbon intensity will require a major shift in macroeconomic policy. In spite of this, macroeconomic policies continue to receive very little attention.

The IPCC reports were conceived in the heyday of neoliberal 'globalization'. It is not surprising to see that they show a strong bias towards 'market-friendly' instruments for policy implementation. This also explains why the reports contain very few references to macroeconomic policies: in the neoliberal world, markets should be left alone and macroeconomic policies should not be used for purposes other than price stabilization (monetary policy) and to prevent crowding out of private investment (fiscal policy).

In fact, this also goes a long way to providing an explanation for the lack of meaningful analysis of industrial and technology policies. As we shall see below, the IPCC reports recognize the fact that technology development is important for climate-change policy but offer a superficial discussion of this. They never mention the fact that many crucial technology and industrial policy instruments (which could be instrumental in implementing climate-change policies) are practically forbidden by WTO agreements. We return to this point below.

The IPCC's AR4 recognizes that climate-change policies can be part and parcel of sustainable development and the two can be mutually reinforcing. Mitigation, for example, can conserve or enhance resilience of forests and other ecosystems, as well as prevent damage to human systems, thus contributing to the overall productivity needed for social and economic development. In turn, sustainable development paths, as noted above, can reduce vulnerability to climate change and cut GHG emissions. The IPCC recognizes this will be affected by the mix of development choices and strategies: making development more sustainable by changing development paths can thus make a significant contribution to climate policy goals. This is recognized in all Third Assessment Report scenarios (Sathaye et al. 2007), and the AR4 accepts the fact that 'changing development paths is not about choosing a well mapped-out trajectory' (ibid.: 693) but rather about 'navigating through an uncharted and evolving landscape'. Furthermore, the AR4 reminds us that 'making development more sustainable by changing development paths can make a major contribution to climate goals' (ibid.: 699).

The AR4 Working Group report (ibid.: 700) also states that

> the literature on long-term climate scenarios […], and especially the SRES [Special Report on Emissions Scenarios], points to the same conclusion. Climate outcomes are influenced not only by climate-specific policies but also by the mix of development choices made and the development paths that these policies lead to. There are always going to be a variety of development pathways that could possibly be followed and they might

lead to future outcomes at global, national, and local levels. The choice of development policies can, therefore, be as consequential to future climate stabilization as the choice of climate-specific policies.

Can a country change its 'development path' without transforming its macroeconomic policy framework? In spite of the recognition that macroeconomic variables are important, the IPCC's AR4 does not make room for a meaningful discussion of macroeconomic policies and how they might affect costs and policy implementation. The IPCC (2007: 721–2) recognizes that macroeconomic policies are important for climate-change policy, but fails to advance discussion of this. In the next section we examine how macroeconomic policies can affect climate-change policies.

One final word on carbon markets is necessary. Carbon trading has been presented in many circles as one of the main instruments that could lead to emissions abatement, more rapidly and at inferior cost. Is this market-based approach a reliable policy instrument? The *Stern Review*, AR4 and several UNFCCC background documents already assign a lead role to carbon trading in the struggle to reduce emissions. Although this may provide an appearance that the challenges of climate change are being addressed, the truth is very different. In fact, carbon markets may prolong the life of an economic structure that remains addicted to fossil fuels and retard the structural transformation required in production and consumption patterns. A comprehensive critique of carbon trading can be found in Lohmann (2006) and Gilbertson and Reyes (2009) and references therein.[9]

Carbon markets rely on a key price, the price of a ton of CO_2-equivalent emissions. This key price is supposed to bring about the reduction of emissions in a short period of time. But there is no historical parallel of a single commodity price bringing about the sort of radical structural transformation of an economy that is required, and during the 1970s acute hikes in oil prices 'did little to wean industrial societies off oil' (Gilbertson and Reyes 2009). In the case of the largest carbon market in operation today (the European Union Emissions Trading Scheme), emissions reductions have not been forthcoming.

The relation between macroeconomics and carbon trading is very strong and can readily be observed in the evolution of prices. The price of a ton of CO_2 plunged from approximately 30 euros in 2008 to 8 euros by March 2009. The collapse in this price makes alternative, cleaner projects less profitable. In addition, the crisis has caused many firms to reduce operations and they now have an excess of allowances. The carbon market is in disarray and will not recover easily. The European Union could change its target for emissions cuts, which is currently a 20 per cent reduction (with respect to 1990 levels) by 2020. If, for example, it raised that target to 30 per cent, then the price of a ton of CO_2 would increase. This would 'artificially' increase the price of CO_2, but the essence of the trading scheme, its rewards to big polluters and its ineffectiveness in achieving sustainable emissions reductions, would not change.

Finally, there is another important problem with carbon markets. The sum of resources generated by this mechanism will simply not be enough to cover the costs of adaptation and mitigation in developing countries that appear in the previous estimates. This is one important reason why macroeconomic policies in these countries need to be redefined in order to generate the resources that are required to meet the objectives of climate policy.

Macroeconomic policies and climate change

The IPCC recognizes that development trajectories are critical for climate change. Adaptation and mitigation are heavily dependent on development paths and on whether sustainable development is being pursued or attained. And since development paths depend on the macroeconomic policy package, it becomes clear that adequate policy space needs to be opened at the macroeconomic level. But if climate-change policy objectives are going to be added to the macroeconomic policy framework, something more than a simple juxtaposition of objectives is going to be required.

The best example of the magnitude of the problem we are dealing with here is found in the case of the Millennium Development Goals (MDGs). These objectives were adopted in September 2000 by the United Nations General Assembly. Two critical targets are to halve the number of people living in extreme poverty and those suffering from hunger by 2015. Another objective is to ensure that children everywhere will be able to complete a full course of primary schooling while eliminating gender disparity. A third goal is to reduce by two-thirds by 2015 the mortality rate of children under five years. Another target is to integrate the principles of sustainable development into country policies and programmes while reversing the loss of environmental resources.

Unfortunately, various indicators are already revealing that these objectives are not going to be met, especially in the context of the current financial and economic crisis. One reason behind this is that although all of these objectives are closely related to public policy intervention, the MDGs were not accompanied by any debates or an attempt to revise macroeconomic priorities. Macroeconomic policies over the past twenty years have had five paramount objectives: price stabilization, fiscal discipline, trade liberalization, financial deregulation and large-scale privatization. The underlying principle of this policy package was that only market-friendly policies would lead to growth and development. Of course, the last three should have been considered instruments instead of policy objectives. The fact is that macroeconomic policies were organized around the needs of financial capital. By the time the MDGs were approved, the record of this policy package was already marked by slow growth rates, higher volatility and a long list of financial crises. And yet the MDGs were defined and decided upon without any reference to the need for reform in the field of macroeconomic policy.

As we have already pointed out, the performance record of neoliberal macroeconomic policies is not bright, with lower growth rates, greater instability and volatility, as well as a string of financial crises almost without precedent in economic history. As Thandika Mkandawire, head of the United Nations Research Institute for Social Development (UN-RISD), stated, 'in light of this experience, one would have expected an interrogation of the macroeconomic policies that formed the basis of the "Washington Consensus". Instead, *one has witnessed a process whereby poverty has been added on to the policy objectives without any fundamental re-examination of the core macroeconomic problems*' (Mkandawire 2005, emphasis added). Furthermore, the countries that have achieved rapid poverty reduction and are better positioned to attain some of the MDGs adopted macroeconomic policies that differed markedly from those promoted by the neoliberal approach.

The problem posed by the MDGs and the macroeconomic policy package they require is comparable to the issues raised by climate change. There is no doubt that meeting the challenge of adaptation and mitigation objectives implies the need to mobilize a vast amount of resources and to be able to carry out deep changes in income distribution, industrial structure, transport patterns and energy (decarbonization) profiles. Clearly, this cannot be left to market-based policies and a passive macroeconomic 'strategy'.

It is a tragedy that the debate on climate-change policies has been boxed into a very narrow discussion that focuses on a triad of options. In the first corner we find tradable permits in all their variants (including the so-called clean development mechanisms and joint implementation schemes of the Kyoto Protocol). The second corner is represented by schemes to directly affect carbon pricing through taxes. And, finally, in the third corner is the set of command-and-control regulations that would impose efficiency standards aimed at affecting the price of carbon emissions. But this leaves macroeconomic policies out of the debate. This is the narrow perspective that the establishment, corporations in the developed and developing world, would like to continue to dominate the negotiating table.

We cannot assume that the agenda of GHG stabilization and adaptation to climate change that involves so many examples of macroeconomic aggregates is going to be satisfied without making important changes in the different components of macroeconomic policies. If we don't redefine macroeconomic priorities as if climate-change policies really mattered, we can't expect that the economic and technological changes that are required will take place.

In the following paragraphs we examine some of the main aspects of the relation between climate-change policy and macroeconomic policies which have been systematically ignored in past discussions and negotiations. Our analysis is limited to five problem areas in which macroeconomic policies need to be reshaped in order to make climate-change policy implementation a reality. These are just examples from a longer list of problem areas, and we are covering just a few of the salient aspects in each item.

Problem area 1: monetary and credit policies The notion that the only objective of monetary policy is maintaining price stability needs to be modified. A half-century of financial crises should help dispel this narrow view of monetary policy. Many other factors demand the attention of monetary authorities: business cycles, bubbles in asset prices, financial regulation and supervision, the structures of several macroeconomic aggregates, as well as capital flows. None of the above will cease to be important in the coming decades. In fact, it may make sense to hypothesize that some of these issues (for example, business cycles) could become more pressing in the future. How they affect the implementation of climate-change policy is an important question that cannot continue to be ignored.

If monetary policy remains unchanged, climate-change objectives will face serious obstacles owing to tight credit and high interest rates. Investment in new plant and equipment in order to reduce emissions needs to be encouraged through adequate credit and financial schemes. Although this may require low interest rates, it may also trigger higher growth rates, and this could offset the gains in efficiency. The problem with monetary policy as it is currently defined and implemented is that it relies on economy-wide effects. Thus, monetary policy offers very little in terms of flexibility and distinctions between sectors.

Reregulating financial and banking activities helps reduce the homogeneity of monetary policy that prevents its use as a sector-level policy instrument (Ffrench-Davis 2000). There is a clear need to restore some heterogeneity to monetary policy. Reregulation, greater supervision and monitoring of lending practices and risk management, all of these may be critical to redirecting credit towards climate-change policy objectives (especially in the case of mitigation).[10]

A good example of why the policy debate needs to be refined is the role of development banks. The IPCC's AR4 makes a reference *en passant* to the fact that 'the retreat of national development banks in some developing countries (as a result of financial liberalization and financial crises in national governments) may hinder the widespread adoption of mitigation technologies because of the lack of financial mechanisms to handle the associated risk'. In fact, what needs to be explicitly recognized is that in many cases development banks were dismantled because they were not compatible with profitability and commercial lending criteria. These became dominant through privatization, liberalization and deregulation of the banking system. In addition, in many instances development banks were simply eliminated because development policy disappeared and was left to 'market forces'. Perhaps this is why a meaningful discussion on macroeconomic policies is carefully avoided by the IPCC.

On the other hand, interest rates are also dependent on international financial flows. In fact, in the context of capital account liberalization, interest rates cease to be exclusively dependent on central bank decisions. This is the theme of the following point.

Problem area 2: financial liberalization and capital movements Financial liberalization and capital flows are critical aspects of the world economy. They introduce important distortions in interest and exchange rates, and they impose a highly pro-cyclical bias on fiscal and monetary policies (Kaminsky et al. 2004). Capital flows may also act as a powerful destabilizing force.[11] With capital flows, the interest rate and the exchange rate cease to be related to domestic macroeconomic forces or determinants. In their new role, they become indicators for speculative capital flows and their role in the economy becomes distorted. For example, a high exchange rate may coexist with a greatly diminished current account.

Capital market activity aimed at speculative profits will not make a positive contribution to new investment, more employment and higher growth rates. Why should it contribute to productive investments in more efficient capital goods with lower emissions? On the contrary, because of the way in which they operate, speculative portfolio investments will continue to have detrimental effects on the economies of recipient countries. They will not translate easily into the generation of new climate-friendly technologies or products. Opportunities for speculation distort investment patterns as they divert resources from productive employments.

It is also important to note that climate change will bring about dramatic increases in risks to life and property, and the insurance market will expand significantly (Whalley and Yuan 2009). One possibility is that financial innovation will be encouraged, primarily in the field of insurance, but also in the diversification of asset holdings (ibid.). As climate-change scenarios worsen, 'the entire global financial structure will undergo major changes with a re-focusing of major financial activity away from intermediation between borrowers and lenders and the facilitation of the accumulation of assets, and towards a focus on insurance arrangements and the diversification of risks associated with climate change' (ibid.: 2). This possibility, together with the financial flows associated with carbon markets (if and when they develop), may constitute an additional cause of instability, and new financial regulation will be needed.

There is evidence that capital controls help stabilize economies, reduce interest rates and cut the cost of expensive sterilization (Ffrench-Davis and Tapia 2004; Ocampo 2003; Ocampo and Tovar 2003). In the context of international funding for adaptation and/or mitigation, capital controls may prove to be a necessary instrument to provide greater stability.

Problem area 3: fiscal policies Adaptation to global climate change will require allocating massive resources on a sustained basis to areas that are frequently in the domain of the public sector. Some of the more important examples are infrastructure in coastal areas, existing transportation and energy infrastructure, etc. Already investments in these areas are lagging behind real needs – one reason for underestimating future investment requirements. In many cases resettlement and relocation of populations will require substantial amounts of fiscal resources. In summary, these items will put significant pressure on fiscal intervention.

But the view that fiscal activism leads to higher interest rates, inflation and/or crowding out of the private sector from financial markets dominates fiscal policy today. In addition, a key fiscal policy objective in developing countries is to generate a primary surplus to cover financial charges. Because there has been a clear tendency to avoid major fiscal reforms, generating a primary surplus has been achieved through the curtailment of public expenditures.[12] This goes a long way to explaining why per capita social expenditures (healthcare, education, housing) have stagnated. Climate-policy objectives may suffer the same fate unless important changes are introduced.

The role of fiscal policies in income redistribution is another important aspect of their potential contribution to climate-change policies. This is an aspect of the relation between fiscal policy and climate change that has been systematically ignored.[13] If adaptation to climate change is enhanced by the reduction of poverty, then distributive policies may go a long way in reducing the burden of climate change. Public investment in infrastructure and municipal services will also have a substantial impact on reducing vulnerability and adaptation costs.

Another aspect of the interplay between fiscal policy and climate policy concerns the role of the public sector in funding basic R&D and technological development, providing subsidies for renewable sources of energy and covering a significant proportion of the costs of adaptation and mitigation. Taxes on carbon fuels are frequently mentioned in IPCC reports and in international negotiations as a mechanism that may help correct carbon prices. However, all of these actions by public agencies and enterprises require redefining fiscal priorities and having a wider perspective on fiscal policy trends.

The issues of subsidies and carbon taxes are important aspects of fiscal policy. To stabilize CO_2 emissions, price changes are considered indispensable (Barker et al. 2007). However, these references to changes in carbon prices do not take into consideration financing of investment or how these changes affect public finances. A comprehensive carbon tax is frequently mentioned as an instrument to correct the price structure and send a market signal that will change consumption patterns and generate systemic technical change. The price hikes that this would generate are supposed to lower demand for fossil energy, to induce energy conservation and foster technological development and the adoption of techniques that are less intensive in fossil fuels. All of this is debatable and has been the object of controversy.[14] But the important point is that whatever the effects that such a measure would bring about, it would also be part and parcel of a comprehensive fiscal policy.

To summarize, the narrow definition of fiscal policy objectives has imposed a severe constraint on public expenditures, making them highly pro-cyclical. This is aggravated in the context of a deregulated capital account. Since expenditures must follow the revenue cycle, budget constraints tend to amplify fluctuations, transforming slowdowns into recessions. This is something that needs to be corrected in order to maintain a stable flow of resources for climate-policy objectives.

Problem area 4: trade liberalization and sector-level policies Trade liberalization is not only about reducing tariffs and getting rid of quantitative controls. It has always included dispute settlement mechanisms and subsidies, as well as other issues that are considered potential trade-distorting measures. When the World Trade Organization (WTO) was born, the trade agenda was expanded to cover a wide gamut of issues, from industrial, agricultural and science policy instruments, to intellectual property and foreign direct investment. The WTO became an international body capable of shaping not only trade policy, but other key sector-level policies. In the context of a heavy bias in favour of free trade, many policies in the realm of agricultural and industrial development were considered to be trade-distorting and were outlawed, becoming the object of retaliation through countervailing measures.

The problem of 'policy space' for development strategies has thus become a critical issue. The restrictions imposed by the WTO deny developing countries the possibility of using the very policy instruments that were used by the developed countries to reach their current development standards. The 'kicking the ladder' syndrome (see Chang 2002) is a theme of great relevance for the discussion of sustainable development and climate-change policies. In Gallagher (2005) several issues highly relevant to climate-change policies are discussed: from the TRIPs (Trade-Related Aspects of Intellectual Property Rights) agreement and its relation to transfer of technology, to industrial policy and investment performance requirements. Many of these essays argue that preserving policy space today is justified on the grounds that these are the policies that allowed developed countries to extricate themselves from the vicious circles of poverty and environmental degradation. All of these themes should be at the centre of any discussion of emissions mitigation policies; instead, they are systematically ignored.

Typically, when discussing things such as technological development and the role of the public sector (Halsnæs et al. 2007), the IPCC fails to mention the fact that technology and industrial policies have been deprived of their more important instruments owing to trade liberalization *à la* WTO. Instead, the IPCC in its AR4 simply repeats several well-known platitudes about market failures, etc. And when it discusses the role of the public sector in technology development, there is no reference to the fact that in developing countries public expenditures on R&D are extremely low (on average, total R&D expenditures in these countries are lower than 0.4 per cent of GDP).

The issue of potential conflicts between multilateral environmental agreements and trade agreements has received some attention in the IPCC reports (see Rogner et al. 2007: Box 13.7). However, the real problem is somewhat different. It is related to the degree of freedom that governments have in important aspects of development policies, some of which are highly relevant for climate-change objectives.

Problem area 5: poverty and vulnerability If vulnerability to climate change is exacerbated by poverty and marginalization, then macroeconomic policy has an important role in climate policy. Although macroeconomic policy objectives were originally centred on full employment, social welfare and distribution, they have now shifted to price stability and fiscal discipline.

Macroeconomic policies have been pushed towards a posture dominated by the requirements of controlling inflation, reducing the external and internal deficits, and deregulating and privatizing as much as possible. It was thought that this would establish the foundations for growth and job creation. However, in the end, after three decades of neoliberal macroeconomics, poverty has not subsided. In fact, this is why the Millennium Development Goals were adopted in 2000. The problem is that the poverty-reduction target was added to the objectives of neoliberal macroeconomics without any meaningful re-examination of the core macroeconomic policy package (Mkandawire 2005). This is a major contradiction: neoliberal macroeconomic policy is based on the repression of real wages, the reduction of social expenditures, the implementation of regressive tax structures that benefit owners of capital assets, etc. In a sense, it would have been a surprise to see the world marching on schedule to meet the MDGs. In fact, even before the global crisis of 2008, all indicators pointed in a different direction.

Deepening of inequality will most probably go hand in hand with increased poverty. This will increase vulnerability to the effects of climate change for millions of people. There are already 3.5 billion people living in poverty. They will bear the full impact of the extreme meteorological events that will come with global warming. A decisive effort to improve income distribution and reduce inequality between and within countries is urgently needed to reduce vulnerability. Focusing and better targeting are not the answer, especially when they serve to reduce fiscal resources that would help reduce poverty. The set of macroeconomic policies that are still being implemented in many developing countries is a heritage of the world in which the TINA (there is no alternative) syndrome dominated economic policy-making. In this policy framework, macroeconomic policies should remain passive and non-interventionist. This is sheer nonsense in the context of today's global crisis.

Concluding remarks

Negotiations towards a successor to the Kyoto Protocol in Copenhagen showed the world that the deep divides between poor and rich countries, as well as between the economies that emit greater amounts of GHG and those countries that will suffer most from climate change, are formidable obstacles to a robust and efficient agreement.

Even as the world economy reeled from the worst crisis in seventy years and recovery seemed a difficult prospect, international negotiations on climate policy were dominated by various carbon-trading schemes. Although some lip-service is being paid to the fact that climate change is such a complex problem that there is no silver-bullet solution, the main policy instrument that appears to be under consideration is some sort of global carbon market. This is most unfortunate and senseless: if the problem of climate change was engendered by the worst market failure in history (Stern 2006), it doesn't make much sense to set up another 'market-friendly' instrument to solve it. Clearly, the roles of the state and macroeconomic policy need to be restored to their proper place in a new social compact committed to the main priorities of climate policy.

4. The Green Economy Initiative

Introduction

The global financial and economic crisis that exploded in 2008 coincided with bad news on several fronts. To begin, food and fuel prices suffered significant hikes in the preceding months, with rather negative effects on the living standards of millions of people around the world. Disquieting news also came from the climate-change front, with constant updates of the IPCC's reports which carried more pessimistic messages. In addition, the Millennium Ecosystem Assessment (MEA 2005) had already shown that over the past fifty years human activity had changed ecosystems more rapidly and extensively than in any comparable period of time in human history, leaving behind a wake of impaired ecosystems and irreversible loss of biodiversity.

The other bad news came from the social front: poverty and inequality have remained pervasive. In fact, today there are more people living in poverty than ever before, and 80 per cent of the world's population live in countries where income differentials are widening (HDR 2007/08). This dismal economic performance and its counterpart in environmental degradation are the best proof that the world is moving along an unsustainable trajectory. When the global financial and economic crisis erupted, many thought it was an opportunity to reorganize things and set the world economy on a new path more in accordance with sustainability objectives.

The most striking example is the Green Economy Initiative (GEI) of the United Nations Environment Programme. Its starting point is the fact that the crisis reveals that the world is moving in the wrong direction, but more important, that the packages of fiscal stimulus that were being approved and implemented in late 2008 and 2009 could be used to reorient the world economy and set it on a pathway bound for sustainability. However, although macroeconomics provides the setting for this unfolding crisis, once again the question of macroeconomic policy is absent. This is something that imperils the objectives of the schemes relating to the GEI. In this chapter we examine some of the main aspects of this problem and advance several proposals to redress this situation.

The Green Economy Initiative

The Green Economy Initiative is a multiple exercise spearheaded by UNEP. It consists of a family of initiatives that include the Global Green New Deal (GGND), the TEEB study (*The Economics of Ecosystems and Biodiversity*) and the Green Jobs Initiative of the International Labour Organization (ILO). The GEI centres on the Green Economy Report, an ongoing study whose main objective is to promote a shift in economic thinking, investment and resource management, raising awareness of the important link between the environment, job creation, poverty reduction and the attainment of the Millennium Development Goals (UNEP 2009a).

The 'overall objective is to motivate governments and businesses to significantly increase investment in the environment as an engine for economic recovery and sustainable growth, decent job creation and poverty reduction in the 21st century'. At the same time, the report attempts to encourage a societal shift away from today's extractive, short-term economy and its wide-ranging market failures in food, fuel and finance. Another objective is to demonstrate that investment in 'green' agricultural and industrial sectors can drive economic recovery and lead to future prosperity and job creation, while at the same time addressing global, social and environmental challenges. The sectors covered by the study include agriculture, buildings, fisheries, forests, industry, energy, tourism, transport, waste management and water.

The Global Green New Deal The starting point of the GGND is the triple crisis witnessed in 2008 in the realms of food, fuel and the financial system. As a result, economic output and trade have diminished and unemployment has increased for the first time in decades. 'Faced with the social and economic consequences of a deepening world recession, it may seem a luxury to consider policies that aim to reduce carbon dependency and environmental degradation. Such a conclusion is both false and misleading' (UNEP 2009b). A critical premise in the overall philosophy of the GGND is the notion that 'rebooting the world economic system' is simply not enough to get the world economy on the pathway to sustainability. If a business-as-usual growth path is resumed the problems that are already weighing heavily on the world's environmental health will be exacerbated:

1. global energy prices will continue to rise (by 45 per cent in 2030) with the price of oil expected to hit US$180 a barrel;
2. greenhouse gas emissions will also increase by 45 per cent in 2030, leading to an increase of temperature of as much as 6°C;
3. ecological degradation and water scarcity will intensify;

4 more than a billion people will be living on less than US$1 per day and 3 billion will live on less than US$2 per day.

According to the GGND, these multiple crises demand the same kind of initiative as shown by Franklin D. Roosevelt's New Deal of the 1930s, but 'at the global scale and embracing a wider vision' (ibid.). The idea is that there is the right mix of policy actions that can stimulate recovery and at the same time improve the sustainability of the world economy. These policies should make up a 'Global Green New Deal' that would spearhead the Green Economy Initiative. The 'expanded vision' refers to the need to reduce carbon dependency and protect ecosystems and water resources while alleviating poverty. Without these new horizons, continues the GGND, future crises will not be averted and 'restarting the world economy today will do little to address the imminent threats posed by climate change, energy insecurity, growing freshwater scarcity, deteriorating ecosystems, and above all, worsening global poverty' (ibid.).

The basic premise of the GGND report is that the current economic crisis has brought governments together to instigate a worldwide recovery and that such an opportunity should also be used to address other important global economic, social and environmental challenges (ibid.: 26). But efforts to revive the world economy should not stop at simply re-creating the same pattern of global economic development of the past. Instead, they should stimulate growth and job opportunities while simultaneously moving the world economy towards sustainability.

The GGND states that although the levels of public spending authorized in 2009 to stimulate the world economy are required to quicken recovery and job creation, they are not sufficient to meet the challenges of sustainability. Instead, what's needed is a package of policy, investment and incentive measures with three fundamental objectives (ibid.: 27):

1 a GGND must contribute significantly to the short-run objective of helping revive the world economy, create employment opportunities and protect vulnerable groups;
2 it must reduce carbon dependency, ecosystem degradation and water scarcity so that by 2025 substantial progress is made in limiting global warming and the damages to major ecosystems;
3 it must also further the Millennium Development Goal of ending extreme poverty in the world by 2015.

In the spring of 2009, the GGND report recognized that governments worldwide were committing US$2–$3 trillion in different stimulus packages for the next couple of years to revive the world economy. However, very few of these policy packages contain all three of the above elements, which are considered to be essential for a Global Green New Deal.

The GGND report recognizes that the scale of investments required for this is large and the timetable is short, but concludes that 'the opportunity for instigating the Global Green New Deal is now. At no other time in recent world history has it been possible to achieve a worldwide consensus over a package of policies that can converge on attaining all three fundamental objectives' (ibid.). In order to take advantage of this opportunity to transform the US$2 trillion or more that was committed by the G20 for the recovery into a powerful lever for sustainability, the GGND examines the range of policies that are needed to complement and coordinate current policies.

One would expect a report that argues in favour of a Global Green New Deal with the objectives that have been outlined here to continue with its deliberations at the macroeconomic level before taking a dive into the intricate details of sector-level analysis. But the GGND report does not feel compelled to examine how macroeconomic issues affect the prospects of implementing its major policy objectives. Instead, it plunges into a sector-level format of analysis and leaves the macroeconomic dimension alone.

Perhaps the GGND is unable to engage in this macroeconomic analysis because it is unaware of the true meaning of the New Deal in the decades that followed the end of the Second World War. And this is perhaps its most important shortcoming. The founding of democratic states, committed to full employment and greater equity, in the wake of the defeat of fascism was the overarching event of the post-war era. It was this which made it possible for capitalist economies to improve living standards and maintain stable growth patterns for the period 1945–75. For all its weaknesses, the Rooseveltian New Deal had at its centre a public compact with social justice as a key desideratum, with growth and development as its instruments. This is what neoliberalism destroyed in the eighties and replaced with the abstract objectives of price stability and responsible finance. This is what was replaced by globalization, deregulation and privatization. The outcome was a combination of stumbling growth rates, increased volatility and more intense inequality. The Global Green New Deal would have to deal with these enormous issues in a meaningful way to make its case.

The New Deal rhetoric: diagnosing the global crisis Although the experience of this 'triple crisis' appears to occupy centre stage in the GGND report, the nature and origins of this calamity are never actually examined in detail. This is surprising in a document that sees in the current global crisis an opportunity to orient the world economy towards sustainability: the crisis itself would need to be examined in terms of its origins, nature and main characteristics.

If the multiple crises are considered to be an opportunity, this analysis is essential. For example, the food and fuel crises are described in terms of the spikes in prices that occurred between 2008 and 2009, but the causes of these price dynamics are never examined. Were they due to short-term increases in demand, drops in supply or speculation in commodity markets? Were they caused by price manipulation by giant corporations that concentrate market power in seeds, grain, agricultural inputs and energy markets? Perhaps they were the result of long-run trends in yields and falling rates of per capita harvested land? Are these price movements related to the exhaustion of global oil reserves or are they more related to factors that intensify volatility in energy markets? The GGND does not give any attention to these questions.

It is difficult to justify the GGND shrinking away from the task of analysing the origins and nature of these multiple crises, while at the same time stating that they provide an opportunity. It's as if a doctor, confronted by a sick man, declares that sickness is a good opportunity to put the patient on the road to a healthy life without taking the trouble to diagnose his disease in the first place.

The final section of the GGND provides further evidence of the urgent need to engage in a serious analysis of the origins of the global economic and financial crisis. In its solitary substantive reference to the origins of the financial crisis, the GGND has this to say (ibid.: 80):

> The existing crisis may have more to do with a failure of governance and a lack of transparency rather than a lack of regulation. The financial system is already governed by many regulations and procedures. Most countries have a multitude of agencies supervising every aspect of financial activity – central and private banks, stock exchanges, securities, mortgage lenders and even other public agencies involved in the system.

This is one of the most astonishing statements contained in the GGND report. It constitutes an important blunder that essentially contradicts the call to set the world economy on the trajectory of sustainable development. The GGND states that the current crisis is an opportunity to redefine the course of the world economy, but when it comes to analysing the origins and nature of the crisis, the GGND clearly prefers leaving things to run in a business-as-usual mode.

In fact, it adopts a point of view that contradicts what has now come to be the most commonly accepted explanation for the financial crisis. The GGND ignores the decisive deregulation of the financial system in the United States that started in 1978 with the Supreme Court's decision in *Marquette* vs *First Omaha* holding that state anti-usury laws regulating interest rates could not be enforced against nationally chartered banks based in other states. This was followed in 1982 by the Garn-St Germain law deregulating the savings and loans industry, a measure that has much to do with the crisis in this sector at the end of that decade. In 1994 the Riegle-Neal law eliminated restrictions on banks' interstate activities.

Two years later the Federal Reserve under Greenspan reinterpreted the Glass-Steagall Act allowing banking corporations to obtain up to 25 per cent of their profits from activities related to investment banking. The Gramm-Leach-Bliley Financial Services Modernization Act of 1999 did away with the Glass-Steagall Act, which had been the backbone of banking-sector regulation since 1933.

The GGND also disregards the effects of changes in the Commodity Futures Modernization Act between 1989 and 1993. During this period, many over-the-counter derivatives and swaps trading operations were classified as ineligible for monitoring by the Commodity Futures Trading Commission because they were considered to be essentially different from futures transactions. They were also outside the radar screen of the Securities and Exchange Commission (SEC), because these operations were not securities. The GGND also overlooks the deregulation that allowed for collateralized debt obligations (CDOs) and credit default swaps (CDS) and other examples of unchecked 'financial innovation', including no controls over predatory lenders. In 2004 the SEC approved a system of voluntary self-regulation on certain aspects of investment banking that allowed banks to operate with smaller reserves and greater leverage. All of these measures were behind the build-up in huge, risky positions whose unwinding has led the world economy into a debt deflation crisis of monumental proportions.[1]

Not content with this viewpoint, the GGND report continues (ibid.):

> There are also independent assessors, such as credit rating agencies and research analysts, and all financial institutions have their own internal credit and audit procedures. In addition, the financial crisis did not originate in poorly regulated emerging markets but in the most heavily regulated markets of Europe and the United States. Thus, reforms of the financial system should focus on better governance and not more regulation. Indeed, simply adding more regulation could reduce transparency and could in fact worsen governance.

It appears that the GGND rejects the enormous amount of literature concerning the revolving-doors syndrome of the financial markets over the past two decades. The credit rating agencies of the private sector have been totally discredited as a result of a system that gives them the power to give high ratings to their clients. As to the internal audit and accounting procedures, the GGND should take note of the incentives to take high risks that were generated by the very essence of derivatives and securitization. To put it mildly, the naivety of the GGND report is disconcerting.[2]

The lapses in the GGND report are not limited to the problem of financial deregulation. It also ignores the vast series of financial crises that took place during the 1990s, from Mexico to East Asia, Indonesia, Thailand, Malaysia, Brazil, Russia and Turkey, to mention a few salient examples. It averts its eyes from the enormous capital flows that concentrate on currency speculation in the world today, and the deep deregulation that has accompanied financial liberalization since the demise of the Bretton Woods system. In brief, the Green Economy Initiative takes as its starting point the notion that 'rebooting the system' will not get us on the road to sustainability, but by not understanding and correctly diagnosing the current crisis, it denies itself the possibility of doing otherwise.

The problem with the GGND diagnosis concerns not only the causes of the crisis, but also its nature. There is ample evidence that this is not only a financial crisis, susceptible of receiving an explanation in terms of Hyman Minsky's analysis of financial instability, but a crisis whose roots go deep into the heart of the real sector of the most advanced capitalist economies.[3] Palley (2009) shows that the post-1980 neoliberal growth model relied on rising debt and asset price inflation to fill the hole in aggregate demand created by wage stagnation and widened income inequality. Minsky's analysis explains how financial markets filled this hole and made the neoliberal model last longer. From Palley's perspective the mechanisms identified with Minsky's financial instability hypothesis are critical to understanding the neoliberal era, but they are part of a broader narrative. The neoliberal model was always unsustainable and would have ground to a halt of its own accord. The role of Minsky's financial instability hypothesis is to explain why the neoliberal model kept going far longer than anticipated. A viewpoint diametrically opposed to the GGND is developed (ibid.):

> By giving free rein to the Minsky mechanisms of financial innovation, financial deregulation, regulatory escape, and increased appetite for

financial risk, policymakers (like former Federal Reserve Chairman Alan Greenspan) extended the life of the neoliberal model. The sting in the tail was this made the crisis deeper and more abrupt when financial markets eventually reached their limits. Without financial innovation and financial deregulation the neoliberal model would have got stuck in stagnation a decade earlier, but it would have been stagnation without the pyrotechnics of financial crisis.

Another study agreeing with the notion that events in the real sector have a lot to do with the origins and nature of the crisis is Dumenil and Lévy (2004). A key element in this analysis is the stagnant profit rates of the seventies and eighties, and the repression of wages as part of an effort to push back the pro-labour conquests of the welfare state. Arrighi (1994) provides a detailed account of the expansion of the financial sector as an expression of capital's response to falling profit rates.

UNEP's Global Green New Deal rejects the need to diagnose the nature and genesis of the current global crisis. By doing so, it denies itself access to a serious analysis of where the world economy is moving and loses the opportunity to offer truly viable policy recommendations to attain sustainability. In the end, and parts of its rhetoric notwithstanding, the GGND embraces the position of mainstream macroeconomics that nothing needs to be done and the best course is to leave markets to act freely.

Sector-level analysis and macroeconomic policy constraints

Dominated by the idea that macroeconomic policies have to remain unchanged, even in the context of a Global Green New Deal, the rest of UNEP's analysis focuses on two key sectors that are considered to be critical for sustainability: reducing carbon dependency and reducing ecological scarcity. In what follows we examine how the GGND deals with the second of these issues and how this interacts with macroeconomic policies.[4] We also take a look at its analysis of market-friendly mechanisms for environmental stewardship, jobs and wages.

Poverty and ecological scarcity The GGND defines ecological scarcity as the loss of ecosystem benefits or 'services' as they are exploited for human use and economic activity (UNEP 2009b: 44). According to the GGND, ecological scarcity is intensifying and the poor in the world are the most vulnerable to the resulting deterioration of ecological services. This is in accord with the results of the Millennium Ecosystem Assessment. But at this juncture, the report makes a surprising assertion: 'a GGND must also tackle urgently the problem of extreme world poverty *caused* by rising ecological scarcity, as well as implement measures that more directly reduce the vulnerability of the world's poor' (ibid.: 44, emphasis added). This is surprising in a document that has made so many references to world poverty and the MDGs. It is one thing to accept that poor people are more vulnerable to environmental degradation and another, quite different, to jump from that fact to a causality by which poverty is *caused* by ecological scarcity. This is plainly wrong and fails to respond to some important questions concerning the economic relations that have been implemented and exist today in the era of globalization. A more serious analysis of the causes of world poverty is required in a document that purports to eradicate extreme world poverty by 2015 while promoting economic recovery. This lack of attention to the root causes of poverty not only threatens the viability of the GGND, it actually transforms it into a vehicle of continuity for the neoliberal regime.

Instead of tackling frontally the central problem of world poverty, the GGND skirts around these difficult issues. Perhaps the reason for this is that any serious analysis of poverty would call into question the economic model that has been implemented almost at the global level during the past three decades. It would entail looking not only at wages and distribution within national economies, but also at the question of terms of trade, debt service and international inequality.

The first policy recommendation is to 'improve the sustainability of primary production'. According to the GGND, much of the population in developing countries depends directly on the exploitation of natural resources and the environment for agriculture, livestock, fishing and fuel. This segment of the world's population includes a significant proportion of people living in extreme poverty. Thus, improving the sustainability of primary production in developing countries would allow developing economies to achieve multiple development objectives.

The definition of primary production is problematic. The document appears to limit this to agriculture, livestock, fishing and fuel-wood collection. In this context, it highlights the effects of ecosystem degradation on the world's poor. Of course, large-scale commercial agriculture is also primary production and frequently has been closely related to some of the underlying root causes of poverty and environmental destruction. The GGND does not address this part of the problem.[5]

How does the GGND think that primary production can be made more sustainable? Because of the heterogeneity of developing countries and the difficulty of formulating a prescription for the policies required by all countries 'to improve the sustainable and efficient use of natural resources', the report stops short of making recommendations that could be applicable in general. It does, however, point towards the need to implement policies that enhance sustainability and which ensure that sufficient financial returns from these activities are reinvested in infrastructure, healthcare, education and skills to guarantee long-term economic development. But insufficient investment in these items has been one of the consequences of neoliberal fiscal policies. In the case of agriculture, it is also a result of the way in which the world's agricultural trade regime has evolved. The GGND fails to make any references to this part of the problem.

In fact, this section is most disappointing because there is already a huge amount of information on technologies for sustainable agriculture which require public support to be implemented and disseminated in developing countries, and the GGND simply ignores this. The International Assessment of Agricultural Science and Technology for Development (IAASTD 2009) is clear about this issue.[6] The difference is that the IAASTD includes a recommendation to develop macro-level policy changes to enable agricultural knowledge and technology linkages with development goals. The GGND is in this view a regression when compared with IAASTD.

The GGND is correct in identifying agriculture as an important area that can make a significant contribution to sustainability and recovery. As it points out, by 2025 the rural population of the developing world will have increased to 3.2 billion people. The involvement of women in direct production and post-harvest activities reaches very high levels (66 per cent in sub-Saharan Africa and 69 per cent in South Asia). Health, education, deteriorating working conditions, deficient access to municipal services and, of course, low income are some of the acute problems affecting rural households.

However, once again the background analysis is weak. Because of its size and strategic importance in environmental stewardship and employment, small-scale agriculture should be at the centre of any effort to launch a GGND. The potential offered by improving livelihoods and food security in small-scale agriculture to attain the Millennium Development Goals is another reason for this. Of course, putting small-scale agriculture in this centrepiece role requires that it be provided with adequate support policies.[7]

There are two obstacles that impede the implementation of these types of policies, and they both pertain to the realm of macroeconomic policy-making. The first is related to fiscal policy: as public investment is curtailed in order to generate a primary surplus, one of the critical areas hurt by cuts in public spending is agriculture. In most developing countries, support for almost all facets of agricultural activities – R&D, extensionism (i.e. the transmission of technological information and in some cases assistance to producers), infrastructure and income deficiency payments – has remained stagnant or has been falling in recent years. In most developing countries the aggregate measure of support for agriculture authorized by the World Trade Organization under the Uruguay Round Agreement on Agriculture (URAA) has simply not been exhausted. In Mexico, for example, total expenditures on agriculture could be quadrupled and still be 100 per cent WTO compatible (i.e. within the limits of the allowed aggregate measure of support).[8]

Tight monetary policies and deregulated credit and banking operations have also contributed to a drastic reduction in credit for small-scale agricultural activities. Because of the reduction in producers' prices, the perceived risk of defaults on loans made to small-scale farmers increases and this causes banks to avoid this sector. The combination of producers' prices reductions, reduced government support in real terms and almost zero credit represents a mortal blow to small-scale agriculture. This is one of the most important negative contributions of neoliberalism.

The second obstacle is trade liberalization. Under the straitjacket that the URAA implies, trade liberalization has led to imports of cheap agricultural products that are heavily subsidized in the developed economies. It must be recalled that rich countries subsidize their economies to the tune of more than US$340 billion a year. In many cases large-scale commercial agriculture and giant corporations controlling the intensely cartelized markets for grains, seeds and agricultural inputs are responsible for price manipulation and for dumping. Agricultural commodities are currently facing a decline in prices, a process aggravated by strong fluctuations. This has destroyed the livelihoods of many small-scale producers in many developing countries. As market concentration intensifies, and global retail chains expand, the winners of trade liberalization have been the large corporations that wield immense market power and dominate key channels of production and marketing of food crops and other critical commodities. The losers in this process are millions of small-scale producers and landless workers in developing countries, already weakened by the global trade regime, an adverse macroeconomic policy package and inadequate bargaining capacity.[9] Against this grim background, food security is likely to worsen if markets and market-driven agricultural production systems continue to grow in a business-as-usual mode (IAASTD 2009: 22).

Agriculture is a powerful instrument for healthy environmental stewardship. It is a large-scale land management system that carries out a multi-functional role and on which 3.1 billion human beings are heavily dependent (UNDESA 2007). Small-scale agriculture has suffered substantial damage due to trade liberalization, fiscal retrenchment and the role of giant corporations in the global market. However, when the GGND touches the issues of trade liberalization, it emphasizes the need to achieve good results in the Doha Round. Although there is a raging debate on the merits and defects of the Doha Round, especially in the context of the global crisis, the GGND avoids mentioning the problems that trade liberalization has brought about: we return to these issues in our final chapter.

One final comment is warranted about labour-intensive agricultural practices that are beneficial from the standpoint of soil conservation and the enhancement of agricultural biodiversity. In many instances the plight of small-scale producers as producers' prices fall and public support is withdrawn, forces households to migrate in search of off-farm income-generating options. This leads to a labour shortage in rural areas and to the abandonment of these labour-intensive agricultural practices. This is one very clear example of why macroeconomic policies have severe impacts on the environment and UNEP in its Global Green New Deal should take a hard look at these issues. Clearly, agricultural policies in many developing countries are responding more to fiscal constraints (primary surplus priorities) than to the plight of the rural poor and to environmental degradation.

Instead of examining this complex problem area, the GGND analyses the role of two other mechanisms for poverty alleviation. One is the payment for environmental services (PES), a policy measure that gained much support in the past decade. This mechanism may be of limited scope, but it offers the possibility of leaving the priorities of neoliberal fiscal policy untouched. Even the GGND recognizes this and states that because the main objective is to generate incentives to landowners for the protection of critical ecosystems, payment systems for ecosystem services cannot be relied upon to act as a large-scale poverty reduction instrument (UNEP 2009b: 51).

In any event, references to PES must also take into consideration two intimately related questions: will they provide for sufficient financial resources and who is going to be required to pay? Of course, each case may be different given the diversity of environmental services and their situational context. However, if the answer to the first question is the government, then we must analyse the structure and priorities of fiscal policy. Once again, if public finance is guided solely by the principle of generating a primary surplus, obtaining the necessary resources to maintain a sustainable scheme of PES may prove to be a difficult task.[10] One example of how fiscal policy priorities affect these programmes of payment for environmental services is found in Costa Rica, where the programme for forest conservation has not been running well. We examine this in Chapter 5.

In 2007 more people were living in urban than in rural areas. Poverty rates in urban areas are high in much of the developing world, and because most goods and services are traded in urban areas, the poor require higher incomes than in rural areas. It is difficult to see how the urban poor would benefit (if at all) from payments for environmental services. On the other hand, vast public investments in environmental renewal and conservation could directly benefit urban poor by creating jobs, even if temporarily. Again, fiscal constraints promise to be a formidable obstacle.

A second policy mechanism considered by the GGND is the direct 'targeting of investments designed to improve the livelihoods of the rural poor, thus reducing their dependence on exploiting environmental resources' (ibid.: 52). The report considers that if this geographical targeting is designed correctly, it can be successful. Furthermore, the GGND report states that 'under-investment in human capital and lack of access to financial credit is a chronic feature of the extreme poor, especially those poor households concentrated on fragile land. These households generate insufficient savings, suffer chronic indebtedness and rely on informal credit markets with high short-term interest rates' (ibid.: 53). The importance of these programmes that target the poor is stressed by the GGND as they are considered to be the backbone of a policy to build a social safety net.

There is one problem with this analysis: targeted anti-poverty programmes are nothing new and they are part and parcel of the neoliberal policy package as it emphasizes the reduction of expenditures to maintain 'healthy' fiscal management. In response to the fierceness of some structural adjustment measures, and realizing that destroying social safety nets could have dangerous consequences, the World Bank was the first to suggest and then forcefully impose the implementation of focalized or targeted anti-poverty programmes. These were considered to be more effective and less costly. As the main priority of fiscal policy became to generate a primary surplus in order to respond to debt management needs, cutting expenditures became critical. Focalized or targeted anti-poverty programmes were seen as a good way to achieve this goal while at the same time providing what appeared to be a social safety net. But these programmes have failed to reduce poverty: according to the World Bank Development Indicators in 2005 there were more than three billion people living below the poverty line of US$2.5 per day and more than five billion were living with incomes equivalent or inferior to US$10 per day! The Global Green New Deal should focus on the origins and dynamics of this problem because it is at the heart of its proposal. Recommending the continuation of a failed set of policies and ignoring the question about the origins of the colossal levels of poverty in the world does not bode well for the GGND.

Environmental stewardship and 'market-friendly instruments' The GGND has faith in the role of market incentives in channelling private investment in accordance with the policy priorities of sustainability. But it seems to forget that market forces have not taken the world economy towards sustainability. In fact, if we are today in a world in which pervasive inequality and environmental degradation coexist, it is in good measure due to the economic model that was implemented over the past thirty years worldwide, a model based on rampant privatization, market freedom and minimum state intervention.[11]

The Global Green New Deal is not alone in embracing this faith in market-friendly policy instruments. According to UNEP's *Global Environmental Outlook 4* (2007),

> natural resources can be seen as a capital asset belonging to a general portfolio, which is comprised of other assets and capitals, including material, financial, human and social. Managing this portfolio in a good and sustainable manner to maximize its returns and benefits over time is good investment. It is also central to sustainable development. A variety of economic instruments exist, including property rights, market creation, fiscal instruments, charge systems, financial instruments, liability systems, and bonds and deposits.

This is the type of reference to the continuation and deepening of the neoliberal policy package that will be closing the doors to a meaningful revision of existing policies. In view of the debate on the monetarization of commodities and futures markets, and their role in the food and energy crises in 2008, this is a most astonishing statement from UNEP. This is the 'Old Deal' with a makeover. The GGND seems to be unacquainted with the theoretical discussion concerning the allocative efficiency of markets (see Box 1.1). The failure to analyse the implications and role of macroeconomic policy, together with these incantations about market-based instruments, is an indication that the GGND report may be closer to neoliberalism than to a new model for sustainability.

The final section on the role of the international community is another salient aspect of the GGND. It is clear that a concerted effort to put the world economy on the pathway to sustainability requires a critical examination of international economic relations. There are many factors that make this an urgent necessity. The world economy was deeply transformed forty years ago, as the Bretton Woods system of fixed exchange rates was abandoned. As we have seen in Chapters 1 and 2, this gave rise to an economy marked by financial liberalization and the colossal expansion of the financial and banking sectors. At the same time, a new regulatory framework for financial flows has been established with important implications for monetary and fiscal policies. The asymmetries between surplus and deficit economies, as well as between rich and poor countries, are another important feature of the world economy. Finally, giant corporations concentrate more market power than ever before, and they are critical economic agents whose role in the structure of the world economy needs to be taken into account. All of these macroeconomic policy aspects of the world economy are highly relevant for the design and implementation of a new blueprint as ambitious as the Global Green New Deal. The UNEP (2009b) report carefully avoids discussing these issues.

Jobs, wages, ecosystems and poverty The Green Economy Initiative is not only about the Global Green New Deal. It also includes the Green Jobs Initiative promoted by the International Labour Organization, and the project on *The Economics of Ecosystems and Biodiversity* (TEEB).[12] These components of the overall Green Economy Initiative are linked in many ways, but one important common thread is poverty and inequality.

The ILO component also lacks the macroeconomic policy perspective that is required to set the world economy on the path to sustainability. This omission is most surprising in the ILO report on green jobs.[13] Although employment creation is one of the key elements of macroeconomic policies, the terms monetary policy and fiscal policy simply do not appear in the ILO report. And here the GEI misses a golden opportunity to start redressing a situation that lies at the root of the current global crisis. Various studies have documented the fact that in the past decades wages have grown at a substantially slower pace than GDP per capita (ILO 2008). In fact, many studies talk about the compression of wages (Galbraith 2000) to analyse this process in which a great number of countries registered a decline in the share of national income that goes to wages, indicating that growth in wages has lagged well behind productivity increases. And these trends and data are from before the crisis: today, as the crisis unfolds, the ILO tells us that 39 million people were added to the ranks of the unemployed in 2009.

Not paying attention to the evolution of wages and to incomes policies in general is an especially important omission of the GEI because the recovery from the global crisis will be very slow and, in many countries, job creation will take a long time. One problem that the world economy confronts is that for every year that a person remains unemployed, the probability that he or she will remain unemployed increases. If on top of that current trends in the evolution of wages continue, then inequality and poverty will increase. In the context of the current global crisis, this is particularly worrying because wages tend to fall at faster rates in times of crisis. Recovery will be slower owing to this additional factor that weakens aggregate demand. And because the emerging pattern of income distribution will be marked by greater inequality, a green and sustainable recovery will be difficult to attain.

In terms of poverty and environmental stewardship, the panorama that emerges from this picture is disquieting. The Green Economy Initiative should explicitly adopt the policy objective of redressing existing inequalities and of establishing the institutions (like collective bargaining) that could help reduce the inequalities brought about by neoliberalism. It is important to understand that inequality is associated with greater pressure on people's livelihoods and the social fabric of communities, something that degrades their capacity for environmental stewardship.

The struggle to arrest loss of biodiversity and ecosystem degradation is another key component of the Green Economy Initiative. In its initial phase the TEEB arrived at the conclusion that 'loss of biodiversity and ecosystems is a threat to the functioning of our planet, our economy and human society' (TEEB 2008: 14). This initiative is based on three premises. First, the destruction of biodiversity is due to market failures and the lack of proper valuation systems for biodiversity. Second, we need to design new market structures capable of determining prices for these ecosystem services. Third, poverty is inextricably linked with biodiversity loss. The TEEB interim report shares the narrow perspective of the GGND as it ignores macroeconomic policies and focuses on market failures. Once again, it would appear that macroeconomic policy priorities have nothing to do with biodiversity loss.

The TEEB report is a strange combination of notions from environmental and ecological economics. Its fundamental premise is that we need to assign prices to the components of the environment that we are losing: ecosystems services and biodiversity. The fundamental premise is that 'we cannot manage what we do not measure', a slogan repeated like a mantra in the TEEB. The associated idea is that the right measure is provided by prices. This faith in prices is not justified: it is not at all evident that management proceeds smoothly when we have prices. In fact, the current global crisis arose in the context of economic spaces where every item had a price (namely, financial markets). Also, price dynamics may have extremely destabilizing effects on the allocation of resources.[14] Why would prices improve management?[15]

Furthermore, what is 'management' in this context? The authors and promoters of TEEB appear to think that management is some kind of neutral social process that ensures things are done correctly. This naive view of things is, of course, completely misleading. We can manage marine fisheries to maximize the rate of return from their depletion. Or we can clear-cut a forest in order to obtain the highest possible return in the shortest period of time. Both living marine resources and forest products have prices, but precisely because they have a price they can be mismanaged to exhaustion. On the other hand, there are things in this world that are best left untouched by the notion that everything must have a price if we are to give it some value. Assigning a price to a captive bottlenose dolphin does not ensure that we will start managing marine ecosystems adequately.

The TEEB report (ibid.: 28) includes a section on 'Economics, ethics and equity' that begins with a remarkable quote: 'Economics is pure weaponry: its targets are ethical choices.' How should we interpret this? The TEEB report is apparently stating that, yes, some questions are ethical, but with adequate economic tools ('weaponry') we can approach them with greater rigour. This is not only false, but is in fact a dangerous proposition.[16] Ethical norms require a deliberative stance from citizens, while economics demands that agents remain ignorant of its anonymous laws. Perhaps this is the tragedy of economic theory, a peculiar discourse on society whose *raison d'être* requires expelling ethics from its core (Nadal 2004b). Only ignorance about the sad state in which economic theory is today can explain why anyone would make such a claim.

Concluding remarks

The Green Economy Initiative is an ambitious enterprise that is lacking a solid foundation. Nobody should deny that we need to set the world economy on the path of good environmental stewardship and sustainability. And yes, we need to reduce greenhouse gas emissions and have better recycling techniques. But the main lesson here is that although transforming our technological base is a necessary condition for sustainability, there are other equally important and unavoidable macroeconomic policy issues demanding attention. These relate not only to the dynamics of key macroeconomic aggregates, but also to distributional questions. It is impossible to 'green the economy' while maintaining at the same time a regime of social exclusion, oppression and inequality. Likewise, there is no access to sustainability if we don't redress the structural imbalances that burden the world economy today. Finally, social responsibility will be a difficult objective to achieve in a world economy ruled by finance capital. We will examine some of these problems in the last two chapters.

A strategy to green the world economy needs to revise the world economy's structure and dynamics, and this implies revising the current model based on the mantra that markets are efficient mechanisms for resource allocation and that macroeconomic policies should not interfere or try to influence aggregate output and employment. The current crisis, considered to be an opportunity by UNEP to launch the GGND, was generated by an economic model that needs to convert everything into commodities, from derivatives to dolphins. UNEP does not seem to be uncomfortable about the fact that the current crisis was brought about by market forces, and continues to preach the advantages of market-friendly instruments.

Finally, when the GEI was launched the most urgent question for UNEP was how to orient the incentives in the fiscal stimulus package to foster sustainability or environmental objectives. By refusing to carry out its own independent diagnosis of the origins and nature of this crisis, UNEP's Green Economy Initiative has, pun not intended, lost the initiative: today (March 2010) the most important issue debated by governments and central banks is how long the stimulus package (including a zero-interest monetary policy) is going to last. Thus, the big question now is not how to use the fiscal stimulus, but rather what the exit strategy is. This question reveals that the political and financial elites are worried about how to reduce the deficit. If the world of neoliberalism survives this crisis, when signs of recovery come the first question is going to be how to reduce the government deficit, and this is going to be done through deep cuts in expenditures. The first to go will be budgetary items related to environmental stewardship.

5 · Latin American focus

Introduction

From Europe or the United States, Latin America is seen as a culturally homogeneous region, closely connected by historical and cultural heritage. This is the land of ancient civilizations, as well as the pan-American vision of Simón Bolívar, the hero who led the struggle for independence at the beginning of the nineteenth century. The region also hosts pristine and unique ecosystems and is perceived as being generously endowed in natural resources. Although it has only 8 per cent of the world's population, it possesses 23 per cent of the world's potential arable land, 10 per cent of cultivated land, 17 per cent of pastures, 22 per cent of forests (52 per cent of tropical forests) and 31 per cent of permanently usable water (Chichilniski and Gallopín 2001).

Eight of the eighteen countries classified as mega-diverse by UNEP are in the Latin American region (Bolivia, Brazil, Costa Rica, Colombia, Ecuador, Mexico, Peru and Venezuela). Together, these countries have a very high percentage of the world's species of reptiles, amphibians, mammals, birds and vascular plants. Endemism is high, and several of the most important biodiversity hot spots are found here, including the Amazon tropical rainforest, the tropical Andes and the Mesoamerican corridor.

Latin America is also marked by common patterns in its development strategies. During the period following the Second World War most of the region's economies followed an import substitution strategy implemented through strong leadership from state agencies. This scheme met with some success until the seventies, when internal and external tensions slowed down growth rates. The debt crisis that exploded in the early eighties (owing to high interest rates and falling commodity prices) spelled the demise of the import substitution strategy, and in some cases of the aspiration to industrialization. This led to significant changes in the development strategies of the most important Latin American countries.

Eventually, import substitution gave way to the establishment of an open economy model along the lines of the Washington Consensus. The economic performance of the Latin American economies under this new strategic approach presents a rather mixed picture, but in general average growth rates were slower than in the post-war years. In addition, the old contradictions and tensions that marked the Latin American economies did not cease to exist and new ones appeared. Finally, during the nineties, several financial crises struck in most of the region, bringing about important changes in the policy outlook of countries like Argentina, Bolivia, Brazil and Ecuador.

Throughout these different phases of economic activity, the environmental integrity of the region has been endangered. The degree of deterioration justifies questioning the effects of this process on the region's future development prospects. It has been continuously affected by the expansion of the agricultural frontier, deforestation, urbanization, irresponsible activities by extractive industries (by both private and public enterprises), as well as various forms of pollution. Although most countries in the region established ministries for the environment, the fact remains that none of them has been able to establish a policy framework that duly integrates environmental stewardship with economic development.[1]

Import substitution as a development strategy

After the Second World War, most of the countries in the region embarked on industrialization strategies based on a set of policies to substitute imports.[2] The new Latin American perspective was inspired by the work of a group of economists at the Economic Commission for Latin America and the Caribbean (ECLAC) who maintained that development and growth would not come simply from capital accumulation and comparative advantages. The new vision had analysed trends of international terms of trade and concluded that they were moving against traditional primary product exports. Thus, domestic production would have to replace non-essential imports through a set of protectionist policies. This called for a stronger role for the public sector.

In general, the import substitution industrialization (ISI) pattern of growth was accompanied by good performance in GDP growth rates in the period 1950–73. But in 1973 international oil markets were severely disturbed by the oil embargo imposed in the aftermath of the Yom Kippur war, and things started to change. The rate of growth of per capita income is a good indicator of the evolution of the region's most important economies. For a sample of twelve Latin American countries, annual growth rates in the period 1950–73 averaged 2.12 per cent. During the period 1973–2000, this average rate dropped to 0.79 per cent. The disparities between these countries can be readily seen in Table 5.1.

Over a twenty-year period, between 1950 and 1970, the ISI strategy successfully brought about the expansion of the manufacturing sector and of employment. Between 1960 and 1965, the manufacturing sector in the region grew at a yearly rate of 7 per cent, with Argentina, Brazil and Mexico leading the way. In most cases, the industrialization process took place without a definite plan or priorities in investment policy.

TABLE 5.1 Growth rates in GDP per capita: selected countries in Latin America

	1950–73	1973–90	1990–2000	1973–2000
Argentina	2.05	−1.24	2.87	0.26
Bolivia	0.90	−0.41	1.60	0.33
Brazil	3.73	1.41	1.22	1.34
Chile	1.26	1.35	4.39	2.47
Colombia	2.13	1.93	0.52	1.40
Costa Rica	3.49	0.56	2.66	1.33
Ecuador	2.50	1.01	−2.27	−0.22
El Salvador	1.99	−0.59	2.51	0.55
Mexico	3.17	1.38	1.67	1.49
Peru	2.45	−1.70	2.24	−0.26
Uruguay	0.28	1.56	1.96	1.71
Venezuela	1.55	−1.43	0.12	−0.86

Source: Urquídi (2005: Table I.2)

The ISI strategy ignored several important aspects of economic change. First, it neglected the assimilation of technological capabilities, a crucial difference with the protectionist policies of Japan and South-East Asia.[3] Second, protectionism in the Latin American experience was unconditional, without time schedules or performance requirements. This has been aptly described as 'frivolous protectionism' by Fajnzylber (1983). This provides a very strong contrast with Japan, Korea and Taiwan, where protectionism and finance were subject to technology, employment and technology performance requirements (Amsden 1989). Third, the industrialization process in Latin America intensified the vulnerability of the external accounts in the region (the manufacturing sector helps explain the chronic external deficit). Finally, the highly unequal income distribution structures in most Latin American countries limited the size of the domestic market.

Macroeconomic stability played an important role during the heyday of the import substitution strategy. Exchange-rate volatility was not a crucial problem, although some countries did experience balance-of-payments difficulties. On the other hand, fiscal policy allowed for the building of infrastructure and social expenditures at adequate levels. Finally, monetary policy relied on banking regulations that maintained credit flows towards productive activities.[4] All of this was to change abruptly during the seventies and with the debt crisis in the eighties.

The import substitution strategy implemented after the Second World War brought about deep changes in the structure of the Latin American economies. But the growth process associated with this strategy came to an end in the 1980s. It also failed to provide the foundations for sound environmental stewardship and healthy natural resource management practices.

Data on environmental deterioration in Latin America for the period 1950–80 are in short supply. However, during the three decades (1945–75) that make up the core years of the ISI strategy, Latin American economies did not give adequate attention to environmental objectives. During these decades the natural resource base was heavily taxed and very little in the form of investment went into what we now call environmental expenditures. Natural resource management practices, cleaning up, reforestation, good practices for soil conservation, water management, urban planning and pollution abatement, as well as other aspects of environmental sustainability, were almost entirely neglected by governments in the region during this period. In fact, in many instances measures that implied heavy environmental degradation were adopted, leading to soil erosion, deforestation, aquifer depletion and pervasive pollution.

To explain the process of environmental degradation, Lopez (2003: 260) develops the key hypothesis 'that environmental and natural resource degradation should be looked at as an integral part of a pattern of growth followed by Latin America, not in isolation'. Although he relies on an analytical framework that concentrates on market failures and property rights inefficiencies, his approach is helpful in unravelling how macroeconomic policies that favoured growth through the accumulation of physical capital also contributed to environmental degradation and social inequality. The most visible aspects of these macroeconomic policies are in the field of credit markets and monetary policy, as well as in fiscal policy (taxation and subsidies). For example, the fiscal deficit remained an intractable problem, in great measure owing to the unwillingness to implement a redistributive fiscal reform. Fiscal revenues were insufficient to keep pace with the growing demands of healthcare, education, housing, transportation, infrastructure and, of course, environmental stewardship. In many instances (examples abound) public enterprises were hard pressed to maximize non-tax fiscal revenues through irrational exploitation of the natural resources at their disposal.

In the end, the internal tensions, together with the negative transformations in the international economy (recession and inflation in the USA during the seventies, high interest rates implemented by Volcker's Federal Reserve and the drop in commodity and oil prices), brought about the demise of the ISI. The international debt crisis of the 1980s was the *coup de grâce* that interrupted the import substitution approach to industrialization and development. After that decade, in which per capita growth stagnated ('the lost decade'), none of the Latin American countries returned to the ISI model. Instead a new approach was undertaken, based on trade and financial liberalization.

Neoliberalism in Latin America: the open economy model

The new approach was based on the idea that the development process had to be left in the hands of free markets. Although the notion that markets allocate resources efficiently lacked any scientific demonstration, the ideological triumph of this belief had been consolidated since the 1970s, especially under the political hubris of Margaret Thatcher and Ronald Reagan.

During the 1980s, the main international financial organizations, the IMF and the World Bank, had used the international debt crisis and the stabilization plans to promote the policy agenda known as the Washington Consensus (Williamson 1990). The five crucial components of the policy package were the following: price stability; balanced budgets for fiscal policy; deregulation of the capital account; international trade liberalization; minimum state intervention in the economy.

Initially, the new open economy model established in most of the Latin American region led to strong positive expectations about investment and growth, as well as a sense of stability. Growth rates improved in the early nineties as inflationary expectations diminished and foreign direct investment started to recover. But this changed quickly as a new crisis exploded in Mexico in 1994. The detonator was a reversal of capital flows and the shock wave affected all of Latin America. This crisis was erroneously interpreted as a foreign exchange crisis and described as a financial crisis. In fact, it demonstrated how the main contradictions of the model would inexorably lead other countries to similar crises.

Towards the last years of the nineties, it was thought that Latin

America could regain some of its competitiveness in manufactures. However, a succession of severe macroeconomic crises (Mexico 1995, Brazil 1997/98, Ecuador 1999 and Argentina 2001) had very negative consequences. The share of manufactures in regional GDP continued to drop and manufacturing value added in the region declined from US$316 to US$285 billion between 2000 and 2004. In international trade, growth of Latin American manufacturing exports lagged behind world average rates. To summarize, manufactures' share in total exports from the region dropped as Latin America moved towards 'reprimarization' with greater reliance on low-value-added and resource-intensive commodities.

In order to understand how macroeconomic policies affect the environment in Latin America, and to follow the country-level studies, we need to analyse how the open economy model functions. This model is marked by essential contradictions that hinder its operations and lead to structural imbalances and, finally, to crises.[5] The first contradiction is related to the role of the exchange rate, which is expected to float freely, maintaining equilibrium in the trade balance.[6] The use of the exchange rate as the anchor of the relative price system imposes severe rigidities on exchange rates. Furthermore, capital inflows lead to currency appreciation and pressure to maintain exchange-rate stability. Typically, the adjustment through the exchange rate is delayed as much as possible, and when the adjustment in the exchange rate is finally carried out, it takes place under conditions of great volatility and unrest in the financial markets. Although the crisis is said to be an exchange-rate crisis, it is really a structural crisis of the open economy model.

The second contradiction is related to the interest rate. In the open economy model a current account deficit is financed by capital inflows. This can lead to the expansion of the money supply, an undesired effect that fuels inflation. To prevent this from happening, monetary authorities sterilize the incoming capital through open market operations. The problem is that sterilization interrupts the adjustment process because the interest rate is kept at an artificial level that is higher than the international rate. Capital inflows continue, reserves grow and domestic investment continues to be confronted with a high interest rate.[7]

The third contradiction is that capital flows can artificially maintain a country's capacity to import goods, without any clear relationship with the country's capacity to export. If the trade deficit is basically due to imports of consumer goods, it cannot be financed by capital inflows for a long period of time. The use of capital inflows to maintain imports may have a contractionary effect on the domestic market and the level of aggregate activity (Bhaduri 1998; Bhaduri and Skarstein 1996). At the beginning of the process the substitution effect leads to a reduction in profits, wages and jobs as the branches affected by increased imports are eliminated. In successive phases, this creates additional cutbacks in aggregate demand. The induced impact does not come from the lack of competitiveness of local industry. Perfectly healthy domestic industries are weakened and put out of action by this indirect effect.[8]

These effects are aggravated because the overvaluation of the exchange rate encourages imports. At the same time, the need to maintain foreign capital inflows requires exchange-rate stability, strengthens overvaluation and fixes high interest rates. This contradiction is resolved by maintaining financial deregulation, and by hoping that it will somehow lead to enough investment to escape from the import trap. The problem of artificial promotion of imports is conventionally ignored; the free flow of capital is simply presented as the ideal manner for a country to access foreign savings, increase productive investment and enter a path of sustained growth.

These three contradictions act not only as a powerful brake on the entire economy, slowing down growth and job creation. They also entail the ingredients of instability, as the balance of several critical macroeconomic accounts is driven farther from equilibrium. In addition, all of these contradictions are aggravated by the fact that financial markets are inherently unstable and that they are driven by expectations in the context of uncertainty. This explosive combination leads to various manifestations of financial and economic crises. In Latin America, the stabilization programmes that followed each crisis involved draconian measures that cut public expenditures, restricted monetary policy and reduced real wages in order to curtail effective demand and control inflationary pressures.

The fourth contradiction of the open economy model arises when an economy attempts to increase domestic savings through deregulation of the bank and non-bank financial sector. When this takes place, domestic restrictions on cross-market access for financial institutions are eliminated, blurring the traditional distinctions between the operations of banks, investment firms, mutual and pension funds, insurance companies and stock exchange brokerage firms. Because of deregulation, a growing proportion of domestic savings can be directed instead towards financial or speculative investments. To the extent that currencies from other economies become more attractive assets, especially if we consider arbitraging opportunities, agents may prefer to speculate on the foreign currency market.[9] As volatility and uncertainty intensify, agents feel increasing pressure to engage in these operations. The need to seek protection from foreign competition, which becomes more intense as a result of simultaneous trade and financial deregulation, compels investors to prefer short-term rates of return.

The standard open economy model also reveals an important contradiction between the goal of achieving an effective presence in the global economy and that of reducing, as much as possible, both the size of the state and the degree to which it intervenes in the economy. This can hinder the ability of a country's industrial apparatus to overcome the barriers to entry that exist in the international arena.

To summarize, one of the main features of the open economy model is that it unleashes the energy of the financial sector and sets the stage for its preponderance in the economy. The role of the state and the structure of the economy are organized around the requirements of the financial sphere, and this has important implications.

Five country-level studies in Latin America[10]

Argentina[11] In the 1970s Argentina embarked on a process of neoliberal economic transformation which resulted in widespread deindustrialization and a reprimarization of the economy, accumulation of a large and periodically unsustainable public debt, and widespread privatizations and deregulation. The military dictatorship sought to radically alter the policy framework that had dominated in Argentina since the 1940s and to do away with the welfare state and the institutions and policies that were a part of the ISI strategy.[12]

The new policy framework was based on trade and financial liberalization and the reduction of state participation in the economy through privatization and deregulation. Financial liberalization was probably the outstanding policy reform, ushering in an era of 'speculation-led development' and massive public debt accumulation.[13] The return to democratic rule in 1983 did not change the policy framework imposed by the military.

In 1989 President Carlos Menem adopted the most far-reaching neoliberal economic programme in Argentine history. It included trade and finance liberalization, and privatization of all state enterprises, utilities and the social security system. The cornerstone of this policy package was a currency board system that pegged the Argentine peso to the US dollar on a one-to-one exchange rate and a requirement that all pesos in circulation be backed by dollars in the central bank's reserves. The peso peg, coupled with a prohibition on the government financing its deficit with monetary emission, meant that Argentina's monetary policy

TABLE 5.2 Fiscal policy priorities in Argentina, 1993–2001 (current pesos)

	1993	1995	1997	1999	2000	2001
Total revenue	50,726.50	50,293.60	55,376.70	58,455.40	56,570.50	51,318.60
Total spending	47,996.00	51,666.90	59,653.30	63,223.80	63,362.10	60,037.90
as percentage of GDP	20.3	20.1	20.4	22.3	22.3	22.3
Interest payments	2,914.00	4,083.50	5,745.00	8,223.60	9,656.00	10,174.60
as percentage of GDP	1.2	1.6	2.0	2.9	3.4	3.8
Deficit or surplus	2,730.50	−1,373.30	−4,276.60	−4,768.40	−6,791.60	−8,719.30
as percentage of GDP	1.2	−0.5	−1.5	−1.7	−2.4	−3.3
Primary spending	45,082.00	47,583.40	53,908.30	55,000.20	53,706.10	49,863.30
as percentage of GDP	19.1	18.4	18.4	19.4	18.9	18.6
Primary surplus or deficit	5,644.50	2,710.20	1,468.40	3,455.20	2,864.40	1,455.30
as percentage of GDP	2.4	1.1	0.5	1.2	1.0	0.5

Source: Alan Cibils, Argentina IUCN–CEESP–TEMTI Country Study

was essentially on automatic pilot, leaving the government very little space for independent policy-making.

Large capital inflows, lured by better investment returns than those offered by weak Northern economies of the early 1990s, fuelled a boom in consumer credit. But the 1994 Mexican crisis led to capital flight, driving the Argentine economy into a deep recession in 1995, with unemployment going over 18 per cent. The neoliberal experiment had increased Argentina's vulnerability. Poverty and inequality increased, steadily reaching unprecedented levels at the end of the century.

Table 5.2 reveals that fiscal spending remained fairly constant as a percentage of GDP, but debt service payments spiralled out of control owing to the fiscal revenue gap left by the 1994 privatization of social security (which was covered by debt) and interest-rate hikes.

In 1999, as the recession deepened, Argentina's fiscal spending cuts needed to bring about a primary surplus acted pro-cyclically, worsening the recession. The country was caught in a downward spiral of falling growth and government income, larger deficits and more austerity. In 2001 capital flight intensified and the government was no longer able to borrow to cover its fiscal gap. In December 2001, banking restrictions were implemented and shortly afterwards Argentina defaulted on roughly US$80 billion of its privately held debt, making it the largest sovereign default in history. The fixed exchange-rate regime was abandoned with a very substantial devaluation and GDP contracted by approximately 20 per cent.

However, owing mainly to the devaluation, the economy began to turn around in the second quarter of 2002. Initially spurred by some degree of import substitution and export increases, the economy began to grow. As the economy grew, so did consumption and investment, leading to six years of strong economic growth until 2008. By the end of 2008, domestic economic problems and the global financial crisis were taking their toll on the Argentine economy and fiscal accounts, causing many to question the sustainability of its debt-service schedule.

Under military dictatorship (1976–83) Argentina's public debt quintupled. However, the latest chapter in Argentina's debt-accumulation process began in 1989, when Carlos Menem was elected president and resumed debt-service payments on Argentina's public debt. This was just the beginning of another cycle of greater indebtedness: by the time he left power, Argentina's debt had more than doubled (from US$58 to 143 billion).

In early 2003 the situation improved and, as a result, the IMF and defaulted creditors increased pressure on Argentina for a solution to its

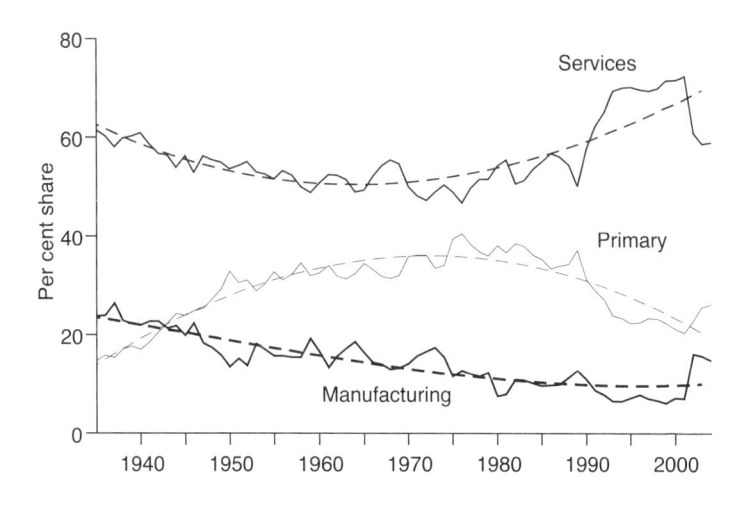

Figure 5.1 Reprimarization: Argentine sectoral GDP 1935–2004 *Source:* Alan Cibil, Argentina Country Study (based on Ferreres 2005)

US$100 billion default debt. After intense negotiations, including two different Argentine official debt-restructuring proposals, a debt swap was opened and concluded in February 2005, with a 76.15 per cent acceptance rate.[14] This agreement included an effective capital reduction of approximately 50 per cent, substantially longer maturity dates and lower interest rates. The debt-to-GDP ratio dropped from 113 per cent at the time of default in December 2001 to 87 per cent after the restructuring. Despite this reduction, Argentina was left with a very heavy debt-service burden. Argentina's debt-service schedule, augmented by new debt issues, implies that the country will have to maintain a primary surplus of 3 per cent of GDP and positive growth rates for the next twenty-five years in order to meet debt-service payments.

Since the 2001/02 Argentine crisis and peso devaluation, soybean production and exports have become a key component of Argentina's macroeconomic balance. Soybean exports have grown considerably and now account for approximately 25 per cent of total exports. Export taxes now represent 15–20 per cent of total fiscal revenue and between 1.6 and 3 per cent of GDP, roughly equivalent to half of Argentina's public-debt-service burden. Soybean cultivation has significant impacts on the environment and on long-term sustainability.

The last thirty years have brought about a radical restructuring of Argentina's economy and society. Abrupt trade liberalization and restrictive credit policies bankrupted much domestic industry and production, turning Argentina into a primary product and service economy. As a result, the process of 'reprimarization' which had begun under the military dictatorship intensified during the last two decades (Figure 5.1). This change in the output mix has critical environmental impacts.

Fiscal revenues: environmental implications Agriculture and cattle breeding have been mainstays of the Argentine economy since the country's early colonial days. But two important transformations took place in the 1970s. First, new seed varieties allowed for year-round agricultural production or double cropping. Second, soybean was introduced and spread rapidly. Crop rotation and cattle breeding were displaced in favour of an intensified agricultural production with widespread use of herbicides and pesticides. Later, in the 1990s, the neoliberal economic policy framework brought about an 'industrial agriculture' model, associated with the expansion of transgenic soybean production. Very soon soybean became Argentina's most important crop. And since 1996 almost 100 per cent of soy planted in Argentina is transgenic 'roundup ready' (RR) soybean, a technological package developed by the Monsanto Corporation. The package includes a soybean variety resistant to glyphosate, a powerful herbicide also produced by Monsanto, and the no-tillage sowing method. Yields have remained constant during this period. But since 95 per cent of the soybean production is exported, this results in substantial foreign exchange inflows and fiscal revenues through export taxes. Soybean production has played a critical role in maintaining fiscal revenues.

The introduction and rapid expansion of transgenic seeds, especially transgenic soybean, have had multiple and profound impacts in Argentina. Impacts include soil degradation, deforestation, land-use concentration, contamination from excessive use of agrochemicals, monoculture and loss of food security, displacement of small and medium-sized producers and increased dependence on transnational agribusiness corporations. Some of these impacts will be examined in the following sections.

Soil degradation The surface cultivated with soybean expanded into marginal lands as short-term considerations became dominant. Also, the introduction of transgenic seed varieties intensified agricultural production: capital intensity increased and year-round agriculture became the norm. With herbicide-resistant soybean varieties, soybean producers have been expanding into less fertile grounds which are far more vulnerable (Pengue 2006: 16). And since crops are no longer rotated with cattle, soil phosphorus content has been significantly depleted (Pengue 2005, 2006).

Biodiversity loss Widespread use of glyphosate has eliminated innumerable plant species from Argentine pampas, with a substantial impact on insect, bird and mammal species. In vast regions of Argentina's most fertile soils, they now speak of '*la primavera silenciosa*' (the silent spring) owing to the disappearance of birds, butterflies and other insects that used to be typical of spring.[15] Herbicide-resistant strains of plants and weeds have appeared, forcing the use of additional or stronger herbicides, deepening the cycle of biodiversity depletion. This also has negative human health impacts (Pengue 2006; Teubal 2008).

Deforestation The rapid expansion of soybean in Argentina's most fertile agricultural areas has displaced other agricultural activities, such as cattle ranching, into areas that were not previously used for agriculture. As a result of the displacement of cattle ranching and the expansion of the agricultural frontier, the rate of deforestation has increased substantially in Argentina's northern provinces.[16] This has resulted in the expansion of the industrial agriculture model into areas where small producers and indigenous communities have lived, with the resulting displacement and marginalization of these populations.

Economic and social vulnerability The industrial agriculture intensification process has contributed to the displacement of small and medium-sized producers from the countryside. This has led to a sustained process of concentration in land use, as larger producers rent the land from producers who, owing to the smaller scale of their productive capacity, cannot afford the machinery required. This may lead to further loss of agro-biodiversity.[17]

The process of land-use concentration is confirmed by comparing the latest available data. Between 1988 and 2002, the number of farming units dropped by 24.5 per cent, while the average surface per unit increased by 28 per cent. Clearly, small and medium-sized producers are being eliminated (Giarracca and Teubal 2006; Teubal et al. 2005; Teubal 2008). This process is aggravated by the fact that large-scale capital-intensive production has lower rural employment ratios (Pengue 2005, 2006; Giarracca and Teubal 2006; Teubal 2008; Teubal and Rodríguez 2002; Cloquell 2007).

The expansion of the soybean industrial agriculture model has also increased Argentina's dependence on imported inputs. Furthermore, over the last decades international commerce in seeds, agrochemicals and crops has become highly concentrated, increasing Argentina's dependence (Pengue 2004a; Teubal 2008). This process not only has environmental and social implications, but it could also severely damage Argentina's food self-sufficiency.

Brazil[18] Brazil started on a path to industrialization through import substitution in the 1930s, but the conditions that allowed for continuity in the industrialization strategy were definitively broken in the eighties. The main priorities after the eighties responded to the need to ensure debt service, to reduce indebtedness and to curtail inflationary pressures. After 1983, Brazil accepted the supervision of the International Monetary Fund and introduced drastic cuts in public spending, a tight monetary policy and high interest rates, as well as financial and trade liberalization.[19]

Another key objective of macroeconomic policy in this period was to eliminate the current account deficit through significant surpluses in the trade balance. In the future, export-led growth would replace the old import substitution strategy. And in the context of this transformation, repressing aggregate demand was enforced through monetary and fiscal policies, as well as the contraction of real wages. The implementation of these policies took place through a drastic contraction of public expenditures, high interest rates and a tightening of money supply, as well as restrictions on credit. In spite of this package of contractionary policies, stabilization remained an elusive goal.

In 1994 the *Plano Real* introduced a new currency, the real, which was pegged to the US dollar.[20] This was designed to stabilize inflationary expectations and thus bring about higher investment rates, spurring growth, fiscal revenues and employment. The new plan included a mandatory balanced budget. The *Plano Real* succeeded in bringing about stability and putting a lid on inflationary pressures.

However, the reduction in inflation was not instantaneous, and this led to a significant overvaluation of the new currency. This damaged the trade balance and the current account deficit continued to be significant, and the currency gap had to be covered through movements in the capital account. The high interest rates had very serious implications for investment and growth rates. Unemployment rates increased and many firms had to close down as they could not compete with the foreign imports that were being buttressed by the overvalued real.

The contradictions of the open economy model examined above started to play a role in the Brazilian economy. Capital inflows artificially contributed to an increase in the exchange rate and the interest rate

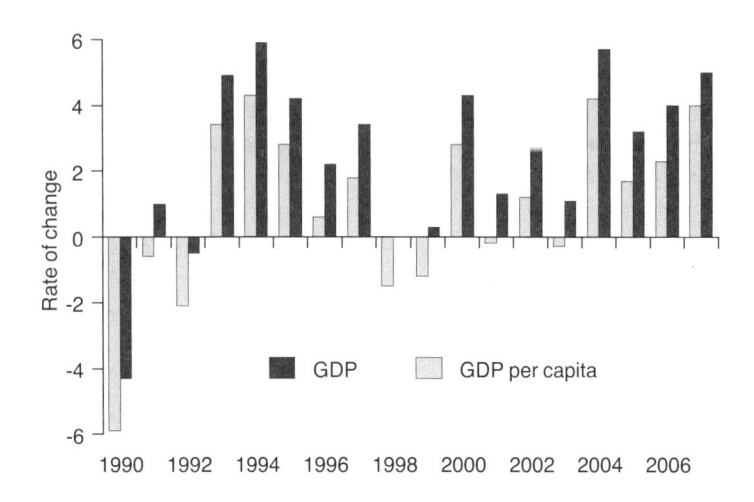

Figure 5.2 GDP and GDP per capita growth rates, 1990–2007
Source: Sergio Schlesinger, Brazil Country Study

remained at a very high level. The probability of Brazil suffering a speculative attack on its currency was increasing and fund managers started to doubt the country's capacity to sustain the real. The reversal of capital flows took place in 1999, bringing about an 80 per cent devaluation.

The historical balance of the *Plano Real* is a mixed bag of results. Hyperinflation was avoided and temporary stability was attained at a very high cost. Figure 5.2 shows how the high interest rates involved in the *Plano Real* slowed down GDP growth.

To summarize, Brazil's macroeconomic policies have been shaped by its debt burden. While monetary policy is obsessed with price stability, fiscal policy is dominated by the short-term objective of generating a primary surplus.[21] This process has shifted resources from the real sectors of the economy (and from the real needs in education, healthcare, housing, transportation, infrastructure and science and technology) to the financial sector of the economy. Consider the following: during the first semester of 2008, Brazil generated a primary surplus of US$55 billion, a sum that represented 6 per cent of GDP and allowed the government to surpass the *annual* goal of 3.8 per cent of GDP. But during that first semester, interest payments on the Brazilian debt amounted to US$56 billion, and this left a total public deficit of 0.14 per cent of GDP. The most dramatic indicator of fiscal policy was that between 2000 and 2007 federal investment, as well as expenditures on education and healthcare, represented only 43 per cent of the total amount allocated to interest on the public debt.

Financial liberalization and fiscal policy: changing the rural landscape In 1992 Brazil deregulated capital flows and profit remittances by foreigners. This was the definitive measure for financial liberalization and established, for the first time in Brazil, the possibility of transferring resources to a foreign country without the need to show that they had an incoming registry or counterpart in the capital account. Institutional investors were allowed to take part in the privatization programme. Portfolio investments could now benefit from arbitraging operations, taking advantage of Brazil's high interest rates and exchange-rate stability.

Financial liberalization allowed banks to obtain external resources and carry out swap operations with foreign entities. In the year 2000 the Cargill Bank, as well as other banks belonging to foreign multinational corporations, initiated operations in Brazil. Their role was to be the financial and credit arms of their operations, pushing for deeper market penetration of their products and strengthening their commercial and industrial presence in the country. These banks were the main instrument for gaining control over primary production and thus the source of its main raw material. This was seen by corporations such as Cargill, Archer Daniels Midland and Bunge as the way in which they could strengthen their industrial, commercial and financial operations.

Contract agriculture was a by-product of the financial predominance of these firms in several regions. A typical contract involves the promise to deliver a certain amount of soybean which is exchanged with the supply of inputs even before sowing. Many of these operations are coordinated by cooperatives, trading companies and input producers. In other cases, especially when harvest is going to take place, other forms of credit with working capital are more common. More than 80 per cent of total output of soybean is now acquired by five or six large trading companies (Cargill, Bunge, ADM, Dreyfus and Maggi are the largest of these).

Brazil was maintaining some of the highest interest rates in the world, and because of price stabilization priorities, credit was scarce and the banks of the large corporations were to play a key role in filling the gap between demand and supply for commercial credit. In addition, in the case of agriculture, the withdrawal of state support had already left a huge vacuum as development banks saw their operations severely curtailed. The loans provided by the banks associated with the big trading companies led to various forms of commercial agriculture in which the key decisions on output and technology mix were taken away from producers. Other policy measures reinforced this trend, including the deregulation of imports for agribusiness and the authorization to harvest genetically modified crops.

This combination of factors made foreign direct investment the main driver for the expansion of a new agricultural model in various key regions in Brazil. Several large multinational corporations took advantage of the new favourable context in order to gain access to alternative sources of raw materials and land. The older MNCs (Cargill, Bunge, Dreyfus) that had been operating in the Brazilian economy since the days of the import substitution strategy reacted to the evolving context and the challenge of the newest competitors (Archer Daniels Midland) by rapidly expanding their operations in order to protect their control over the supply of the most profitable commodities.[22]

As a direct consequence of this evolution soybean production underwent a dramatic expansion. In the period 1991–2005, the area devoted to soybean tripled and by 2006 it was occupying more than twenty-two million hectares, an area that was roughly equivalent to that devoted to the other four main staple foods grown in Brazil (rice, wheat, beans and millet). Total output of soybean reached 58 million tons, approximately 25 per cent of world production. The West Central region in Brazil experienced the most rapid rates of growth, advancing on the vegetation of the *cerrado* biome, where 40 per cent of Brazilian soybean production is taking place.

It is important to underline that these macroeconomic policies combined have also favoured the expansion of speculative capital in Brazil's agribusiness. Crops such as sugar, for example, have expanded at even faster rates than those for soybean in some regions owing to expectations of ethanol price rises in the near future. The problem, of course, is that if these expectations are not confirmed by market trends and prices go down, producers will likely get stuck in a very difficult situation. The experience of these boom and bust cycles in agriculture is well known, but when liquidity abounds in international markets, the speculative tendency actually worsens. The social and environmental impact of these attacks on entire agro-ecosystems parallels the effects of financial crises when reversal of capital flows occurs.

Environmental effects There are several important environmental impacts from this process. The first is the loss of agro-biodiversity, as the expansion of monoculture takes place. This is also associated with the intensive use of chemical inputs that pollute soils and aquifers.

The second type of damage comes from the destruction of the *cerrado*, a sprawling savannah of more than two million square kilometres in central Brazil (about 24 per cent of its territory). The region hosts forty ethnic groups (with 45,000 indigenous people), several of which face the threat of extinction. In terms of biodiversity, this is one of the richest savannahs in the world, with 12,000 plant species and 2,000 animal species, many of which are endemic to the *cerrado*. Rates of destruction of the *cerrado* remain at very high levels.

This vast region does not have a system capable of monitoring environmental degradation and resource management practices.

A third problem is related to the deforestation of the Amazon rainforest. Direct destruction of the rainforest through the expansion of soybean has been documented by several studies. In 2008, Blairo Maggi, the 'King of Soy', even declared that deforesting the Amazonian basin could help solve the food crisis.[23] However, soybean expansion is contributing indirectly to the destruction of the Amazon forest as previously deforested areas that were used for ranching are converted to soybean production.

The pressure from monoculture crops (soybean and sugar cane) is having a critical impact in displacing cattle production from the states in central-west, south and south-east Brazil into the regions of Legal Amazonia. This is confirmed by official data showing the number of cattle in the north and central-west of Brazil, precisely where the Amazon rainforest is located. Table 5.3 reveals that the fastest growth rates of cattle production, with all of its environmental impacts, are precisely in these fragile regions.

TABLE 5.3 Brazil: cattle by region, 1995–2005

	1995	2005	Variation (%)
Brazil	161,227,938	207,156,696	28.5
North	19,183,092	41,489,002	116.3
Central-west	55,061,299	71,984,504	30.7
South-east	37,168,199	38,943,898	4.8
South	26,641,412	27,770,006	4.2
Northeast	23,173,936	26,969,286	3.4

Source: Sergio Schlesinger, Brazil Country Study

This appears to be a 'logical' step because the land in the Amazon basin is not suitable for harvesting commercial monoculture crops such as soybean and sugar cane. Ranching is expanding in areas where land is cheaper and competition with commercial crops can be evaded. Ranching is and will continue to be the main driver for deforestation in

Amazonia, representing 80 per cent of total deforested land, and this is being intensified by its displacement from land reallocated to soybean and sugar-cane production.[24]

Thus, soybean production is already causing some deforestation directly, but its main impact on Brazil's forests is indirect. Fearnside (2006) shows that as soybean farms are set up in land that has already been cleared, or in savannah and transitional forests, they displace ranching and slash-and-burn farmers deeper into the tropical forest. New highways and other infrastructure projects accelerate the deforestation process.

Macroeconomic policies have set the stage for this tragedy: in the context of intense inflationary pressures, high indebtedness, a restrictive monetary policy, financial liberalization and a fiscal policy preoccupied solely with generating a primary surplus, the vacuum left by the withdrawal of support for small-scale agricultural activities has been occupied by large consortia. These have brought about a radical transformation of the rural landscape in Brazil, with deep and long-lasting environmental consequences, threatening not only the Amazon rainforest itself, but the last remains of the unique biome of the *cerrado*.

Costa Rica[25] This small Central American republic is perceived as having one of the most advanced environmental policies in the region. Although this country has a tiny fraction of total landmass, it has 5 per cent of the world's biodiversity. Its varied terrain, situated in an isthmus, and its tropical and subtropical climate regimes make it ideal for biodiversity. Costa Rica also has a unique social welfare system providing health and education services.

The renewed emphasis on eco-tourism may help make Costa Rica a showcase of development strategies that are sustainable. But the beauty and ecological variety of this country represent a small fraction of what used to be its treasure. Costa Rica has been deforested and its soils degraded: only 15 per cent of the original forest remains and most of its soils have been seriously affected by agricultural practices. Fortunately, national protected areas have multiplied and government appears to be seriously committed to preserving what's left. However, these remaining riches are seriously threatened by new patterns of growth and several economic forces.

In the early eighties Costa Rica had already entered a pattern of high indebtedness, and 60 per cent of its export earnings were devoted to debt service. It underwent a process of structural adjustment supervised by the IMF and the World Bank, but severe imbalances persist and inflation continues to be a problem. Managing Costa Rica's large public debt

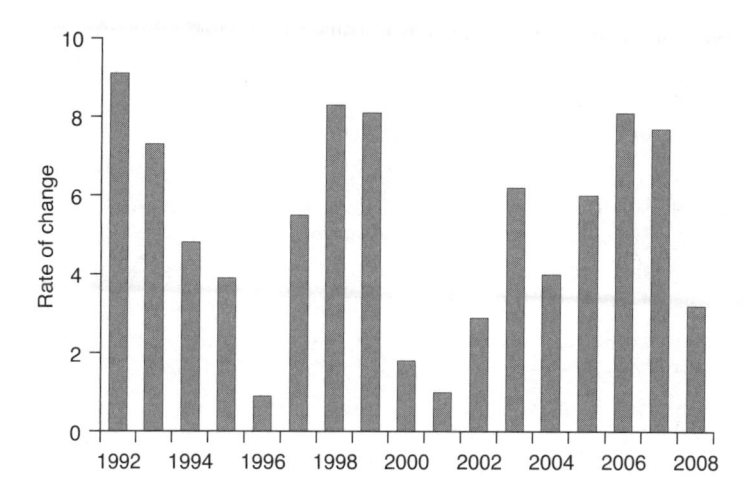

Figure 5.3 Costa Rica: evolution of GDP, 1992–2008 *Source*: Carlos Murillo, Costa Rica Country Study

has weighed heavily on the stability of macroeconomic policy, growth and social welfare.

On the social front, real wages have maintained a disquieting downward trend. Income inequality has worsened recently. In rural areas, many small-scale producers have been left out of official support programmes that promote exports rather than food security. Because some export-oriented crops require large-scale investments, this has also led to some land concentration and greater inequality in rural areas.

Figure 5.3 shows GDP growth rates for the period 1992–2008 and reveals an inconsistent stop-and-go pattern. This is the consequence of structural problems that remain unsolved under the new strategic approach: concentration of exports in a few agricultural products, lack of adequate productive linkages between sectors, etc.

In the new strategy, exports were supposed to be the main growth engine. The free trade zones have made a substantial contribution to the manufacturing sector, but in-bond industries by themselves will not lead to industrialization and technological development. The concentration of exports to the US market remains a serious problem. Finally, in several commercial crops (macadamia or pineapple, for example) the concentration of production in big foreign-owned firms also implies high profit remittances. In any event, the economy appears to be incapable of sustaining adequate growth rates and good years are inevitably succeeded by periods of mediocre performance, with a growing deterioration in the trade balance.

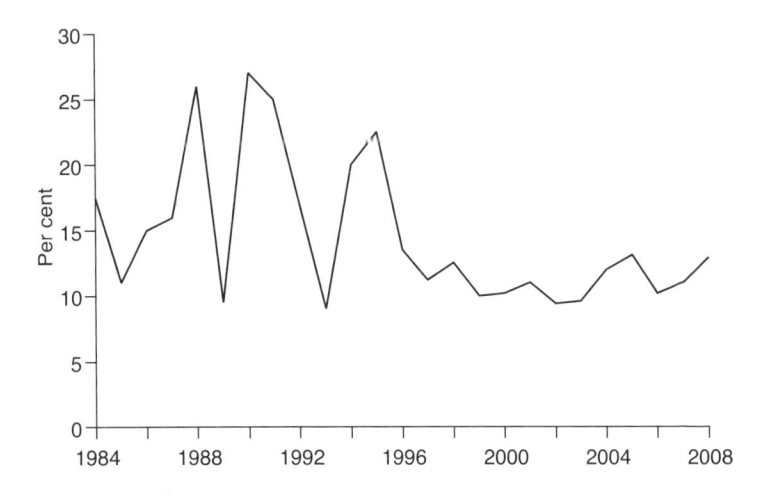

Figure 5.4 Costa Rica: evolution of inflation rates, 1984–2008
Source: Carlos Murillo, Costa Rica Country Study

Although free trade zones are providing a significant proportion of the country's hard currency needs, Costa Rica's export base continues to rely heavily on the natural resource base and low-cost labour. The country continues to be the region's most important beef exporter to the USA. In 2008, 52 per cent of exports came from free trade zones where in-bond industries are based, but commercial crops remain important. These crops have their own environmental costs (and human health costs) owing to their use of agrochemical inputs. Tourism has now become the second-largest source of foreign exchange.

Monetary policy After the crisis of 1980–82 Costa Rica was marked by severe macroeconomic disequilibria, both on the domestic front (high inflation, unemployment, high and unsustainable fiscal deficits) as well as in the country's external accounts (current account deficit, deteriorating terms of trade, high indebtedness, exchange-rate volatility). The new strategy based on exports and economic openness required a different approach to monetary policy. The struggle against inflation had mixed results in the 1980s, owing mostly to the currency devaluations. It showed better results in the 1990s, with less volatility, although it still remained at a two-digit level. The new policy approach included the deregulation of the capital account, and the modernization of the financial sector was pursued as a high-priority objective.

In 2006 Costa Rica adopted a new approach to monetary policy. The sole objective of the central bank's posture is to maintain price stability and reduce inflation to single-digit levels. A system of bands within which the exchange rate could vary was established, allowing the central bank to intervene within that range to maintain stability and order in the currency market. As a result, the exchange rate appreciated by 10.7 per cent. Interest rates dropped as the bank chose not to create incentives for speculative capital inflows.

Fiscal policy The country has maintained a chronic primary deficit that has been basically covered through new public debt at increased servicing costs. This puts pressure on interest rates and has generated distortions that act as incentives for speculative investment. The primary deficit in Costa Rica has been the result of a weak and skewed tax system.

Recently, tax reform has focused on changes in income taxes and in the transformation of the sales tax into a value-added tax. Improved tax collection systems have increased fiscal revenues significantly (24 per cent and 27 per cent growth in 2006 and 2007 respectively). This had favourable repercussions, but the international crisis in 2008 brought about slower growth and fiscal revenues dropped by 28 per cent in twelve months while expenditures increased by 4 per cent. The small primary surplus observed in 2007 was rapidly wiped out.

Poverty and inequality Until the 1980s Costa Rica's history was one of an egalitarian system; real wages kept increasing and income distribution was among the best in Latin America owing to its social welfare programmes. The structural adjustment programmes (SAPs) of the eighties brought about a reduction of 17 per cent in real wages (1980–90) and increased economic polarization in Costa Rican society. And although employment started to improve, the jobs that were created at the time were of poor quality, with greater instability and few benefits. Clearly, the burden of the adjustment process fell unduly on the poorest segments of Costa Rica's society.

Also as a result of SAPs many small-scale farmers were reluctant to give up their traditional crops, which provided food security, and lost access to government support for export crops. The non-traditional (i.e. commercial) crops that were favoured at the time required infrastructure investments; many farmers were caught in a difficult situation and either sought off-farm income-generating activities or even sold their plots.

Poverty has remained at a constant 20 per cent level, and recently inequality started to increase. Although the Gini coefficient maintained a low level during most of the 1990s, it started to deteriorate after 1997 and peaked in 2001. Some progress was made after that but things went wrong again in 2005, and it is likely that austerity measures to counter the effects of the 2008 global financial crisis will lead to further deterioration in this indicator. The environmental implications of poverty cannot escape policy-makers. Rural poverty will undoubtedly undermine the long-term viability of all national protected areas. A sustainable conservation policy based on the creation of biodiversity islands in a sea of rural poverty is not a good idea.

Payments for environmental services and macroeconomic policy In 1997 Costa Rica started a new Programme for Payment of Environmental Services (PPES) aimed at protecting and developing forested areas. This instrument is also an important tool in attaining the carbon-neutral position defined as a national goal by 2021. Finally, the programme is being dovetailed with policies in the context of the UN Programme on Reducing Emissions from Deforestation and Forest Degradation in Developing Countries (REDD). The programme is based on the environmental services supplied by forested areas (including plantations) instead of a direct subsidy to investments in this sector. The programme is aimed at predefined priority areas covering more than 29,800 square kilometres, an area equivalent to 80 per cent of Costa Rica's territory.

Payments are made by the implementing agency FONAFIFO (Fondo Nacional de Financiamiento Forestal) to landowners who adopt healthy forest resource management practices, including agro-forestry and sustainable forest management. The programme covers four types of environmental services: carbon emissions mitigation, hydrological services, biodiversity conservation and scenic values. A parallel objective is poverty alleviation. Priority is given to projects that are located in natural protected areas, biodiversity corridors and land belonging to indigenous groups. Small and medium-sized producers have precedence over others and the area per project cannot exceed 300 hectares.

The PPES allowed for the reforestation of 400,000 hectares in more than 8,300 projects between 1997 and 2008. The government has already allocated US$90 million to this programme. In the beginning, payments in the programme oscillated around US$22–42 per hectare a year. In more recent years, payments have varied depending on the type of contract. In the case of conservation projects, payments amount to US$816 per hectare, with a schedule of payments. Protection projects involve payments of US$320 per hectare for five years, and owners cannot modify the use of their land. Only 9 per cent of payments in the PPES are allocated to these projects. Finally, projects for natural regeneration in former grasslands involve payments of US$205 per hectare.

This programme is financed through a special 3.5 per cent tax on sales of hydrocarbon fuels. This is an environmental tax explicitly directed towards the improvement of forests. Average annual revenues generated by this tax amount to US$13.8 million. These resources are insufficient to cover the demand from the owners of forested lands. An estimated 38,000 applications have remained unattended. In 2004 applications covering more than 800,000 hectares were pending (Engel et al. 2009).[26] Clearly, unless resources for the PPES are increased significantly, the long-term perspective is bleak.

The PPES is still a small venture. To become a core element in a long-term strategy for sustainable development, it has to increase its coverage. As of today, resources from international agencies and the private sector do not appear to be able to cover the costs of expanding this programme. To meet the challenges of an expanding PPES the country's fiscal priorities will have to be redefined. Thus, the relationship between debt sustainability and fiscal policy is at the heart of the future of the PPES.

As a response to the global crisis and the downturn in the economy (which reduces tax and non-tax fiscal revenues), the Ministry of Finance is cutting spending. It remains to be seen whether appropriations for the PPES remain untouched or whether they can increase. The combination of fiscal constraints and the contraction of credit may prove dangerous for the programme and for Costa Rica's forests. Today, the competition between alternative land uses is clearly disadvantageous for forests. A comparison of cost structures and profits associated with diverse land uses reveals that commercial crops and cattle are substantially more profitable than forested land.

Ecuador[27] Ecuador is a highly diverse country with a varied landscape and a rich tapestry of ecosystems, from tropical rainforests and intermountain valleys to the famed marine ecosystems of the Galapagos Islands. But environmental problems abound in this beautiful country. Ecuador has shown the highest deforestation rates in decades, with a tremendous impact on biodiversity. These deforestation rates have intensified in the past decade. It is estimated that logging and oil exploration have contributed to this loss of forested land: only 15 per cent of Ecuador's primary rainforests remains.

Ecuador started to rely heavily on oil exports as a source of fiscal revenues in 1970. In 1982, with the international debt crisis, Ecuador was one of the first countries to start implementing a neoliberal policy package. The discovery of oil in the seventies opened the door

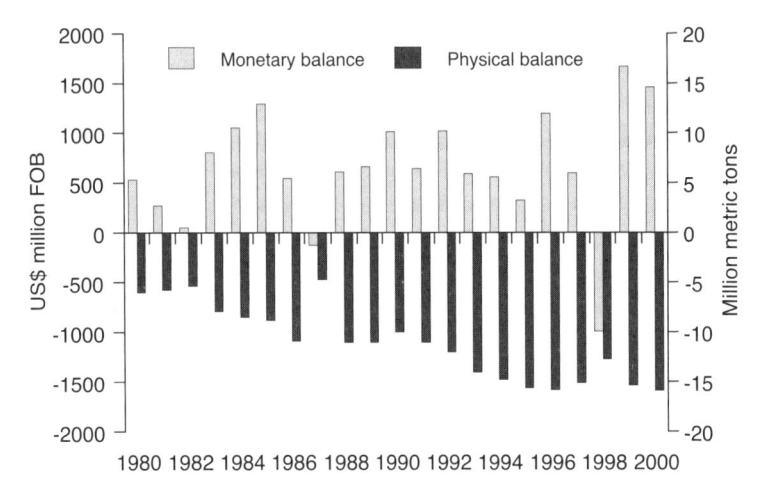

Figure 5.5 Ecuador: trade balance in monetary and physical terms
Source: Pablo Samaniego, Ecuador Country Study

to an industrialization strategy, but the Dutch disease syndrome struck Ecuador's economy: the exchange rate remained overvalued by an average of 40 per cent between 1970 and 1987. Severe economic problems subsisted with a fiscal structure marked by inefficiencies. As the mismatch between revenues and expenditures intensified, Ecuador's debt increased as international loans rose from US$300 million in 1971 to US$8,000 million in 1985. Ecuador was forced to undergo a dramatic adjustment and deep cuts were implemented in fiscal spending. The role of the state as driver and regulator of the development strategy unravelled and its capacity to provide basic social services also started to crumble.

In 1986 the sector-level policies for industrial development started to be dismantled and a growth model based on extractive practices was implemented. The environment started to suffer the impact of this intensification of usage and extraction rates in the old commercial crops and in new sectors such as shrimp, fisheries, flowers, African palm trees, etc. The expansion of shrimp aquaculture destroyed mangrove forests at alarming rates.[28] All industrial activities declined during this period. The reprimarization of the economy was clear: the economic structure of Ecuador in 1995 resembled that of 1970.

During the eighties and nineties privatizations proceeded, banking activities were deregulated and, most important, the capital account was liberalized. Trade liberalization was driven by the macroeconomic policy objective of price stabilization. In that period some progress was made with respect to the Ecuadorean version of the 'twin deficits' – the external accounts and public finance – but inflation remained at very high levels (50 per cent). Interest rates remained high also, and thus financial charges could be covered only in activities with very high profitability levels. All of this led to a greater weakening of the real sectors of the economy, especially those related to manufacturing industries.

In 1997 a strong El Niño event took place, affecting crops in the coastlands and severely damaging the country's physical infrastructure. Non-performing loans to agricultural firms increased significantly, affecting the financial position of banks. Because new and extraordinary expenditures had to be undertaken to repair the country's damaged infrastructure, a new 1 per cent tax was established on all financial transactions. This led to a further decrease in bank deposits and weakened the banks' position as a full-blown bank crisis developed.

Contracting real wages and reductions in public spending on social services were unable to stabilize the economy. GDP dropped by 6.3 per cent, the exchange rate suffered a devaluation of 196 per cent and inflation reached 78 per cent in 1999. In terms of per capita income, the country moved back ten years. With a weakened industrial sector the economy had to rely more than ever on its natural resource base. The comparison of the monetary and physical trade balances shows how the external sector responded to these years of crisis (Figure 5.5). The measure in physical terms provides an idea of the effort deployed in an economy's natural resource base to maintain its level of exports.

In January 2000 Ecuador adopted the US dollar as its national currency, its domestic medium of exchange and its official unit of account. This measure was the response to the deep contraction of the real economy, hyperinflation, a large fiscal deficit and the meltdown of the sucre. The immediate effect of dollarization was that Ecuador lost control over monetary policy. The price level and interest rates now depended on the net balance of the current account. Although monetary policy could not be used in a counter-cyclical manner, inflation slowed down. Interest rates remained at a very high level for a longer period of time with extremely negative effects on productive investments.

One of the critical problems of dollarization in Ecuador is that stagnant or declining productivity is compensated by extra pressure on natural resources and the environment.[29] Land-use patterns changed, intensifying agricultural practices that increase pressure on soils and biodiversity. Dollarization led to a greater reprimarization of the economy and of exports (Falconi Benítez 2005) in order to *increase the monetary base*.

The decision to adopt the US dollar as the domestic currency was accompanied by legislation on maximum ceilings for the growth of public expenditures and a reduction of the public sector's external debt. In this manner, fiscal policy became 'legally' pro-cyclical, and together with dollarization became one of two constraints on aggregate demand. Although Ecuador's external and fiscal accounts improved, this was due to four factors: oil prices, remittances by migrant workers, the depreciation of the US dollar vis-à-vis other currencies and the flows of foreign direct investment. These factors contributed to the elimination of the country's twin deficits, but this is a temporary and unsustainable achievement.

Data for 2000–08 show that, in physical terms, exports are dominated by fossil fuels and biomass. The structure of exports by weight in 2000–08 shows that 86 per cent of these exports are primary raw materials and only 9.4 per cent semi-manufactured products. Other products, mostly biotic in origin, increased their share. All of this means that Ecuador's dollarization policy is based on the continuous flow of increasing doses of raw materials and primary products, with their severe ecological footprint.

Evidence suggests that Ecuador may have fallen into the trap of low productivity and static comparative advantages that leads to irrevocable environmental degradation. In the future, this weakening of the physical environment may even put a brake on the economy's growth. Of course, this is a delicate subject and over-dependence on the extraction of raw materials for growth may play out differently if, instead of fossil fuels, for example, the process relies more on biomass. After all, fossil fuels are non-renewable and biomass is a renewable resource. But even here there needs to be caution: certain biomass resources, such as fisheries or forests, can be abused and over-exploited, sometimes to the point of collapse, and recovery may take a long time. Also, high biomass extraction rates can have negative effects on biodiversity and on the long-term survivability of natural protected areas.

The Ishpingo-Tambococha-Tiputini project Today, Ecuador is at a crossroads. Abandoning dollarization will not be easy and there are many political and economic costs that need to be considered. On the other hand, if Ecuador maintains the dollar as its domestic currency, it will need to intensify exports of agricultural products and of extractive industries. In this case, heavy environmental costs will be incurred, endangering the future viability of the economy.

An innovative project suggesting a way out of this dilemma is the Ishpingo-Tambococha-Tiputini (ITT) or Yasuní project, which is simultaneously pursuing the objectives of economic development and environmental sustainability. The project consists of a scheme to leave a significant amount of Ecuador's oil reserves underground. These reserves are located in a highly diverse region covered by pristine tropical rainforest that is home to several indigenous peoples. By leaving these reserves underground Ecuador would contribute to the fulfilment of three critical objectives: biodiversity conservation, the reduction of CO_2 emissions (both from deforestation and the burning of fossil fuels) and conservation of cultural diversity. The counterpart of this would be a flow of income that would be disbursed by international donors, governments and anyone willing to support the project. The scheme would allow Ecuador to reduce the physical deficit of its economy, and reap the benefits of its endowment of natural resources as a reward for this contribution to environmental sustainability.

The area covered by this project is in the Yasuní National Park, located in Ecuador's Amazon region. This area is the homeland of the Waoram[30] and Tagaeri-Taromenane people. The latter live in voluntary isolation from the rest of the world. These people are nomads and have defended their territory for centuries. Some have been forcibly displaced by oil explorations in the Yasuní National Park.

This area is a hot spot of biodiversity, with a rich concentration of insects, amphibians, reptiles and freshwater fish. In one hectare of Yasuní forest 644 different species of trees have been found, a number larger than the total number of tree species in all of North America.[31] The Yasuní National Park was declared a biosphere reserve by UNESCO in 1989. However, owing to lack of resources, the resource management plan has not been designed and was never implemented.

The ITT oil exploration block involves 412 million barrels of proven reserves of (heavy) crude oil and, taking into account probable reserves, the total amount could reach 920 million barrels. Total proven reserves in Ecuador amount to 4,500 million barrels, which means that the ITT fields would account for 9–22 per cent of the country's reserves. The economic importance of the fields located within the ITT block is undeniable, both from the viewpoint of the external sector (and monetary policy) and from the perspective of fiscal revenues. Petroecuador and Sinopec (China Petroleum and Chemical Corporation) are two firms currently developing plans for ITT. The first would initiate operations with 130 wells and the second with 214 wells and an investment of approximately US$5 billion (Oilwatch 2007). If this output were to be exported it would increase Ecuador's crude oil exports by 31 per cent with respect to 2008.

Initially, the Yasuní project was based on a payment-for-environmental-services scheme, but later this was considered to be impractical. The new project has a different financial architecture and is contained in the National Development Plan, based not on forgone damage but on the benefits generated by the project:

1. Effective conservation of forty natural protected areas (4.8 million hectares) and adequate resource management plans for 5 million hectares in natural zones, the property of indigenous and Afro-Ecuadorian peoples. The conservation of Yasuní would also allow the Tagaeri and Taromenane people to continue in voluntary isolation if they so desire.
2. Reforestation, natural regeneration and adequate management of 1 million hectares of forests belonging to small landowners on soils currently threatened by erosive processes.
3. Improved energy efficiency and energy savings in Ecuador.
4. Social development in the areas covered by the project through education, training, technical assistance and productive employment in sustainable activities.

The central ideas of the Yasuní project could go a long way to transforming the economic logic of production and conservation. First, oil kept underground would reduce emissions significantly: it is estimated that the emissions from proven reserves in Yasuní would equal the emissions of Brazil (332 million metric tons [MT] of CO_2 equivalent), France (373 million MT) and Ecuador for thirteen years. Second, funds would be obtained from 'CO_2 avoided emissions' certificates (already the German parliament has agreed to allocate US$50 million to these certificates). Third, the funds would also contribute to developing energy-efficiency projects, helping in the transition to a sustainable fossil-free economy.

Project funds would be related to the market value of the avoided CO_2 emissions. Taking as reference a quotation of US$17.66 per MT for certified emissions reductions (CERs) in the European market, this has a net present value of US$5,195 million (using a 6 per cent discount rate). This is less than the net present value of US$6,979 million that would correspond to the output from these fields at a price of US$61.21 (WTI – West Texas Intermediate, the reference oil type used in price quotations) and using the same discount rate. The income would accrue to a special fund that would issue Yasuní Guarantee Certificates. If Ecuador decided to exploit the ITT fields, it would have to reimburse these funds. The Yasuní initiative is a bold project designed not only to initiate a structural transformation in Ecuador's economy. If correctly implemented it could lead the way out of the dilemma imposed by dollarization and serve as a rallying point for the international community in its quest for a sustainable future.[32]

Mexico[33] Mexico is a highly diverse country with a rich tapestry of varied ecosystems covering its landscapes, including tropical rainforests, temperate forested areas, cloud forests, semi-arid and arid environments. Mexico's coastline extends for some 11,000 kilometres and its exclusive economic zone covers reef barriers and well-endowed marine fisheries. This combination of ecosystems allows Mexico to be home to more than 200,000 different species or approximately 10–12 per cent of global biodiversity. According to the National Biodiversity Commission, Mexico ranks first in biodiversity of reptiles, second in mammals, fourth in amphibians and fourth in flora.

One of the most important strategic objectives of Mexico's environmental policy is the conservation and management of this endowment in biodiversity. The most important policy instrument to attain this objective is the national system of Natural Protected Areas (NPAs). Already more than 170,000 square kilometres are NPAs, with 34 biosphere reserves, 64 national parks, 26 areas of protected flora and fauna and 17 sanctuaries (CONABIO 2007). This wealth of environmental diversity is at risk, and there are alarming signs in almost every environmental dimension.

<u>Macroeconomic policy and Mexico's economic performance</u> During the period 1950–70, Mexico's economy maintained an average yearly rate of growth above 6.3 per cent. This allowed for a substantial increment in per capita income and was associated with its import substitution industrialization strategy. The difficult international economic context of the 1970s led to drops in capital formation rates, inflationary pressures, unsustainable fiscal deficits and growing indebtedness. In 1982 high interest rates and collapsing oil prices led to Mexico's default on its international financial obligations.

The stabilization plans of the 1980s gave way to deeper structural reforms and the adoption of the neoliberal policy package. Accordingly, the main objectives of fiscal policy were redefined in order to generate a permanent primary surplus directed towards debt service. The pro-cyclical bias was incorporated in a federal law establishing the obligation to maintain a balanced budget. As a percentage of GDP, public expenditure stagnated and remained at a very low level after 1990. This affected several environmentally sensitive sectors, from small-scale agricultural production to Natural Protected Areas.

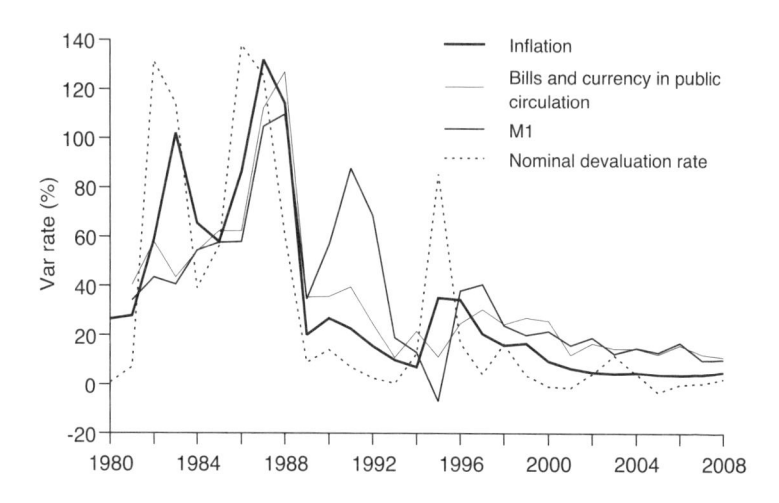

Figure 5.6 Mexico: monetary policy and money supply *Source:* Marcos Chávez, Mexico Country Study

Monetary policy was radically transformed, first by providing complete autonomy for the central bank. Price stability became the main objective of monetary policy. Finally, monetary policy was also charged with the task of maintaining exchange-rate stability in order to generate a favourable climate for foreign direct investment and international capital flows.

After 1989 Mexico underwent an intense process of privatization, deregulation of markets and the shrinking of state intervention in the economy. This was accompanied by the complete deregulation of the capital account, creating the conditions that would lead to international capital flows. This process culminated with the negotiation and completion of the North American Free Trade Agreement (NAFTA) between Mexico, the United States and Canada.

In the early 1990s exports from the manufacturing sector created the impression that Mexico could abandon its dependence on oil and continue with its industrialization strategy. However, the in-bond industries in the maquiladora sector behind the expansion of industrial exports were disconnected from the rest of the economy: thus, although exports attained very high growth rates, the economy remained stagnant and high unemployment continued.

Inflation was controlled through the repression of aggregate domestic demand. A tight monetary policy and high interest rates inhibited productive investment, although they attracted capital inflows. This in turn contributed to an overvalued currency that was also used as an anchor for the price system and contributed significantly to the reduction in inflation. But the trade balance continued to deteriorate, and soon Mexico found itself relying increasingly on capital inflows to sustain its growing trade deficit. Another aspect of the anti-inflation strategy was containment of the growth of wages.

The government and monetary authorities shuddered at the cost of any adjustment and postponed it until the financial community started having second thoughts about Mexico's ability to fulfil its commitments. In December 1994 the crisis exploded, a macro-devaluation took place and the temporary gains in the struggle against inflation were wiped out. As 1995 advanced, the economy went into a tailspin, with a drop of 6.5 per cent in GDP. The severity of the crisis can be gauged by its impacts on the world's financial markets.

The economy's performance under the neoliberal policy package has been disappointing. Not a single strategic objective has been attained. Growth remains mediocre (with an average 2.2 per cent per year) and is insufficient to meet the requirements of the labour market. The country's external accounts remain fragile, with an extreme concentration of trade in a single market (the United States). There is a large surplus in the country's trade balance with the United States, but this is the result of oil and maquiladora exports, so that in the final analysis Mexico's trade structure is relying on cheap labour and its natural resource base. This is problematic for several reasons. One is that the maquiladora exports are based on low labour costs and generate tremendous environmental pressures along the border areas. In addition, oil exports in volume terms will likely start diminishing because of Mexico's dwindling reserves. The important surplus observed with the United States is not enough to compensate for the deficit in Mexico's trade with Europe and Asia (especially China).

Finally, the balance of payments is also improved by the remittances of migratory workers who have crossed the border in search of stable employment opportunities. Mexico has exported an average of 400,000 migrant workers to the United States every year since 1994. Their remittances have been a positive contribution to the balance of payments, but their personal experience is testimony to the failure of the Mexican economy to provide adequate job opportunities for its people.

Today the model that brought about the 1994 peso meltdown continues to operate without much change. Inflation targeting remains the paramount objective of monetary policy (aiming at levels as low as 2 per cent). This is operated with the same tools as before: an overvalued currency and the containment of domestic aggregate demand. This, in

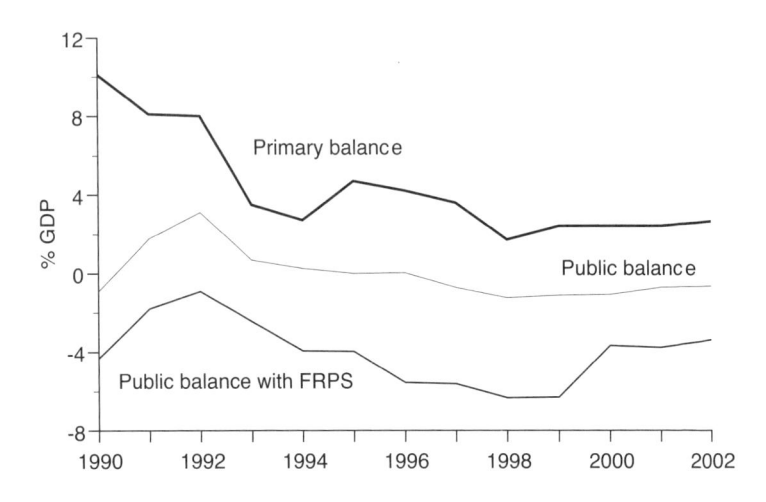

Figure 5.7 Mexico: fiscal policy and Financial Requirements of the Public Sector Source: Marcos Chávez, Mexico Country Study

turn, is achieved through tight monetary and fiscal policies. Domestic demand is also contained through the repression of real wages, and this brings about an unsustainable situation.[34] In 2009 70 per cent of the *employed* workforce earned up to five minimum wages or the equivalent of US$631 at the going exchange rate (half of the employed workforce earned less than three minimum wages or US$380, a level of income just on the poverty line). These data reveal that the labour market is more a battlefield than a space for orderly determination of one of the main distributional variables in any economy.

Mexico's fiscal accounts appear a good basis for sustainable debt management. But, here again, generating a primary surplus without a comprehensive (and progressive) tax reform continues to dominate fiscal policy. This has been achieved through pro-cyclical measures such as increasing value-added taxes, as well as the curtailment of expenditure in real terms rather than through increased revenues. Social expenditures (healthcare, education, housing, municipal services) have also been drastically affected by this approach to fiscal policy. The impact of this on the allocation of resources for environmental stewardship has been rather negative.

But this approach cannot hide the true state of public finance in Mexico. To the traditional elements of the public debt, we must add the Financial Requirements of the Public Sector (FRPS). As a result of several bailout operations, first for the sugar-cane industry (which went bankrupt in the 1980s), then for the failed system of privatized toll roads (early 1990s) and finally for the rescue package for the country's banking system (1995–97), the FRPS represented more than double the normal public balance deficit. In addition, if we add the government's commitments associated with the reform of the pension system, the real deficit becomes significantly higher. Servicing this deficit is a problem that remains unsolved and leads to a heavy mortgage on public resources and on the capacity to invest in environmental stewardship.

The evolution of fiscal policy traced in Figure 5.7 reveals the burden of debt service on fiscal policy. Fiscal revenues from value-added taxes and a regressive tax system are not being invested in the future of this country, but are siphoned off to cover the debt from a dark past of corruption and mismanagement. The impact of this process, which has been going on for three decades, will compromise the future of Mexico's development.

Stagnation and environmental degradation Mexico's recent economic history is a picture of stagnation, increased poverty and severe environmental degradation. At least Mexico has managed to implement a system of satellite (national) accounts, and we can attempt to quantify the economic impact of this environmental decline. Figure 5.8 shows that net environmental domestic product (NEDP) is 20 per cent less than GDP. This means that the Mexican economy has been eating away at the environment at a very high rate of exploitation in order to maintain an economy that feeds the priorities of financial capital.

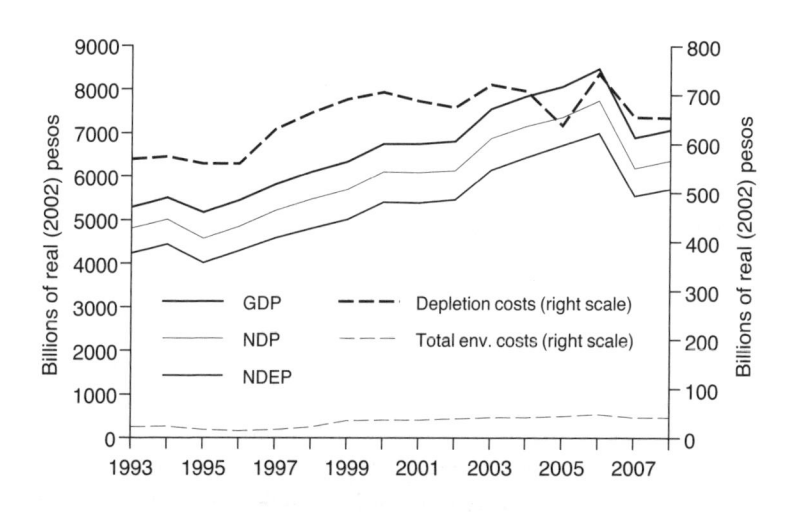

Figure 5.8 Mexico: GDP and environmental costs

The future of Mexico's economy will continue to be compromised by this heavy environmental burden. Today deforestation is proceeding at a very fast rate, with an estimated one million hectares being lost every year to illegal logging and the expansion of the agricultural frontier. Soil erosion, loss of topsoil and the reduction of soil fertility continue to haunt the rural landscape.[35] More than 35 per cent of the country's underground aquifers are being exploited at rates higher than those of natural replenishment. Most commercial fisheries are over-exploited and some are on the verge of total population collapse. Pollution of soils and water bodies is also proceeding rapidly, with no end in sight to the accumulation of toxic waste. Greenhouse gas emissions per unit of GDP dropped slightly in the past decade owing to the collapse of the petrochemical industry, not through any genuine progress in energy efficiency. If the macroeconomic framework we have described here is maintained, these negative trends will not only subsist, but may even worsen.

Concluding remarks

The successive financial crises during the nineties and their impact in Latin America finished by spelling the decline of neoliberalism in the region. By the end of that decade several countries had experienced important political changes and enough new leaders had sufficient strength to challenge the economic doctrines inherited from the Washington Consensus. The Kirchner governments in Argentina, together with the Lula government in Brazil, Chávez in Venezuela, Correa in Ecuador, Evo Morales in Bolivia and more recently the new governments in Paraguay and Uruguay, share enough of an anti-imperialist platform to reconfigure the patterns of economic integration in the region. More than a turning point in terms of traditional political fault lines, the new political landscape permitted envisaging the emergence of a new framework for development policies. It is perhaps too early for us to venture a forecast about the economic strategies that will be followed. But one thing is clear – new policy space has been opened for a strategy seriously committed to sustainability objectives.

The problems and structures inherited from the past still weigh heavily on the new emerging policy structures. Argentina and Brazil, for example, in spite of all their rhetoric about change, have maintained the same basic trajectory they had in the nineties, except for some significant (but not revolutionary) changes. Venezuela and Bolivia, on the other hand, have signalled their will to implement truly important and deep social, political and economic changes.[36] The current global financial crisis will contribute to the definitive demise of neoliberalism in Latin America, but at the same time it will not facilitate the implementation of reform. A window of opportunity in perilous times is not the easiest opening for sustainable development. The new emerging political structures need to understand that social and environmental sustainability must now be at the centre of their macroeconomic priorities. Some of the changes that need to be implemented are discussed in the next two chapters.

6 · Guidelines for macroeconomic policy and sustainability

Introduction

The subordination of social and environmental considerations to macroeconomic policy imperatives has been the dominant mode of policy-making under neoliberalism. Once macroeconomic objectives are determined, every other policy target is formulated in accordance. In this sense, social and environmental policies are being shaped in central banks and ministries of finance. The dominant notions of a primary surplus, very low inflation rates and free capital flows are the macro policy objectives to which all other considerations must submit. Whether soil erosion or biodiversity, health or education, mainstream macroeconomic policy-making is adamant: these are sector-level issues that need to be disciplined by macroeconomic imperatives.

Of course, the central idea is that stability will lead to growth, and this will benefit all sector-level objectives. A safety net, specifically extended under particular social groups, would take care of the rest. But under neoliberalism, growth has been mediocre, stability has been elusive and crises became more common. Inequality intensified and environmental degradation deepened. Policy priorities concerning the eradication of poverty, education or environmental stewardship were put on the back burner for the sake of balanced budgets and macroeconomic equilibrium. Clearly, we need to modify the relation between macroeconomic objectives and sustainability.

Redefining the central objectives of macroeconomic policy

Is macroeconomics a science or is it politics? asks the macroeconomist William Barnett (2006). For some, this may appear to be a good starting point for thinking about the scientific status of this field of economics. But in fact, it may turn out to be a rather simplistic question. Perhaps things need to be put in a wider perspective.

Macroeconomic theory was born in response to the needs of developed, rich capitalist economies.[1] All of its main tenets are an attempt to reply to perceived *policy* needs of these economies. From ways and means to counter unemployment to the mechanisms required to curtail inflationary pressures, macroeconomic theory developed as a field dominated by the short-term policy considerations of developed countries.[2]

This does not mean that macroeconomics was all policy and no analytical infrastructure. John Maynard Keynes and Michael Kalecki had an analytical view of how a modern capitalist economy worked. So, in a sense, we can say that from a policy-oriented perspective on how to restore full employment, macroeconomics had to ask how capitalist economies work. From this angle, the work of these authors was closer to a theoretical discourse about markets, capitalist accumulation and financial systems. The same can be said about post-Keynesian macroeconomists and structural macroeconomics.

A slightly different evolution is provided by so-called development theory, a field of work concerned with the economic problems of countries that had gained their independence just as the European colonial empires were being dismantled, particularly in Africa and Asia. In Latin America, development economics was concerned with the way in which these economies redefined their new roles in the world economy. Balanced growth, public finance, duality in economic systems, the role of agriculture, the process of industrialization, international trade issues, distribution of income and the size of the domestic market were some of the issues that preoccupied economists working in development economic theory. Most of the problems defined in this field were also policy oriented and belonged to what had already become the field of macroeconomics.

The crucial point is that these policy questions are marked by political choices, not dictated by the conclusions of scientific analysis. And this makes a big difference. To answer Barnett's question, macroeconomic policy is politics; its priorities are not defined by scientific necessity. This is something we need to take into account when redefining the main objectives of macroeconomic policy. If there is no 'science *diktat*' and the priorities in the agenda are not science-driven that's because the agenda is driven by political choices, and that leads us to an entirely different ballpark.

The world economy, or any given national economy for that matter, is not a giant mechanism whose 'laws' dictate the strategic priorities that need to be pursued or that events have to take this or that particular trajectory.[3] Yes, there are important functional relations that exist in our economies, but they do not reveal why stabilization should be more important than full employment. And the conclusion of this is that there is absolutely no reason why sustainability should *not* be a key priority or, for that matter, the paramount objective of macroeconomic policy.[4]

This is a political and ethical choice that a modern, well-informed global society should make. Fiscal and monetary policies are capable of having significant impacts on the environment. Nothing stops us from turning things around to have sustainability shape fiscal and monetary policies.

If macroeconomics is politics, does this mean that we can engage in irresponsible macroeconomic populism? Clearly, a distributive policy that can lead to hyperinflation, for example, will not take us to sustainability. But, on the other hand, IMF-sanctioned policies that lead to slow growth, volatility and financial crises are just as foreign to sustainability as macroeconomic populism. In fact, in many cases these policies did not lead to fiscal strength or stable external accounts. The ability of a given macroeconomic package to achieve a certain policy agenda depends on the adequacy of the policy instruments being used, as well as their consistency. And the neoliberal policy package lacks this internal coherence.

It is possible to maintain a debate on the precise level of the interest rate, or the exchange rate, or the level of expenditures required, or how much fiscal pressure should be put on capital gains. But we need to recognize that all of these things are instruments, not objectives per se. The truly important question is what priorities are being targeted. The performance of the policy package needs to be assessed in terms of the overall strategic objectives. And if these objectives are related to reducing poverty and inequality, and to putting a brake on environmental deterioration, then the evaluation of the policy package needs to be carried out in those terms.

The previous discussion reveals that there is a greater space for alternative policies than what was preached in the heyday of neoliberalism. And this applies to both developing and developed countries. In working to harness macroeconomic policies for sustainability, we have to reject the widely publicized approach that sees in public policies (particularly in anti-cyclical policies) the main source of market distortions.

Clearly, one first step is to abandon the TINA mindset and its corollary, the one-size-fits-all economic policy recipe. There are too many idiosyncratic parameters and specificities at the national level to think that a single policy model can take all of them into account. On the other hand, because we are talking about the role of the state in guiding societies towards the goal of sustainability, this also involves delicate political questions about democracy, transparency and governance. The painful experiences of inefficiency and corruption in state-run firms are too important to be ignored. Likewise, the recent evidence of corporate greed and irresponsibility in sectors such as banking and finance, as well as in natural resources (offshore drilling is a painful reminder of this), shows that these problems are not monopolized by the public sector. These questions are beyond the scope of our analysis, but they must be taken into account.

There are alternatives, and we need to go beyond the supposedly international constraints of globalization and interdependent markets. If a country establishes capital controls, regains its control over monetary policy and interest rates, and if it also rediscovers the powerful instrument that fiscal policy can become, then all sorts of alternatives start to appear on the policy horizon. We need to reform the international trading system, but we need also to commence spelling out the reforms at the domestic level. Obviously, designing alternatives and implementing reforms should not be done in terms of the old priorities. The new policy space needs to be oriented towards social and environmental sustainability.

Of course, there are macroeconomic balances that we need to keep in mind. But it is crucial to understand how these balances are obtained and what they involve. In particular, we need to know whether they are the result of irreparable social sacrifice or whether they are attained at the cost of irreversible environmental destruction. Also, we need to understand that they can be reached through different policies. Now we know that unregulated markets, extreme privatization, primary surplus and tight monetary policies can lead to slow growth, greater inequality, fragile public finance and, on top of this, environmental degradation galore.

To begin, environmental policy itself should be thought of as macroeconomic policy. This is not only a question of according additional importance to the so-called green national accounts. It goes beyond this and implies that all other objectives and policy instruments must be aligned as a function of sustainability objectives. In practice, this means that monetary and fiscal policies, for example, must go through a process of redesign and redefinition in order to comply with the paramount objective of sustainability, not the other way around. Just as macroeconomic policy-making was dominated by full employment between 1945 and 1970, and just as it was ruled by the imperatives of price stability after the seventies, today macroeconomic policy has to obey the dictates of full sustainability. If the full-employment priority was the result of the bad memories of the Great Depression, and if price stability was the result of the inflation rates of the seventies, then sustainability goals can be the result of an increased awareness that the environment, our home, is being destroyed at a rate that imperils humankind's chances of survival.

Critical issues in macroeconomics and sustainability

Macroeconomics and structures Macroeconomics focuses on aggregates, but this does not mean that the *composition* of these aggregates is unimportant. In fact, macroeconomic policy for sustainability makes sense only when the *structure* of these aggregates is taken into account. For example, the outstanding balance of the trade account may show a surplus, and this is judged a positive result by any macroeconomic standard. However, if exports are heavily biased towards goods that are natural-resource intensive, or if they are produced by cheap labour (as in the case of maquiladora industries), then that surplus may not be sustainable. A trade surplus that is achieved by depleting non-renewable natural resources, or at the expense of irreplaceable ecosystems or social equity, will not be sustainable.[5] Should the disaggregated components of macro accounts be taken into account by macroeconomic policy-making for sustainability? The answer is a resounding yes.

Suppose an economy or a region shows acceptable results in its struggle to control inflation. This may sound right for many, but the obvious question is how this was attained. If the answer is that this achievement is the result of the containment of aggregate demand via a restrictive incomes policy (i.e. wage controls), cuts in public spending, high interest rates and a tight monetary policy, or that it is related to an overvalued exchange rate, then we can start worrying. Stagnant real wages will intensify inequality and slow growth due to high interest rates will not help poverty. Reductions in public spending typically affect social expenditures and will have a negative effect not only on social equity, but also on productivity. One of the first items to be affected by cuts is the set of environmental expenditures. Typically, expenditures on items such as the development of resource management plans for biosphere reserves are the first to go (Nadal 2003). All of this will conspire against the social sustainability of this apparently healthy result. Thus, the structure or the composition of macroeconomic aggregates provides a relevant indicator for social and environmental sustainability.

In addition, macroeconomics cannot abstract itself from the social relations that exist in modern economies. As Taylor (2004) says, the structural approach to macroeconomic theory has it that an economy's institutions and distributional relationships across its productive sectors and social groups play essential roles in determining its macro behaviour. In fact, this poses a deep theoretical question. Macroeconomics should take into account causal and functional relations between aggregates, and this can be approached with some sense of accuracy only if the *structures* of these aggregates are taken into consideration.

Working with homogeneous aggregates should not hide this fact. The implications for the environment are important.

Macroeconomic policy and heterogeneity One feature of macroeconomic policy is that it relies on macro or economy-wide prices or variables to carry out adjustments and send signals to every sector and every agent in the economy. Herein lies one of the informational advantages of macroeconomic policies: that through one single variable – for example, the exchange rate – economy-wide adjustments take place at great speed and without the need to adjust all the individual prices of the myriad goods in that economy. The same could be said about the interest rate or even about some key prices such as those of energy inputs, when public firms control energy supplies.

However, economies are made up of heterogeneous sectors (industry, agriculture), different branches of activity and a great variety of actors. Heterogeneity may be defined in terms of physical features (agricultural produce versus synthetic fibres), type of goods being produced (machines versus consumer goods) or by the final destination of goods (exports versus domestic demand). And although this is true of all economies, some forms of heterogeneity may be extreme in developing countries where distribution of productivity gains between sectors is extremely unequal. This diversity is also present in the asymmetries of income distribution, although most mainstream macroeconomic theory assumes that this is irrelevant (for example, the IS–LM model rests on the assumption that monetary and fiscal policy measures do not affect income distribution). In addition, the business cycle itself is made up of a set of heterogeneous boom and contraction phases (Ffrench-Davis 2000).

A very important aspect of heterogeneity that needs to be taken into account by monetary policy is the type of circulation that takes place in finance and industry. Recognition of this played an important role in the evolution of Keynes's thinking about monetary policy (see Moggridge and Howson 1974 and Howson 1973). The differences in the supply and use of credit by different types of agents have profound macroeconomic implications in terms of growth and stability. In his *Capital*, Marx was to give a central role to the different types of circulation in capitalist economies, an analysis that remains highly relevant for the study of how rates of return impact on the environment.

There is another form of heterogeneity that is relevant here: the environment is a composite dimension in which air, soils, water and biodiversity are linked in a very complex web of relations. The environment is made up of a diverse set of ecosystems and dimensions, many of which are related to different industrial sectors or branches. Agents maintain diverse relations with these heterogeneous environmental dimensions, and they are affected by macroeconomic policy signals in quite diverse ways.

For macroeconomic policies this poses a well-known problem. The downside of the informational advantages of using economy-wide tools is that these signals do not discriminate among sectors or agents. They may carry unfair and/or distorting messages to different groups and firms, and there are winners and losers when these general policies are implemented. Because these signals will affect the productive and investment strategies of all agents (starting with their decisions to invest and/or consume), and ultimately this has implications for their use of resources, the impact on the environment is an important parameter that needs to be taken into account. Because the environment is a multidimensional heterogeneous object, a special effort is required to restore some flexibility to macro policy instruments.

From the perspective of expenditures, fiscal policy has the ability to discriminate by sectors as funds are allocated in the country's budget. Different environmental considerations can be introduced when preparing a country's budget. For example, priorities can be defined in terms of specific projects for water conservation or a set of biosphere reserves, or preventing marine pollution. So, from the viewpoint of environmental heterogeneity, fiscal policy may have its own mechanisms that allow for fine-tuning and adequate targeting. But the advantages of this flexibility disappear when everything is shaped by the macroeconomic imperative of a primary surplus. Once this dominating goal is defined as the top priority, everything else is expendable.

From the viewpoint of fiscal revenues, heterogeneity can also be reinforced. After all, an old principle of taxation is the respect for equity, an idea that is related to preventing a regressive tax structure. The notion that the wealthier groups in a society should receive tax breaks and support a low fiscal burden has been justified on the grounds that this promotes investment and creates favourable expectations. In reality, this is not supported by data on capital formation over the past decades. What did happen is that inequality increased in most OECD countries (Galbraith 2000).

It is well known that the impact of a flat income-tax rate will have a regressive effect as it has a disproportionate impact on the poorer social groups. To restore some equity to tax polices, governments have traditionally opted for a differentiated structure of tax rates, as a function of income. In the case of indirect or value-added taxes, which have been promoted in some circles as an alternative to income taxes because they are seen as an instrument that would increase coverage of fiscal contribution (including the so-called informal sector), the regressive effect is even stronger. But some form of flexibility can be attained by having different rates for different goods and even exempting some categories of goods (medicines and food) or putting greater pressure on commodities that pose health hazards (such as cigarettes). Environmental taxes can be another important source of revenue, and they can help increase pressure on 'bads' instead of goods.

Discriminating between sources of revenues is one way of introducing heterogeneity into fiscal policy. One important source of revenues can be found in financial transactions. Today the astronomical quantities of resources exchanged daily in the stock exchanges of the world, or in the global currency markets, to mention just two examples, offer a valuable opportunity for taxation. Even a modest tax on financial transactions can go a long way to generating an adequate flow of resources that can be used for social expenditures as well as for environmental conservation and restoration. The empty rhetoric about distortion of financial markets has to be rejected and a more realistic approach to the role of finance in capitalist economies has to be introduced into macroeconomics for sustainability.

What about monetary policy? In general terms, monetary policy appears to be more homogeneous in its effects than fiscal policy. If monetary authorities want to increase the money supply and relax interest rates, this policy will affect all economic agents. Of course, wealthier agents with more assets will have better access to credit; if weaker agents are to benefit from monetary policies, special measures need to be adopted. If differential impacts are desired, some form of flexibility needs to be introduced: heterogeneity for monetary policy must be restored (Ffrench-Davis 2000). This can be done through selective credit policies, something that requires regulatory changes because, by itself, monetary policy is incapable of doing this.[6]

Deregulation exacerbated the non-discriminating posture of monetary and credit policies. Many developing countries had regulations on banking activities that constrained banks to lend for activities that were judged to be strategic, such as agriculture. Also, differential margins for interest rates were frequently part and parcel of these regulations. Thus, in addition to capital reserve requirements and other prudential regulations, the banking sector was surrounded by regulations that affected the composition of its loan portfolio. In order to use monetary policy as a more effective instrument, it will be useful to re-regulate banking activities in this direction.

The need to re-regulate the banking business becomes clearer once it is understood that banks now have the capacity to create money and that the relation between deposits, savings and loans is not what standard textbooks claim. One of the most important contributions of post-Keynesian economics is the notion that banks can create money as demand requires and that 'loans create deposits' (see Chick 1983; Lavoie 2006; Tily 2007). The implications of this are critical in many ways. For one thing, the money supply is not regulated by the central bank, deposits are not a prerequisite for loans and savings are not needed for investments. Loans are made in response to demand (as long as banks think the recipient is creditworthy).

Monetary policy cannot be redirected towards the objectives of sustainability if we don't take into account the crucial fact that banks create money. Once the fractional reserve banking system was introduced, private banks had the power to create money. This is now called endogenous money by theoretical economists and is usually ignored in the theoretical models used in the academic establishment. This does not mean that central banks have no role to play. On the contrary, they remain the main source of liquidity for the economic system. But the ability of banks (private agents with a profit-making motive) to create money through credit cannot be ignored. Perhaps the crisis that we are witnessing today is in good part the consequence of this privatization of one of economics' most important public domains, the dimension of monetary creation.

Short of making the banking sector a strictly public venture, which makes sense from many perspectives, re-regulating banking is a strategic option. Issues such as capital reserve requirements, prudential conduct of business, and the prohibition on engaging in risky speculative investments are some of the issues that come to the forefront. But, in the context of sustainability, re-regulating banking means ensuring that adequate resources are made available for agents that play a key role in environmental sustainability (for example, small-scale agricultural producers). It also means putting in place regulations that prevent financing environmentally destructive projects (for example, in the extractive industries).

To summarize, we need to restore some degree of heterogeneity to macroeconomic policy in order to improve its effectiveness as a policy for sustainability. This is an important issue that requires more attention. But we also need to reconsider the most basic elements of the way in which banking takes place. Should banking be a business? Does it make sense to run the monetary system through private agents seeking profits when we are discussing sustainability objectives?

Macroeconomics and sector-level policies Sector-level policies are crucial, and without them macroeconomic policies may never attain their objectives. This applies to industrial and agricultural policies alike. But in order to achieve a better integration of macro and sector-level policies for sustainability, we need to reject today's straitjacket imposed by the 'kicking away the ladder' syndrome (Chang 2002). This is just another aspect of the perverse hierarchy that puts macroeconomic imperatives at the summit.

The idea that there are 'technical' constraints on policy interventions at the sector level is one of the most negative aspects of neoliberalism. For over two decades this has denied developing countries access to sector-level policy instruments that were used by developed countries to attain their current levels of per capita GDP. As a result, agricultural and industrial policies that were important to modifying economic structures in developing economies were banned, something that was sanctified by WTO prohibitions and forcefully implemented through its system of countervailing measures.

What happens at the sector level has enormous implications for macroeconomic policy objectives. An important point here is that 'sector level' does not mean 'secondary level'. If this is not understood, we run the risk of always having environmental policies dominated by the biases of macroeconomic policies. For example, without productivity gains in agriculture and industry it may be difficult to attain a healthy balance in a country's external accounts or the national budget. But improving productivity levels may require the implementation of industrial and technology policies. Important elements of these policies are simply not compatible with the international trade regime established under the WTO. The wide scope of issues that came under the aegis of the WTO after its creation, from investment rules to intellectual property, needs to be revised if we want to advance in our quest for sustainability.

The process of deindustrialization that has affected so many developing countries has dismantled the matrix of inter-sector and inter-branch linkages in the industrial system. This has contributed to the 'structural deterioration in the links between GDP growth and the trade balance' (Ocampo 2004/05: 296). These linkages need to be rebuilt if we want to ensure that sector-level policies contribute to the goals of sustainability.

One example that comes to mind here lies in the relation between fiscal expenditures for agricultural development and sector-level policies. Suppose a country approves an explicit policy to rely on small-scale producers in agriculture to strengthen soil conservation practices and recover agro-biodiversity but, on the macroeconomic policy side, implements a rigid fiscal policy that requires the generation of a primary surplus (while invoking the mantra of a balanced budget). Typically, the primary surplus will be brought about through cuts in public spending and support for small-scale producers will not be forthcoming. The number of examples can multiply: an ambitious policy to open and maintain natural protected areas may be completely obliterated by the overwhelming priority of a primary surplus.

Greater consistency between the macro and sector levels will help integrate the short-term preoccupations of macroeconomic policies and the pressing goals of long-term sustainability.

Short and long run: another form of heterogeneity? Macroeconomic policies have always concentrated on the short run. This is one of the key characteristics of mainstream macroeconomic theory. A significant part of academic debate over macroeconomic policy-making revolves around the validity of the assumption that in the long run the economy converges to equilibrium but in the short run some kind of public intervention is needed. So, for mainstream analysis events that take place over long-term horizons fall outside the scope of macroeconomic policy. This poses a new problem for sustainability objectives.

Policies for sustainability need to operate in a combination of time horizons. Soils take dozens if not hundreds of years to recover, forests take decades to recuperate, fishery stocks may take one generation to replenish, etc. How we can reorient policies that are designed to deal with short-term problems to take care of these problems is a fundamental issue that has not received enough attention. Debates about discount rates emphasize the differences in results when long time horizons are involved, and they have been used essentially to try to settle issues concerning the rationality of investing now in conservation so that the welfare of future generations is improved or at least not diminished. High discount rates seem to indicate that we need to invest more today in order to prevent damage tomorrow, and vice versa.[7] This is why a lot of the debate over long-term environmental issues, such as climate change, has revolved around the level of discount rates, while macroeconomic policies are mostly ignored. These debates systematically overlook the problem of how we can articulate short-term policy considerations concerning economic activity, trade or fiscal imbalances with the long-term effects on the environment.

Investment decisions that are affected by short-term considerations can have long-lasting effects. For example, investments in large-scale projects in the extractive industries (open pit mining or large commercial forestry projects) or big infrastructure investments respond to expectations of what is going to be happening to demand over the period that is relevant for recovery of the original investment. However, the environmental impact of these large projects may be felt over a much longer time horizon. Macroeconomic policy has to stop being a device to take care of short-term issues as if the future literally didn't count.

National environmental accounts already exist in several countries, with different methodologies and coverage. This is a good start, but something that needs more resources to improve accuracy and the coverage of sectors and activities. Above all, we urgently need to identify ways and means of effectively integrating the main results from these accounts with macroeconomic policy-making. Achieving this will go a long way to integrating the diverse time horizons involved in sustainability policies.

Counter-cyclical macroeconomic policies and sustainability The critique of the Keynesian approach to macroeconomic policy-making gradually destroyed counter-cyclical objectives. This was only natural. If Keynes had a clear message, it was that in the downward phase of a business cycle, macroeconomic policy had a role to play. Full employment and stable economic growth were objectives recognizable in their direct relation to the real sectors of the economy. When in a business cycle investment and activity slacked, both employment and growth suffered and the obvious conclusion was to push against that phase of the cycle. Even in the world of the neoclassical synthesis, public policy had a role to play, at least in the short run.

But in the realm of rational expectations and the new classical macroeconomics, macroeconomic policies have no role to play, even in the short run. This was translated into specific policy goals through the Washington Consensus, where fiscal balance, a tight money supply and a balanced set of external accounts (with a surplus in the capital account) became the core components of the macroeconomic position in both developed and developing countries. The importance of these balanced accounts implied the extinction of counter-cyclical policies and an almost complete disregard for what happened in the real sectors of the economy. This had critical implications as policy shifted its attention to the results of macroeconomic accounts and left market forces to rule the dynamics and determine the structure of the real sector of the economy. As monetary policy concentrated on price stability and fiscal policy on a balanced budget (in reality, generating a primary surplus), a pro-cyclical stance was adopted.

All of this was aggravated in the neoliberal (open) economy model through financial and trade liberalization. One of the contradictions of the neoliberal (open) economy model is precisely this pro-cyclical bias in macroeconomic policy-making. Given the impetus of trade liberalization, perhaps one of the most important pro-cyclical biases in the neoliberal macroeconomic model lies in the prohibition on using standard measures to redress the trade balance. The extreme example of this is NAFTA's prohibition on using standard balance-of-payments measures (such as tariffs and surcharges) to redress a balance-of-trade deficit. And although the exchange rate can be used as a counter-cyclical instrument, in the context of financial liberalization, capital flows generate significant rigidities in exchange-rate adjustment (Nadal 1996). All of this is aggravated if the exchange rate plays an important role in controlling inflation as authorities will postpone any adjustment as long as possible. In the end, a large-scale devaluation takes place and a full-blown crisis explodes.

A macroeconomic policy stance that has sustainability as its core objective has to involve a counter-cyclical stance that implies reworking monetary and fiscal policies. It has to be accompanied by the re-regulation of the financial sector and some form of control over capital flows. It also has to integrate the fact that in the boom phase of the cycle agents' expectations tend to favour increased risk adoption, the overestimation of assets' values and high leveraging (Minsky 1992). This is why financial markets exhibit strong pro-cyclical trends. As Ocampo (2004/05: 304) has shown, this has important implications for the role of international financial organizations, and we return to this in the next chapter.

Full financial liberalization had disastrous consequences for developing countries. This policy posture, together with the volatility associated with capital flows, distorted investment patterns, encouraging defensive investment (oriented towards protecting a firm's assets) instead of more expansive outlays (designed to expand market shares and generate growth). The combined effect of these policies promoted speculative behaviour and caused a long string of financial crises and deepening inequality. Increased poverty sometimes put additional pressure on the environment. The need to step up exports of raw materials increased environmental stress caused by extractive industries, etc. All of this generated very negative effects on the environment. The economic and environmental costs of this in the developing world have been staggering. Reorienting macroeconomic policies in the direction of sustainability objectives implies a radical transformation in this vision of macroeconomic policy-making.

Guidelines for macroeconomic reform

Today narrow macroeconomic priorities rule everything else. Once they are decided upon, all the other policy objectives fall into line in complete submission. Social and environmental policies, labour market considerations, sector-level policies for industry and agriculture, all are defined in their respective state agencies and are subordinated to the dictates of the policy priorities defined at the central bank or the treasury. This hierarchy needs to be carefully evaluated if we want to make any progress.

How do we start thinking about specific reforms in macroeconomic policy? The following paragraphs identify and briefly explain some of the most important elements that must be taken into account in order to correct the trajectory of macroeconomic policy-making. We include here a list of items that need to be explicitly incorporated as key policy objectives.

1 Inequality This is perhaps the worst enemy of sustainability. Inequality is not the result of a bias in technological skills or of disparities in the contribution of each person or group to social production (the marginal productivity theory). Inequality is a political event and macroeconomic policy should have as its core objective the reduction of income disparities and social inequality. Sustainability is antithetical with a world in which 48 per cent of the total population live on less than two and half dollars a day.[8] We know that inequality involves asymmetric vulnerability as the poorest groups in a society are exposed to higher environmental risks. At the same time, these groups are the ones that suffer most in economic terms from long-run disasters such as soil erosion or depletion of water sources. To close the circle, these groups may feel pressure to expand the agricultural frontier through deforestation, intensifying environmental destruction.

A macroeconomic policy stance with sustainability objectives at its core involves parting with the notion that inequality will disappear as trickle-down effects set in. It also means abandoning the idea that it is enough to build social safety nets and to improve targeting of anti-poverty programmes. Social policy cannot be replaced by these limited policy objectives. The experience of the past two decades shows this is simply not enough. Social and environmental objectives need to be put at the centre of macroeconomic policy-making right from the start, not as an afterthought. Together with this, we need to recover the redistributive role that fiscal policy can play, with a truly progressive tax reform and an intelligent structure for expenditures on sustainability items (i.e. all those items that are related to social welfare policy, as well as the environment). Among other things, incomes policy must cease to be an instrument to control aggregate demand by forcing negotiations to focus on expected instead of real inflation. Finally, price structures should be monitored to make sure that the price system does not conspire against poor agricultural producers.

2 Resources for sustainability A macroeconomic policy for sustainability has to ensure that an adequate flow of resources is allocated to environmental stewardship and restoration. This objective pertains to the amount of resources that a society should invest in strengthening environmental health and resilience. A fiscal policy posture committed to the goals of social and environmental sustainability (SES) should respond to intimately related objectives: distributional equity and generation of sufficient resources for environmental repair and conservation. These two objectives complement each other. Macroeconomic policy has to make sure that a sufficient amount of resources flows from the economic system into social welfare and the physical environment. This is an objective that can be attained in a number of ways.

In developing countries the most important channel for allocating resources to the environment at the scale that is required for sustainability is fiscal policy. But for this to operate adequately several important changes must be introduced. First, a new programme needs to be designed and implemented that will increase tax revenues by levying higher taxes on high-income brackets, capital gains and financial transactions. This has to be accompanied by a comprehensive tax reform that will eliminate incentives for evasion as well as windows for elusion, especially in the corporate tax regime. This does not necessarily mean that fiscal pressure will be increased to the point of discouraging investment and capital formation. There is ample evidence that taxes on high-income groups are low and there is room to accommodate higher levels of taxation. This is the outcome of two decades of a fiscal policy based on a Laffer curve type of reasoning.[9] It is also the result of the notion that taxes on capital gains and financial transactions were best avoided lest capital flight take place or financial chaos ensue. But at the tax levels that are typical of developing countries, this is something that demands a closer look.[10] On the other hand, levies on financial transactions exist in the United Kingdom and they have not provoked capital flight (we return to this point in the next chapter).

Furthermore, the principle of generating a primary surplus must be replaced by a better policy objective. This is a perverse posture that ultimately implies transferring resources from the real sectors of the economy to the financial sphere. In addition, generating a primary surplus has been typically attained by reducing per capita social expenditures (healthcare, education, housing, etc.) instead of increasing fiscal revenues through progressive tax regimes. Thus, in the long run, this policy posture undermines the capacity of a country to attain sustainability objectives, sacrificing everything for the sake of satisfying the appetite of a voracious financial sector. Only with a better policy objective will public finance be able to channel sufficient resources to environmental repair, conservation and stewardship. Debt management has to occupy a secondary position and cease to be the regulator of fiscal policy. We will examine the international constraints that may be an obstacle here in the next chapter.

Of course, primary surplus policies are directly linked to what is called debt management. One thing that has to be recognized is that the magnitude of the debt and its burden continue to weigh heavily on the developing world. In fact, even though the debt of developing countries has been 'managed' through this type of policy for more than two decades, the problem has not been solved. The external debt has been replaced in importance by domestic public debt, but in an open economy this distinction becomes almost superfluous.[11] The question of debt relief and cancellation, as well as its macroeconomic effects, will be addressed in the next chapter. The important point here is that debt management through primary surplus fiscal policies has been a complete failure from the perspective of sustainability: this is why there never seem to be enough resources for environmental stewardship or for social expenditures. This is one very powerful reason why the Millennium Development Objectives are not going to be attained.

Subsidies have been stigmatized under the neoliberal regime. However, we should recognize that there are many cases in which subsidies play a very important role in correcting problems that the market economy is not only incapable of redressing but may in fact be provoking. In addition, a measure of hypocrisy has marked fiscal policy in the past: as social expenditures have been curtailed, subsidies for activities in the financial sector or for energy companies have channelled billions of dollars to bailout schemes and environmentally detrimental activities, such as deep-sea fishing and extractive industries. In many cases, special interests and lobbyists have hijacked fiscal policy and misdirected public resources. These subsidies must be redirected to sustainability objectives. If they are well planned, one advantage of these subsidies for environmental objectives is that they will increase the value of assets related to these activities. For example, land belonging to small-scale farmers will experience an increment in its value and this will convince owners of the long-term commitment of public policies directed to sustainability.

Not all of the resources for environmental stewardship have to come from public sources. Other sources can be relied upon to generate and allocate these resources for environmental health. The first is the creation of incentives for firms to cover the costs of any environmental damages they cause. The debate on market-friendly schemes versus command-and-control regulations needs to adopt a more rigorous perspective and leave ideology aside. The second is through payments for environmental services, especially to communities that engage in healthy environmental stewardship. One good example here is provided by small-scale agriculture that provides services by maintaining healthy soil management and water administration practices, as well as bio-diversity conservation.

3 Monetary policy, exchange rates and the capital account If monetary policy is going to contribute to sustainability objectives, it needs to escape from its subordination to the needs of financial capital. This can be done in a number of ways, but one sine qua non condition is financial re-regulation (the object of the next subsection). A key principle here is that the financial system must serve the real economy and not the other way around. Emphasis is placed on the need to redefine the strategic objectives of monetary policy.

Some of the implications arising from the objectives of monetary policy have already been discussed. The shift from full employment and growth to price stability during the seventies implied enormous changes. This shift brought about slower growth rates and important structural transformations at both the domestic and international levels. Today, when monetary policy is pursued in the context of an inflation-targeting regime, a deflationary bias is imposed on the economy. Typically, central banks are given a lot of recognition when their inflation targets are attained, while sluggish growth, sagging aggregate demand and unemployment are attributed to other factors. The effects of monetary policy posture and its effects on the real economy need to be fully recognized.

The capacity of monetary authorities to pursue expansionary policies is severely curtailed as inflation targeting induces a potent bias in favour of high interest rates. This of course has a depressing effect on growth and employment. It also has important implications for environmental stewardship: 'rentier' economics is not a healthy recipe for environmental sustainability. Monetary policy may entail high interest rates in the interests of stabilization or to maintain a 'competitive' level and attract capital flows, but this imposes restrictions on rates of return and rates of extraction of natural resources. In the context of a monetary policy that incorporates sustainability objectives, a wise balance will have to be maintained between short-term rates and long-term rates that aim at fostering development.

In an open-economy setting, monetary policy has to be analysed as it interacts with the exchange-rate regime and capital account liberalization. There are at least two fundamental points here. The first concerns the need to recover control over the role of the interest rate as a reference for domestic monetary matters and not simply as a reward for external capital flows. The second issue is that the exchange rate must also recover its role as an adjustment variable for a country's external accounts. In order to recover the role of interest and exchange rates it is important to establish some form of control over capital flows. There is a vast literature on this, and there are various national experiences that have been quite successful in reducing volatility and the negative impacts of capital flows (Ocampo 2003; Ffrench-Davis and Tapia 2004).

In order to rely on monetary policy to further the goals of long-term sustainability, we need to restore a higher degree of heterogeneity in order to increase selectivity with policy objectives. We can do this by re-regulating the banking sector, and also by recovering some kind of social control over finance and money supply in view of the fact that banks create money. The notion of independence of the central bank should now be re-examined in the context of its role in the rescue packages.

Central banks must expand the horizons of their radar screen. Full employment, growth and achieving a healthy pattern of income distribution can be part of the core objectives, but they have to be accompanied by several other goals. Monitoring the formation of asset bubbles, the structure of the external sector's accounts, and the evolution of the business cycle are factors that need to be incorporated in the mission of central banks. The evolution of macroeconomic aggregates affects expectations of all economic agents, and this in turn has implications for the way in which they assess risks or the value of their assets. The importance of this cannot be ignored from now on, as the global crisis of 2008/09 has shown with utmost clarity.

4 Financial regulation Today the discussion about the origins of the crisis leads in the direction of re-regulating the financial sector. Because the crisis is perceived as originating in the financial sector, the logical conclusion is to prevent this happening again through a robust regulatory framework. This is not entirely accurate because this crisis has strong roots in the real sectors of the economy. This can be seen through the evolution of profit rates and the compression of wages since the seventies. Nevertheless, it is true that the volatility in financial markets is something that demands closer monitoring and scrutiny by regulators. Although reversing three decades of deregulation will take some time, awareness of this requirement offers an opportunity to introduce sustainability as a key issue in the debate.

Today it is evident that protection of customers and the prudential behaviour of banks, for example, are not enough to prevent systemic failure of the magnitude that brought about the crisis. Micro-prudential regulation has to be complemented by macro-prudential regulation that guarantees the stability and integrity of the financial system in order to avoid loss of output in the real economy.

The need to establish new rules for the financial sector has now been recognized. In fact, in some cases the issue is not so much innovation in regulatory schemes, but bringing back old rules that were irresponsibly eliminated. The Obama administration has recently unveiled a series of reforms that it wants to be approved soon. They are basically related to restrictions on the operations (so-called proprietary operations) that banks can carry out. This is still a far cry from the reforms that are needed, but it is a step in the right direction. The struggle to rein in the worst excesses of the financial (banking and non-banking) system is truly international in scope. The G20 has been the scenario of the dispute. Whether the financial lobby will allow governments and parliaments to approve the required legislation remains to be seen. Here is a list of items urgently required in this reform of the financial system at the national level.

First, there are certain activities by firms in the financial sector that need to be prohibited. To begin with, all off-balance-sheet transactions must be outlawed. In 2007 and 2008, Lehman Brothers Holdings, Inc. used these off-book operations to understate its leverage and deceived shareholders about its ability to withstand losses. The complex financial operations that took place were compatible with the Generally Accepted Accounting Principles and, from this perspective, were not illegal. But these practices are on the fringes of deception and speculation, and they allow agents to escape regulations, constituting a negative incentive to engage in fraudulent operations that can lead to the collapse of the entire financial system. Stealthy operations are incompatible with healthy regulation.

This is one of the most important problems that need urgent attention. Some financial practices that are not strictly illegal, but border on unfair business practices, may accelerate or intensify environmental degradation. The linkages between financial transactions and environmental degradation may not be obvious to a casual observer. However, the linkages are real. A dramatic example provided in Daly (1994) establishes the relation between hostile takeovers, junk bonds and the destruction of the giant redwood forests in California. Pacific Lumber was a family-run business that had the reputation of being one of the most environmentally sound companies in the USA. It refused to practise clear-cutting and left a natural canopy in harvested areas that stabilized soils and increased forest growth potential. But in 1985 Pacific Lumber was taken over by MAXXAM, another company engaging in forest products and real-estate transactions. The takeover was financed by the issuing of short-term junk bonds in the context of questionable business practices. To make the junk bonds more attractive, MAXXAM announced it would increase Pacific Lumber's cutting rate to pay for the bonds. After the takeover, Charles Hurwitz, MAXXAM's CEO, raided the pension fund and ordered a doubling of the rate of cutting to pay off the loans and junk bonds used to finance the operation. Hurwitz was quoted as telling Pacific Lumber's employees: 'This is the story of the golden rule: he who has the gold rules.' And the moral of this story is that natural assets can be sold and turned liquid if this is what is needed in corporate strategy.

Second, regulatory arbitraging must come to an end. In today's financial systems, market participants can select between operations that lie within the shadow banking system and thus escape minimal regulatory oversight. This distorts investment flows and creates opportunities for speculative pursuits. The macro-prudential regulatory regime for the financial sector has to cover investment banks and hedge funds, in addition to the traditional commercial banking sector. Restrictions on risk-taking, leveraging and capital adequacy, for example, need to be enforced on the entire financial system and not just on traditional banking operations. Similarly, over-the-counter operations must be banned as they contribute strongly to the lack of transparency that marks the financial sector today: clearly, every contract needs to be publicly traded and reported to all jurisdictions.

Third, financial regulations need to take into account interdependencies not only between firms and instruments, but also with monetary and fiscal policy, as well as the dynamics of the business and financial cycles. Financial re-regulation needs to move beyond micro-prudential considerations and take macroeconomic and sustainability considerations into account. In Brazil the combination of financial deregulation and retrenchment of public spending (the result of a fiscal policy geared to generating a primary surplus) led to the expansion of large-scale commercial soybean production, the displacement of ranching and, finally, increased deforestation in the Amazon basin. This is one of the clearest examples of how finance and grave environmental problems can be intimately linked. Re-regulation of the financial sector has to incorporate these lessons, forbidding downright financial support of activities that lead to large-scale, irreversible damage to the environment.

Fourth, futures and commodity markets need to constrain (perhaps even ban) operations by agents that have no interest in the underlying (physical) operations. In addition, the amount of resources going into these markets needs to be limited. This can be done through direct regulations or through a special tax on transactions in these markets above certain limits. Speculative 'investments' and hedging practices in futures and commodity markets were the main drivers of the price hikes that affected the world economy and the food security of hundreds of millions of people in 2007/08. Because futures prices affect spot prices, the spectacular expansion of resources involved in futures markets brought about price increments in spot markets (UNCTAD 2009).[12]

Several classes of financial operations and instruments need to be prohibited. Their nature and effects call for this. The list of examples is probably headed by over-the-counter derivatives, as mentioned above, but other instruments and financial innovations have surpassed the capacity of regulating agencies to maintain adequate surveillance. Some of these derivatives have been aptly called 'financial weapons of mass destruction', and their destructiveness is comparable to the effects of nuclear weapons.[13] Although they have played a key role in providing profits for some, they simply do not fulfil any useful economic role. In general terms, financial regulations should prevent these instruments from distorting investment and should replace them with incentives to create and operate instruments that will benefit long-term sustainability. In this sense, re-regulation should go beyond simple market oversight and aim to provide financial support for underprivileged groups and for environmental stewardship. It should also promote the creation of institutions that seek long-term development impacts rather than the short-term capital gains that have been the central focus of so much of the financial market (UN Financial Reform Commission 2009).

The notion that 'natural resources can be seen as a capital asset belonging to a general portfolio, which is comprised of other assets' and that 'managing this portfolio in a good and sustainable manner to maximize its returns and benefits over time is [a] good investment' (UNEP 2007: 30) is one of the most scandalous statements issued by the most important UN agency for the environment. When natural resources are stamped with a monetary sign and can become objects of speculation, trouble is just around the corner because they can be acquired with leveraged money with a view to appreciation rather than long-term conservation. In today's financial markets, where regulation is weak and the innovative capacity of money managers outstrips the supervising capacity of regulators, recommending that natural resources and the environment be treated 'just like another asset' is a recipe for disaster.

Concluding remarks

After thirty years of having a single macroeconomic policy package imposed on most of the world's economies, the global crisis of 2008 has brought home a different message. Its core elements are that there is room for more than one set of policy priorities. This has been the main signpost for this chapter, where we have attempted to lay down a set of general principles and guidelines that are useful while redefining macroeconomic strategies that pursue sustainability as a central objective.

There are many components that need to be redesigned in order to make macroeconomic policy a truly faithful instrument for sustainability objectives. An attempt has been made to highlight the most important ones. Others include the role of the public sector, which can be a powerful tool but has been strongly stigmatized by the supporters of neoliberalism. This is a point closely related to the need to regulate foreign direct investment. Finally, the role of the national environmental (or green) accounts has to change. Up to now, the so-called green national accounts have been designed and organized in order to measure the cost of environmental destruction. These national accounts have a restoration purpose. They assume a function that only makes sense *ex post facto*, once damage has been incurred. This makes it difficult for them to play a more active role in policy-making.

Recovering control over key macroeconomic policy parameters, such as interest and exchange rates, is related to questions of international macroeconomics and needs to be examined in the larger context of international economic affairs. Thus, while many of these policy guidelines are issues to be tackled at the level of individual countries, arriving at an adequate solution is also of concern to the international policy community. This leads to the next and final chapter.

7 · International macroeconomic reform for sustainability

Human activity is transforming the face and health of the planet. The magnitude of these changes is such that scientists are beginning to consider the possibility that a new geological era has been ushered in by anthropogenic forces (Zalasiewicz et al. 2010). Although this may remain controversial for some time, the truth is that the direction of the extraordinary environmental changes that are taking place does not bode well for our immediate future. Humankind must change these trends in environmental degradation soon or face disagreeable surprises down the road. The previous chapter dealt with reforms at the national or country level that will help integrate sustainability with macroeconomic policy-making. This chapter is concerned with a different angle of the same problem. It looks at macroeconomic reforms at the international level.

International economics and sustainability

The world economy is marked by several traits that condition our ability to change course and embark on a trajectory of sustainability. These are characteristics that escape the boundaries of a single nation and they are crucial to our analysis of why we are *not* moving in the direction of social responsibility and environmental stewardship. They also have serious implications for any attempt to harness macroeconomic policies and sustainability.

Expansion of the financial sector One of the most notable features of the world economy is the overgrown financial sector and the weight of capital flows. This spells out what has been called the *financialization* of the world economic system. Several indicators reveal that financial activities are the single most important sector in the world economy today, with an estimated value of assets several orders of magnitude above GDP and trade flows. It is no exaggeration to say that finance has become separated from the real sectors of the economy. But that is only one part of the story: in fact, finance has become the dominant activity, subordinating everything else to its priorities.

The financial sector is particularly prone to instability: because money and elaborate financial assets do not have any intrinsic value, their acceptance depends on confidence and trust. Their value is particularly vulnerable to changes in how people perceive economic conditions: expectations may weigh more than objective analysis and herd behaviour instead of rational management may be the dominant pattern. This is why crises are so frequent in economies with oversized financial sectors. The consequences of these crises are not limited to the financial sector: bankruptcies, destruction of plant and equipment, protracted unemployment and sharp falls in living standards are the debris of these explosions. If financial activities are so prone to instability and crisis, and if their effects are so disastrous, why should we expect them to contribute to the general objectives of social and environmental sustainability? Clearly, concerns about how to achieve social and environmental sustainability must pay special attention to the presence of financial gigantism in today's economy. If we want to reorient macroeconomic policy-making towards sustainability, it is important to understand the origins and nature of this process.

The genesis of this expansion of the financial sector and its activities has been traced to the long-term evolution of the world's capitalist economy. Braudel (1982, 1984), Wallerstein (1974) and Arrighi (1994) provide the historical and theoretical framework for this analysis based on the notion of systemic centres of capital accumulation. From this analytical perspective, 'financial expansions are symptomatic of a situation in which the investment of money in the expansion of trade and production no longer serves the purpose of increasing the cash flow to the capitalist stratum as effectively as pure financial deals can' (Arrighi 1994: 8).

When in a long-term cycle of capital accumulation the rate of profit associated with industrial and commercial enterprise declines, capital seeks different channels to prop up profitability. Typically, periods of declining profit rates are also associated with increased uncertainty, so capital seeks not only higher profit rates, but also the security of greater mobility. These two goals are met through greater liquidity and this leads to a greater preference for ventures in financial activities. The expansion of the financial sector in the second half of the twentieth century is not a unique phenomenon in the history of capitalism.[1] But it is perhaps accurate to say that the financial expansion experienced since the late 1960s is unique in that it truly encompasses the entire (geographical) world and has succeeded in subordinating all of macroeconomic policy-making to its needs.

This process of financial expansion starts with the demise of the Bretton Woods (BW) system of fixed exchange rates in 1971. When this system disappeared, new risks and opportunities for private agents emerged. As Eatwell and Taylor (2000) describe this process, flexible exchange rates brought about the privatization of risk: under the BW regime, governments maintained fixed exchange rates and private sector agents had no need (and no incentive) to engage in large-scale currency transactions. The privatization of exchange-rate risk that ensued carried with it the need to hedge against the costs of fluctuating exchange rates. The deregulation of the capital account to allow international capital to flow freely was associated with this need for greater protection.

In a system of floating exchange rates, private agents have an incentive to take advantage of arbitraging opportunities. Speculative transactions in foreign exchange markets can generate profits as capital enters and leaves different economic spaces taking into account inflation and interest-rate differentials, as well as exchange-rate fluctuations. As the capital account of the most important capitalist economies was deregulated, free flows of capital led to the expansion of the financial sector.

The expansion of finance has taken place through the creation of new families of financial instruments, most of them belonging to the class of derivatives. This and off-balance operations allowed different components of the financial sector at the international level to be connected through extremely opaque operations. In addition, financial speculation took by assault several other critical economic spaces, such as commodities and futures markets. Through the network of interdependent financial markets, contagion has taken the crisis to every nook and cranny of the global economy.

Capital account and financial market liberalization was pushed not only by the IMF, but also by the WTO through several agreements, such as the General Agreement on Trade in Services (GATS) that covers financial services. These measures were promoted without any consideration of their macroeconomic implications or their effects on the vulnerability of an economy open to capital flows.[2]

The linkages between financial liberalization and a macroeconomic policy stance that is contrary to sustainability stem from four interrelated problems. First, the combination of floating exchange rates and free capital flows distorts the role of interest rates throughout an economy. The rate of return implicit in exchange-rate variations disrupts the structure and role of interest rates in an economy (Eatwell and Taylor 2000: 189). Interest rates cease to be a simple reference for domestic investments in an economy where short-term financial capital flows take place. They become another variable in speculative allocations to diversify risk in financial portfolios and cannot play a constructive role in long-term investments for sustainability.

Second, financial liberalization fuels volatility and contagion. Volatility arises from the role of opinion and expectations in financial markets. Contagion comes from the interdependence of financial markets. All of this generates economic inefficiencies and distorts investment patterns. The nature of capital flows frequently leads to rapid expansion of banks' liabilities, and this has brought about unscrupulous loans, typically associated with booms in real-estate 'investments'. Unless this is corrected, how can we expect investment flows to be allocated for sustainable development?

Third, the exchange rate in a context of financial liberalization and free capital flows is not a price that adjusts to equilibrate markets. In the words of Eatwell and Taylor (ibid.: 75), 'portfolio adjustments do not provide a way for a "fundamental" external deficit to generate an exchange rate adjustment that will make the deficit disappear'. Why should we expect floating exchange rates in a context of deep financial liberalization to help move the world economy in the direction of sustainability?

Fourth, addiction to free flows of capital has limited governments' ability to impose taxes on capital. This brought about more regressive tax structures and enhanced inequality. At the same time, this has had a negative effect on fiscal revenues and therefore on expenditures. The allocation of adequate amounts of resources for environmental stewardship is hampered by this vicious structure of fiscal policy.

One of the most important aspects of capital flows is related to their effects on monetary policy, particularly to the fact that they expand money supply as demand for assets denominated in the domestic currency increases. In theory, the adjustment works automatically: capital flows bring about the appreciation of the exchange rate, and a drop in the interest rate. This reduces the flow of incoming capital and equilibrium is restored in the balance of payments. But the expansion in the money supply can bring about inflationary pressures. This can be curtailed by sterilizing the added resources through open market operations.[3] However, sterilization interrupts the adjustment process, keeping the interest rate at a higher level. Capital flows continue with sterilization and a higher interest rate, leading to chronic overvaluation, further damaging the trade balance and creating an atmosphere that promotes volatility and fuels negative expectations once fund managers start having doubts about a country's capacity to maintain the exchange rate. Macroeconomic policy-making needs to tackle this problem in order to implement sustainability policies.

Financialization of commodities markets The current global financial crisis was preceded by a series of abrupt hikes in prices of several basic commodities in international trade. This caused a great deal of stress and food crises in many developing countries in 2007/08. These price dynamics in commodity markets are related to the growing presence of financial investors in commodity futures exchanges (UNCTAD 2009; ITUC 2009). This financialization of commodity markets is brought about by the action of financial agents that use primary commodities as another class of assets to be included in their investment portfolio. In other words, an asset intended primarily for use becomes increasingly treated as an investment vehicle. The result of this has been a series of speculative bubbles that have deleterious effects on a great number of people, as witnessed by riots and turmoil in countries as diverse as Egypt, Bangladesh, Mexico and the Philippines.

Mainstream economists have attributed these price movements to fundamental changes in supply and demand. For example, biofuels production or the change in diet in China as per capita GDP increases have been considered some of the main causes of these price dynamics. But other studies point in a different direction (UNCTAD 2009; Suppan 2009). One important indicator here is that price variations took place at a point in time when fundamentals did not justify this variation. Trading volumes in commodity exchanges experienced sharp increases during the period of price hikes. For example, futures and options contracts on commodity exchanges rose from an average of 13 million contracts between 2000 and 2005 to more than 35 million contracts on average in 2006/08. The peak was reached in 2007 with 45 million contracts, according to data from the Bank of International Settlements. During that period the value of over-the-counter contracts in commodities increased by 1,300 per cent, surpassing US$13 trillion. Some of these financial investors who act as traders in commodity markets command a huge amount of resources, and their operations are capable of having important effects on prices. The increased presence of financial investors for whom commodities are just another class of assets to be used in hedging and profit maximization strategies has had a significant impact on spot prices.[4]

Commodity exchange and futures markets have existed for a very long time and they have been used to provide stable market signals and help producers meet the uncertainties of agricultural activities. Futures markets allow for price discovery and reduce price volatility. These instruments allow producers to hedge against price fluctuations that may have negative effects on production (thus ensuring activity levels close to capacity utilization).

In these specialized markets participants have been limited to producers, farm processing agents and traders. Until recently, other agents were prevented by law from entering these markets in order to prevent speculation. In the United States, for example, where the largest mercantile exchanges function, restrictions on trading in maize, soybean, wheat and other crops prevented speculation and price manipulation from the beginning of the twentieth century. But these restrictions were gradually relaxed, and in 2000 the US Commodity Futures Trading Commission (CFTC) deepened this deregulation process (with the Commodity Futures Modernization Act) on trading in maize, oats, wheat and soybeans.[5] The end result was increased trading and price hikes.

In the past there was some speculation in commodity exchanges and futures markets, but it was based on how agents perceived the evolution of supply and demand. Speculation in futures and mercantile exchange markets was simply the act of taking advantage of a system of relative prices. Carrying costs, delivery dates and inventories were critical in deciding how much to buy and when to sell. This changed when financial investors responded to risks in financial markets and went on to diversify their portfolio structures in order to search for optimal investment structures. For these agents, commodities become the physical support for a new investment that is not different (from the viewpoint of portfolio structures) from other financial assets. As futures contracts involving commodities became more common and were the object of complex securitization (Frankfurter and Accomazzo 2007), the normal price–inventory relationship was altered. To a financial investor securitized *commodity-linked instruments are now considered an investment rather than a risk-management tool*. This alters price dynamics and brings into commodity markets some of the negative traits of financial markets: herd behaviour and self-fulfilling prophecies that can engender higher prices until markets break down.

Financialization of commodities is a problem that extends well beyond the walls of the mercantile exchange and has direct impacts on output mix, technology choice and resource management practices. When they enter into a commodity market and start pushing prices upwards, financial operators may pull agricultural production chains into the space of financial transactions, risk management and speculation.

Because of the size of the resources at their disposal, their transactions in futures markets have direct effects on market (spot) prices.[6] But more than that, these effects are relayed through the workings of contracts that link agribusiness (with their own credit and marketing facilities) to direct producers in the field. Banking deregulation, tight monetary policies (with scarce and costly credit), recessive fiscal policies and the withdrawal of support for small-scale agriculture all combine to leave this space for large agribusiness.

International monetary disarray The world's current monetary system, based on the US dollar (and to a lesser extent on a few other strong currencies), is plagued by serious problems that affect sustainability in many ways. The system generates instability and diminished credibility of the value of the US dollar and has been unable to correct the external imbalances existing between surplus and deficit countries.

So far, the US dollar has been able to maintain the lead role but at a very high cost for the world economy. Countries issuing reserve currencies are constantly confronted with the Triffin dilemma between achieving domestic monetary policy goals and meeting other countries' demands for liquidity. This dilemma (first identified by Robert Triffin in the 1960s) states that when a national currency plays the role of international reserve currency, the source of liquidity in the country issuing that currency is its own trade deficit. In order to maintain liquidity at an adequate level, the issuing country must maintain a deficit, but this gradually destroys the value of the reserve currency. This is exactly what has been going on in the world economy: substantial fluctuations in the US current account have been accompanied by significant variations in the dollar exchange rate (see, for example, the fall in the dollar's exchange value between 1985 and 1995). In addition, there is significant risk of loss of value as US trade deficits reach gigantic proportions. Thus, countries issuing reserve currencies cannot maintain the value of these currencies and, at the same time, provide liquidity to the rest of the world. The consequence of an arrangement based on this scheme is a set of deep global imbalances.

In March 2009, the governor of the Chinese Central Bank, Mr Zhou Xiaochuan, called for the creation of a new international currency that would eventually replace the US dollar as the world's standard, reserve asset and means of international settlements (Zhou Xiaochuan 2009),[7] allowing for global financial stability and facilitating world economic growth. This international currency should have no links with economic conditions and the sovereign interests of any single country, and he recommended use of the IMF's special drawing rights scheme as the new reserve unit.

This would of course imply a monumental overhaul of the world's financial and monetary system. It also revealed the unhappiness of many developing countries (which currently own massive reserves in US dollars and dollar-denominated assets) with the role of the United States in the world economy.

The source of China's discontent (as well as that of other emerging economies) is that the value of the assets that it has chosen to keep as reserves against an emergency depends on US economic policies. In the context of the current global crisis, policies in the USA to limit the damage inflicted by financial problems and to stimulate the economy could lead to significant dollar depreciation.

In fact, the Chinese official made a compelling case for the reduction of the dominant role of a few hard currencies (such as the dollar, the euro and the yen) in international finance and trade. Moving to a reserve currency that belongs to no individual nation would make it easier for all nations to manage their economies better, he argued, because it would give the reserve-currency nations more freedom to change monetary policy and exchange rates. It could also be the basis for a more equitable way of financing the IMF, Mr Zhou added.

According to IMF data, in 2009 64 per cent of the world's official foreign-exchange reserves were held in dollar-denominated assets. The euro comes in second place, with 26.5 per cent, and the British pound and Japanese yen come in third and fourth places with 4.1 per cent and 3.3 per cent respectively. This is accompanied by a very strong role in international trade and in the international currencies markets: in 2007, approximately 88 per cent of daily foreign exchange trades involved dollars.

The world lacks a truly international currency: today's international monetary system consists of a set of currencies competing with each other to act as international reserve assets and means of international settlement. In the years 2005–08, the euro appeared to be a serious contender for this role. Chinn and Frankel (2008) examined in some detail how the liquidity and breadth of the European financial markets were approaching those of the US dollar, and how as a result the euro was eroding some of the advantages that historically supported the pre-eminence of the dollar in its role as leading reserve currency. However, the collapse of the Greek economy in early 2010 cast a dark shadow over the credibility of the European currency (and even over its future). The fact that the euro lacks its own treasury and the Treaty for the Functioning of the European Union (TFEU) includes a no-bailout clause (Article 125) does not help assuage creditors and financial markets. The situation in Spain, Portugal and Italy in early 2010 does not bode well and could trigger a crisis for the euro. Today, in the midst of the global financial and economic crisis, there is clearly no stable international currency.

But what does all of this have to do with the environment? The answer relates to the capacity of the world economy to maintain well-remunerated jobs and rising living standards and to allocate sufficient resources for environmental stewardship. It is also related to the need to set the world economy on a low-carbon trajectory, and to redirect agriculture and other activities close to the natural resource base on a path leading to sustainability. The world's monetary system, in its current mode of restrictive monetary policy-making, is not only incompatible with full employment objectives, it also deepens inequality and asymmetries, and leads to recurrent financial crises that undermine governments' efforts to achieve stable growth, destroy people's livelihoods and are accompanied by severe environmental degradation. The time for reform has come.

Export-led growth and aggregate demand The WTO is now fifteen years old. Its structure and philosophy reflect the heyday of neoliberalism. The long succession of crises, culminating in the global crisis of 2008, should provide enough impetus for the international community to seriously rethink what it has been trying to achieve through deep and non-discriminatory trade liberalization. A look at the structure of world trade and the relative shares of different groups of countries provides a sobering backdrop for the assessment of the accomplishments of the WTO. Although exports from developing countries have increased, the structure of world trade remains heavily lopsided. Formidable tariff and non-tariff barriers remain in developed countries, preventing true market access for developing countries' exports. The big winners of globalization *à la* GATT–WTO have not been the world's developing or poorest countries.

Trade liberalization has been clearly associated with greater trade deficits in developing countries (UNCTAD 2003). All of this has serious negative implications for developing countries' current accounts, indebtedness and environmental sustainability. In addition, there is a disturbing trend towards divergence instead of convergence in several critical domains. For example, in manufacturing industries the tendency is for a higher concentration of total exports in a small number of countries. Lall (2004) points to this trend and explains it as being a result of the greater disparities among countries in their ability to attract, master and improve on new technologies. The greater international disparity is not a temporary adjustment to liberalization, and it will not correct itself automatically.

Between 1945 and 1980, most developing countries embarked on a strategy based on building their own manufacturing capabilities through import substitution. During the 1970s, there was a shift in macroeconomic policy, as slower growth rates and inflation affected many developing economies. The import substitution model was abandoned and exports became the development strategy of choice for many developing economies. The new thrust in export promotion was also associated with the shift in thinking about macroeconomic policy and the role of markets. The triumph of free market ideology sounded the death knell for the policy instruments associated with import substitution (protectionist tariffs and controls, subsidies). Also, macroeconomic policies designed to promote full employment came to be seen as sources of inflationary pressure and market distortions and fell from grace. Import substitution was closely associated with industrial and technology acquisition policies that were judged to cause market distortions. The opportunity to push forward an agenda of deregulation came in the 1980s as the global debt crisis exploded and drove many developing countries to the doors of the IMF seeking help. The dismantlement of the import substitution policy apparatus was accompanied by structural adjustment that brought about the cuts in social and environmental expenditures so characteristic of the lost decade of the eighties.

A very important factor that promoted exports as the road to development and prosperity was the demise of the neoclassical synthesis in macroeconomic theorizing. As a result of this shift in theoretical macroeconomics, policy-making adopted the view that application of domestic stimulus to prop up aggregate demand was inefficient and would only cause inflation. In this context, export-led growth became the only alternative for the expansion of domestic employment. As Keynes (1973: 335–6) wrote, when a country has 'no direct control over the domestic rate of interest or the other inducements to home investment, measures to increase the favourable balance of trade were the only direct means at their disposal for increasing foreign investment'. But Keynes also warned that the advantage which one 'country gains from a favourable balance is liable to involve an equal disadvantage to some other country', and this 'means not only that great moderation is necessary, so that a country secures for itself no larger a share of the stock of the precious metals than is fair and reasonable, but also that an immoderate policy may lead to a senseless international competition for a favourable balance which injures all'. He added in a footnote that the remedy of a reduction of wages would hurt trading partners.

The experience of the Asian tigers and China can be reinterpreted in this new perspective. The most important example is China, where new records in export performance have been based on depressed wages and undervalued exchange rates. The problems caused by insufficient aggregate demand were shouldered by everybody's trading partners. As competitors in the world markets resorted to similar practices, the trend towards the reduction in growth rates in the global economy was strengthened. On the other hand, serious global imbalances accumulated and threatened to destabilize the world's economy.

As wages deteriorate in a race to the bottom, the environment also suffers the consequences. In Latin America, for example, the combination of increased pressure to export and the abandonment of industrialization policies led to an increasing share of non-processed commodities and raw materials in total exports. This additional pressure on the environment was exacerbated by two factors. On one hand, there is the drive towards deregulation of all spheres of economic activity. On the other, the fiscal policy priority to generate a primary surplus led to sustained cuts in resources for environmental stewardship, aggravating ecosystem degradation.

Transnational corporations and concentration of market power Another feature of the world economy is that giant corporations with considerable market power have become key actors in international economic affairs. These mega-corporations play a very important role in international trade and investment: more than 66 per cent of world trade takes place through transnational corporations, and 40 per cent of this takes place within companies (UNIDO 2002). They concentrate enormous market power in sectors that are close to the natural resource base (the crises in energy and food prices in 2007/08 can be traced to the actions of these corporations). According to members of a congressional investigation into the Deepwater Horizon disaster (see *Huffington Post*, 14 June 2010), the dramatic explosion and sinking of a BP drilling platform in the Gulf of Mexico were due to cost-reducing practices that sacrificed safety to profits.[8] If these allegations are true, they reveal what many already knew: these mega-corporations are doing what they want to the environment far away from adequate supervision and monitoring. Deep-water oil drilling is but one example. But there are many other instances in the extractive industries, commercial logging, fisheries, agriculture, etc.

There is a big difference between the agents that sign the agreements within the WTO system (i.e. governments) and the agents that actually perform trading operations (i.e. firms and large multinational corporations). It is no exaggeration to say that these economic giants have considerable political clout and are able to direct international trade negotiations in their own interests. For example, in the old days UNCTAD had a clear mandate to monitor markets and patterns of market concentration, but developed countries destroyed this in the 1980s. Today there is a serious disconnect between the overarching WTO objective of reducing or eliminating market distortions and the presence of intense market power in most branches.

Market distortions are not always related to government subsidies but may be due to market concentration. Perhaps the single most important lacuna in all WTO agreements is this lack of reference to market concentration, oligopolies and anti-trust enforcement measures. Free trade has become the equivalent of a world in which international market prices are affected by collusion, unfair business practices and market concentration. And the WTO has left this reality untouched. Leaving these problems to the obscure workings of international commerce arbitration boards is not the solution because their scope of competence does not include mandatory anti-trust measures applicable to general cases. Although this problem is screaming for attention, it has not been addressed by the WTO. The impact on the environment is enormous as the livelihoods of peoples that have lived in forests or managed water bodies for centuries are destroyed through these 'market forces'.

Vertical and horizontal integration in global commodity markets is a primary cause of market distortion. Possible policy responses include an international review mechanism on mergers and acquisitions (M&As) that involve transboundary transactions. At a minimum, transparency requirements should be imposed on transactions between agents that have more than 20 per cent of a regional or global market. Similarly, M&As and joint ventures involving cross-licensing and capitalization of patent rights should receive better scrutiny. These operations can be used to engage in serious business malpractices and unfair competition that distort market operations.

Not only has the WTO failed to regulate and look into the unfair business practices of large MNCs in the world's markets, it has established rules that protect these firms. The Trade-Related Investment Measures (TRIMs) agreement of the WTO forbids host governments from imposing any type of performance requirements on these firms. This eliminates one very important tool from the arsenal of industrial and technology policies that were critical in achieving the economic success that is now attributed to free and unregulated markets (Chang 2003). Although the lobbying of MNCs failed to get a multilateral investment agreement from the OECD and WTO in the nineties, they are still protected by an array of bilateral investment agreements that shield them from government intervention. In some notorious cases (for example, NAFTA's Chapter 11) MNCs are protected from the effects of environmental rules and legislation.

International income disparities Inequality between developed and developing countries has increased in the past two decades. The World Bank estimates that 48 per cent of the world's total population lives on less than US$2.50 a day. Approximately 80 per cent live below the 10-dollar figure. Inequality intensified within many developing countries and within developed countries as well. It is now recognized that in most advanced industrial countries, median wages stagnated during the last quarter-century, while income inequalities surged in favour of the upper quintiles of the income distribution. In effect, money was transferred from those who would have little to spend on basic needs to the richest groups, thus weakening aggregate effective demand.

How did this growth in inequality come about? First, fiscal policy was dominated by a regressive posture in which social expenditures suffered and tax cuts were implemented for the richer groups. This contributed greatly to the dismantling of social safety nets and was part of a 'market-friendly' stance favouring a strong primary surplus and small or zero fiscal deficits. Free capital mobility also had the effect of limiting governments' ability to impose taxes on capital.

Second, in a competition to attract foreign investment, many developing countries dismantled the institutional network that had contributed to better wage levels in the past. Unions and anything that was perceived as an obstacle to wage flexibility came under attack or were neutralized. This resulted in increased disparities between workers' compensation and the income of the richer strata.

Third, the struggle against inflation in developing countries frequently involved repression of aggregate demand. In many cases, this was achieved by shrinking real wages. In negotiations with unions, typically the expected inflation rate was used to determine wage increases, so that when actual inflation surpassed this target, the real wage was reduced.

The increase in public debt in some OECD countries was partly the consequence of the evolution of the distribution of income. In some advanced countries such as those in the European Union, social protection systems that provided partial compensation for stagnating income were financed through increased public debt. In countries where the social protection system is much weaker (e.g. the USA), increased household borrowing may have postponed a decline in living standards in tandem with the decline in real wages. Finally, inequality is also exacerbated by price dynamics, because poor households spend proportionately more on food and energy consumption. The crisis caused by price hikes in food and energy in recent years had a greater impact on lower-income brackets of the population.

Inequality is a curse that a sustainable economy needs to eliminate. It is perhaps difficult to think of a world with perfect income distribution, and this is why this objective is dismissed as too close to nirvana to be feasible. However, it is clear that a world in which approximately 50 per cent of the population live below the poverty line is moving on a trajectory that is contrary to sustainability and leading to disaster.

This increase in inequality is not unrelated to environmental degradation. Poor people rely more on so-called environmental services, and under duress they may put more pressure on the natural resource base. The global financial crisis threatens to hasten this prospect. The policy response to the crisis should aim at reducing, instead of intensifying, social inequality. While developed countries pursue counter-cyclical policies, most developing countries are constrained to pursuing pro-cyclical policies. This will exacerbate international and intra-country inequality.

Debt bomb The debt of developing countries has long been recognized as a critical obstacle to development. It is also one of the most important connections between macroeconomic policies and environmental sustainability. Considering the data and the dynamics of debt servicing, it is amazing that debates on the MDGs, the Green Economy Initiative or the recommendatrions for mitigation and adaptation to climate change in the IPCC's AR4 pay no attention to this huge problem.

For example, the total public external debt of developing countries increased between 1970 and 2007 from US$70 billion to US$3,360 billion. Total debt service payments by developing indebted countries to developed creditor countries during the period 1980–2007 amounted to a staggering US$7,150 billion. These numbers tell a dramatic story about the evolution of the world economy.

In 1970, the world's poorest countries had a total debt of approximately US$25 billion. In 2002, these countries' debt had risen to US$523 billion. In the case of Africa, in 1970 its debt was US$11 billion, but thirty years later this was US$300 billion. The poorest nations in the world owe multilateral institutions about US$70 billion. On top of this, US$550 billion has been repaid in both principal and interest during these past three decades on loans of US$540 billion, and still we have an outstanding debt for these countries of US$523 billion! By 2008 developing countries had reimbursed the equivalent of 102 times the amount of their debt in 1970; in that period their outstanding debt was multiplied by a factor of 48 (Millet and Toussaint 2009). It is clear that this process of multiplication of debt needs to be halted if anything approaching sustainability is to be attained.

For the creditor countries, the amounts involved in debt statistics are small. However, for poor developing countries these amounts are of critical importance and may spell the difference between life and death: as many as five million children and vulnerable adults may have lost their lives in sub-Saharan Africa since the late 1980s as a result of the debt crunch (Shah 2005). Through a series of instruments and different forms of pressure, creditor countries have forced these indebted countries in the developing world to sacrifice healthcare, education and environmental stewardship and to prioritize debt repayment in their fiscal policies.

The history of developing countries' debt goes back to the period of decolonization in the fifties and sixties. Guissé (2004) shows that in 1960, at the peak of the decolonization period, a debt of US$59 billion was imposed on the newly independent countries by the outgoing colonizing states. At a rate of 14 per cent the debt accumulated rapidly. Before the newly independent states had had a chance to set up their economies, they were laden with the heavy burden of an external debt that had no economic or legal justification whatsoever. For many developing countries the ordeal of this odious debt was just beginning.

The notion of 'odious debt' is a well-established legal concept (Howse 2007). Legally, odious debt results from loans to an illegitimate or dictatorial government that uses the money to oppress the people or for personal purposes. Moreover, in cases where borrowed money is used in ways contrary to the people's interest, with the knowledge of the creditors, the creditors may be said to have committed a hostile act against the people. They cannot legitimately expect repayment of such debts. The best example of an odious debt is the case of South Africa, where the debt acquired during the apartheid regime has been a terrible burden on the country since the termination of that period in its history. This ugly situation was aggravated for some of the poorest countries as acceptance of partial debt cancellation in the context of the Heavily Indebted Poor Countries (HIPC) initiative is accompanied by conditionality imposed by the IMF on trade liberalization, financial deregulation and restrictions on fiscal policy (generation of a primary surplus through curtailment of social expenditures).

In addition to the transfer of resources that the debt problem implies, major sovereign debt crises have constituted a serious obstacle to growth and development during the past thirty years. These crises have been extremely harmful: their costs in social and environmental terms have been overwhelming. Unemployment, poverty and greater inequality are associated with greater pressure on natural resources, soil erosion, deforestation and loss of biodiversity. Clearly, any discussion about resources for sustainability must involve an analysis of the constraints that the debt time bomb imposes on macroeconomic policy (especially fiscal policy) of developing countries.

Reforming international macroeconomics for sustainability

An economic regime based on unfettered free markets and financial liberalization is taking us away from long-term environmental sustainability. The set of issues raised in the previous section clearly shows that neoliberal globalization implies a race to the bottom in social and environmental standards and may lead to irreversible catastrophic situations unless we act now. This final section deals with reforms to the international economic regime required to make room for a more proactive macroeconomic policy posture.

The agenda for international macroeconomic reform is obviously very large and encompasses many aspects of the world economy. Here we highlight those aspects directly and indirectly related to long-term social and environmental sustainability, focusing on the following dimensions: a) changing the international monetary system; b) regulating international finance and capital flows; c) solving the sovereign debt predicament; d) reforming the international trade regime; e) financing global environmental stewardship.

a) Changing the international monetary system An international monetary system built for sustainability should have three main objectives: to guarantee sufficient liquidity and prevent deficiencies in aggregate demand; to avoid structural imbalances between deficit and surplus countries; and, finally, to ensure that adequate financial resources are allocated for global environmental stewardship. To meet these objectives there are two levels of reform that need to be considered. The first requires a deep transformation of the world's monetary system and involves a new international reserve currency. The second implies a thorough overhaul of existing institutions and of their role in money creation. Both approaches would need a serious regulatory regime for international finance.

The world's monetary system urgently needs to undergo a deep transformation if sustainability objectives are to be attained. John Maynard Keynes recommended the creation of an international reserve currency issued by an International Clearing Union. This currency would be 'governed by the liquidity requirements of world commerce and would be capable of deliberate expansion' (Keynes 1980: 163). It would also be accompanied by a system to get rid of the imbalances and asymmetries that mark today's global economy. This implies 'a method by which the surplus credit balances arising from international trade which the recipient country does not want to employ can be set to work without detriment to the liquidity of these balances' (ibid.). The post-Keynesian tradition has been at the forefront in developing the structure of these reforms proposed by Keynes many decades ago. The proposal for an international currency is based on the need to prevent a lack of aggregate demand at the global level due to nations holding excessive idle reserves or draining reserves from the world economic system. This issue is closely related to the problem of resolving international trade imbalances.[9] It is a required step if we want macroeconomic policies to be compatible with a strategy for long-term sustainability.

There have been several proposals in this direction (see Davidson 1999 and UN Financial Reform Commission 2009). A first question concerns the responsibility for managing the global reserve currency. Because the IMF is an institution so committed to neoliberal ideology, it clearly should not be given this responsibility. Captivated by the ideology of financial liberalization, it was caught asleep at the helm when the 2008 crisis exploded. In its current form, the IMF is unlikely to be able to play a constructive role in monetary reform. Clearly, it would have to undergo a major overhaul if it were to be given a new mission. This would make it, literally, a new institution.[10]

A new unit of account and ultimate reserve asset for international liquidity is needed. A scheme such as the one described in Davidson (1999) could be followed. The system would be endowed with a trigger mechanism to encourage a creditor nation to spend what are deemed to be 'excessive' credit balances accumulated by running current account surpluses. These excessive credits could be spent in three ways: a) on the products of any other member of the union; b) on new foreign direct investment projects; c) to provide unilateral transfers to deficit members. Surplus countries would have considerable freedom to adjust in ways they consider beneficial to their interests. The system could be oriented towards investments that ensure environmental sustainability. Deficit countries would no longer have to adjust painfully because they would be able to remedy their imbalances through increased exports.

This scheme could still allow for persistent export–import imbalances, but in the case of poor nations where a current account deficit persists over a certain period of time owing to heavy debt service obligations, clearing union officials would foster negotiations between the debtor and its creditors for debt restructuring, as well as partial or total debt cancellation. This scheme needs a strong regulatory regime for international capital movements but could be compatible with blocks of nations that would like to permit free capital flows.

As of today, the dollar will continue to be a reserve currency only if others are willing to hold it as such, but as risk increases, doubts about the dollar will intensify. The USA has embarked on a response to the crisis involving large domestic and external imbalances with unpredictable implications for the international reserve system. Thus, both the United States and countries holding foreign exchange reserves may actually find it acceptable to introduce a new system. The former would be able to take policy decisions with less concern about their global impact; the latter would be less concerned about the impact of US policies on their reserve holdings. This is the solution to the conundrum of holding huge reserves in US dollars and offers the opportunity to channel significant resources to environmental stewardship.

Interestingly, with a supranational reserve currency the United States would recover its control over monetary policy. Everyone would benefit from the reduction in global risks associated with aggregate demand deficiencies. Failure to carry out this transformation will impede stable growth and will continue to promote instability, weighing heavily on our ability to attain sustainable development.

b) Capital flows and regulations for international finance The global financial crisis of 2008 forces us to recognize that the time has come to seriously debate and put in place a robust regulatory system for international finance and for capital flows in particular. Capital controls can contribute to smooth cycles in the capital account, and reduce overall economic vulnerability (Furman and Stiglitz 1998; Ocampo 2003). In Chile, unremunerated reserve requirements shielded the economy from overabundance of short-term capital at times of surges and helped attain higher growth rates (Ffrench-Davis and Tapia 2004). They also protected the economy from contagion at a time of great volatility caused by the

Mexican financial crisis of 1994/95. In Colombia, capital controls also allowed for better handling of maturity periods of external debt (Ocampo and Tovar 2003). In both cases, capital controls allowed policy-makers to regain some autonomy for a counter-cyclical monetary policy. This is also consistent with the historical record of developed countries, which shows long periods of capital controls and only gradual liberalization of capital flows (Eichengreen 1996). The experience of the past twenty years demonstrates that premature and abrupt liberalization of the capital account was totally inappropriate for developing countries.

Capital controls should not be seen as a panacea. Their central mission is to smooth the cycles of the capital account, enhance stability and allow for a greater degree of independence in monetary policy. This objective can also be attained with the use of balance-of-payments provisions within the WTO framework. These provisions can provide a constructive response to external accounts crises (Nadal 1996) and should be reconsidered as an important tool in the intersection between trade and financial flows. The world's trade regime needs to be revised in order to make it compatible with country-level counter-cyclical policies and with regulations directed at crisis prevention. In addition, trade agreements such as GATS need to be reviewed in terms of their balance-of-payments effects, their impacts on macroeconomic stability and the scope they provide for financial regulation.

Regulations for the world's banking sector are another critical aspect of this problem. The Bank for International Settlements (BIS) in Basle has thus far been unable to prevent crises. The Basle I and II accords it promoted to regulate capitalization and risk management were unable to function as early warning signals.[11] However, the Basle Committee on Banking Supervision could help identify and design new policies that would bring the banking industry closer to the needs of social and environmental sustainability. One way to get started in this area is to establish a working group within the Policy Development Group charged with the task of identifying and reviewing emerging supervisory issues and proposing and developing policies that promote a sound banking system. Social responsibility and environmental sustainability are certainly two extremely important emerging issues that have been systematically neglected.[12]

Several important initiatives involving self-regulation in the banking system have failed. For example, the Wolfsberg Group, an association of twelve big banks with global operations, developed a set of anti-laundering principles. But this initiative is from an interest group and is simply aimed at reducing legal risks for banks, and it is utterly inappropriate to think of this as a healthy approach to regulation. The Equator Principles are another voluntary initiative focusing on project finance whose members provide loans only under nine principles that cover such things as social and environmental assessments. Unfortunately, the Equator Principles have not been very effective.

c) Solving the debt predicament The world lacks a system to deal with the debt problem. Past negotiations with unfair and inefficient risk-sharing schemes provided only temporary relief and were dominated by creditors. Typically, debt negotiations have emphasized the notion that strong pressure is needed so that debtor countries do not feel tempted to default. Needless to say, the emerging solutions haven't been in the general interest. Debt rescheduling and relief cannot continue to depend on the negotiating capacity of individual debtor countries.

As long as developing countries are weighed down by the debt burden, sustainable development will be an elusive goal. Every year, developing countries in all regions are forced to generate a primary surplus to cover their financial charges, a significant proportion of which is related to the original or 'old' debt. This is why resources have been siphoned from the developing world for more than fifty years, with terrible social costs and very negative environmental consequences worldwide. Today's global financial crisis puts even more pressure on indebted countries. It is perhaps the single most important macroeconomic obstacle to the allocation of resources to social and environmental sustainability.

Debt relief and policy space Generating a primary surplus is the key process by which developing countries have diverted resources to service debt. Macroeconomic adjustment programmes imposed by the IMF typically contain fiscal policy restrictions aimed at bringing into being a primary surplus, making debt management the main priority.

The primary surplus has been one of the main causes of environmental deterioration in developing countries. Cuts in expenditures to generate this primary surplus usually involve reducing appropriations for social and environmental sustainability. They prevent the allocation of sufficient resources to budgetary items such as sustainable agriculture, biosphere reserves, education in general and environmental education in particular, as well as the many other things on which sustainability relies. Instead, precious resources have been shifted towards debt service, with the net result that the overall government budget is in deficit once these financial charges are factored in.

A different approach to debt management is required. It needs to go beyond the simple notion that fiscal policy has to generate funds for debt service. A concerted effort to help debtors and creditors reach common ground must be launched by the relevant international organizations based on the premise that effective debt relief is essential. In the past, real debt relief has been extremely weak and has usually been linked to rather optimistic projections about future economic performance. Another round of simple rescheduling of obligations is clearly not desirable.

In the context of today's crisis, sustainable debt dynamics has to be redefined for the recovery of debtor nations. The sense of urgency arises from the fact that the poorest and most vulnerable countries will certainly face difficulties in meeting external debt service. The UN Commission for Reform of the International Financial and Monetary System does not exclude debt moratorium and, where appropriate, debt cancellation. In other cases, negotiations must recognize economic, social and environmental objectives and not just the right of creditors to recover. Public and private creditors should recognize that a rapid solution to the problems of debt overhang can improve recovery. Social and environmental sustainability can be imperilled if these problems are not addressed effectively.

Equity considerations suggest that poor countries should benefit from immediate debt cancellation together with concessional funds in order to engage in counter-cyclical policies. The HIPC initiative has been insufficient to solve the debt problem of this group of countries. In 2005 a new Multilateral Debt Relief Initiative was launched. But these efforts have been implemented without due consideration to the macroconomic policy regime in the debtor countries, and these debt relief packages are embedded in a pro-cyclical policy framework. This aggravates inequality and poverty and impedes the allocation of adequate resources to environmental stewardship. Total and unconditional debt cancellation for the poorest countries would liberate resources for social and environmental sustainability in countries rich in biodiversity.

Major debt negotiations today take place under the informal and imperfect coordination of the debtor and its creditors by the IMF, under the guidance of the G7 major industrialized countries, which set the overall policy directions for the IMF and other involved institutions, such as the Paris Club, where debts owed to governments are restructured. This system has failed to solve the debt problem. A new framework should recognize that debt crises and failure to achieve efficient debt relief incur great costs in terms of social welfare and environmental destruction.

It is evident that the institutional architecture governing international debt needs to be fundamentally overhauled so that debtors and creditors are placed on an equal footing. The priorities of social and environmental sustainability should be the organizing lines for equity in solving debt problems. International civil society organizations, as well as several UN commissions, have proposed the creation of a new International Debt Court. The rationale for this is similar to that for national-level bankruptcy courts: it would organize priority of claims, debt cancellation and overall debt relief according to previously agreed criteria that would ensure equity and sustainability. Most important, this court would differentiate between countries and between types of indebtedness. In particular, it would be able to distinguish between bona fide inability to cover debt service, odious debt and *force majeure*.[13]

d) Reforming the international trade regime Reducing trade barriers is not an end in itself. The dynamics of trade negotiations should stop being dominated by this fallacy. The goal is sustainability and development, not free trade per se. So, before the world embarks on a new round of multilateral trade negotiations, the WTO should begin to assess carefully how the existing agreements are being implemented and how they are performing.

This section takes a look at some of the reforms needed in the world's trading system in order to guarantee its contribution to the objectives of sustainable development. The issues discussed below are agriculture, special and differential treatment provisions, foreign investment, international commodity agreements and, finally, the balance-of-payments provisions.

Agriculture What we do today to the agricultural system of the world will determine the history of our future as a species. Yet the world has been unable to reconcile adequate food production and distribution systems, improving living standards, and the environmental sustainability of the agricultural system. Although global agricultural production has continued to outstrip total population, the rate of growth of yields has been slowing down and today barely accounts for a third of its level twenty years ago (IAASTD 2009). The per capita cultivated area has begun to contract, indicating that we have reached the limits of the agricultural frontier in many key areas of the world. Consumption rates of irrigation have led to over-exploitation of aquifers, and heavy use of chemical inputs contributes to pollution of underground and surface water bodies. All of this coincides with a situation in which close to a billion human beings suffer from malnutrition.

The Uruguay Round Agreement on Agriculture (URAA) contributed to trade liberalization in this key sector, but left untouched the capacity of developed countries to channel resources to the agricultural sector. The URAA did not open up market access for the products of developing countries, while global agricultural commodity prices suffered severe reductions and volatility increased. After fifteen years of operations, the URAA has failed to solve the complex questions of food rights, economic development, social responsibility and environmental stewardship. The current approach, based on the false premise that we need to let markets operate freely, is unacceptable. It has spelled trouble for small producers in developing countries as dumping practices destroyed their markets and livelihoods.

The question of subsidies requires closer scrutiny. The world needs adequate crop prices that contribute to a healthy and vigorous worldwide agricultural sector (Ray et al. 2003). The old system needs to be replaced with an institutional and legal framework that blends sound supply-management policy measures with adequate support mechanisms in developing countries. A new institutional arrangement, perhaps a new framework convention, needs to tackle the issues of sustainable agriculture, small-scale producers, biodiversity, food security and access to genetic resources, not on a piecemeal basis, but as part of a single undertaking. The new convention should restate the fundamental right of nations to defend themselves from dumping practices and from the market distortions brought about by the concentration of corporate power.[14]

Special and differential treatment Special and differential treatment (SDT) is based on the idea that fairness is an important guiding principle in international economic relations. It is also linked to the recognition of existing international asymmetries in the functioning of markets and generators of inefficiencies. In the context of the WTO it is linked to the idea that developing countries are not obligated to reciprocate the full trade concessions made by developed countries because they need more time to adjust to the economic forces unleashed by trade liberalization.

SDT was recognized by the original GATT and its principles were incorporated in several of the WTO agreements. The actual implementation of special and differential treatment relies on various types of mechanisms: limited time derogations; exceptions and preferences in disciplines; lower commitments in tariff reductions; technical assistance commitments, etc. But SDT failed to provide the conditions needed by developing countries to adjust. A few extra years in certain transition periods, or a few tariff points below developed countries' concessions, have not been able to redress asymmetries that took decades or even centuries to crystallize. The lopsided structure of world trade indicates that SDT has been a failure in establishing a level playing field.

The main problem is that SDT has been accompanied by a severe contraction of the policy space of developing countries. As a result of structural adjustment policies, several WTO agreements and some regional and bilateral trade agreements, control over macroeconomic policies has been drastically reduced. In addition, the array of industrial and agricultural policy instruments has shrunk to the bare minimum. Ironically, precisely at a point in time when economic theory recognized asymmetric market configurations as the source of market failure, the world's trading system has turned its back on the notion of SDT as the key guiding principle to eliminate asymmetries.

The first component of a new framework should be the recognition that the world's trading system must open for developing countries the possibility of resorting to the industry policy instruments that developed countries used at one point and which late industrializers also used. These are especially important for accessing dynamic competitive advantages that are skill and technology based. Without these policy instruments, developing countries run the risk of remaining for ever in the low productivity trap of the natural resource exporter. The second component is that financial assistance is essential to attain a level playing field. Today we are far from the required levels of development aid. It is sometimes argued that foreign direct investment (FDI) flows have picked up and that they are preferable to aid. This is misleading because FDI is heavily concentrated in a few developing countries, and because a significant portion of total FDI is made up of mergers and acquisitions (M&As) of already existing companies. Financial assistance is a different instrument with a rationale of its own, oriented towards long-term investments under preferential conditions, and should be part and parcel of sustainability policy.

Foreign investment The Trade-Related Investment Measures (TRIMs) force developing countries to forgo the use of important industrial policy instruments. Policies aimed at increasing local content in value-added, or limiting imports to a certain proportion of exports, are not allowed under the current version of TRIMs. Even this was not considered sufficient, and developed countries engaged in a big diplomatic effort to strengthen these provisions as part of the multilateral investment agreement (MIA).

Thus, instead of protecting developing countries against the effects of market concentration, the TRIMs ended up shielding powerful multinational corporations against public policies in host countries. The policy instruments that are eliminated by TRIMs are important in the context of industrial policy. Some of them are critical in order to develop technological capabilities and aim for higher-value-added exports. They are essential to building forward and backward inter-industry linkages capable of transmitting economy-wide multiplier effects. Without these instruments, developing countries are condemned to remain in a low productivity trap and to rely on exports of primary and raw materials that have a greater ecological footprint.

Chapter 11 of the North American Free Trade Agreement (NAFTA) has the best example of how trade policy can put commercial concerns above environmental and health objectives. In a perverse twist of priorities, special and differential treatment is accorded to private multinational firms to the detriment of the public interest in host countries. This restricts policy options and forces countries into remaining at a sub-industrial stage.

The WTO should allow developing countries to impose performance requirements on foreign direct investment. Particularly important are requirements in terms of greater local value-added, trade balance restrictions, employment generation, regional growth and technological development. Also, a revision of the TRIMs is required to incorporate the need for greater market transparency through the monitoring of the operations of multinational corporations.

International commodity agreements International commodity agreements (ICAs) are an important paving stone on the road to greater market transparency and less volatility. In the past, UNCTAD's mandate was to use them to arrest the deterioration of terms of trade and to stabilize markets whenever there were large fluctuations. Several agreements were set up (coffee, cocoa, rubber, sugar, tin and tropical timber), but this provision was abandoned in the 1980s in the aftermath of the debt crisis and was never restored.

Over the past century, real prices of primary products have experienced a significant declining trend (Ocampo and Parra 2003). The vulnerability of many countries that rely on one or a few basic products for exports puts undue pressure on people and the environment. ICAs could help change this situation. The need for a second generation of ICAs as a relevant policy mechanism stems from market failures caused by price volatility and long-term trends of declining prices for many primary commodities. In addition, ICAs can reduce distortions due to market concentration and reinstate more transparency in trade through the supervision of multinational corporations.

A new generation of ICAs could explore ways and means to increase value-added of raw commodities, providing developing countries with assistance to take advantage of new economic opportunities, from processing to packaging. Adding value to these commodities will create forward and backward industrial linkages that generate more employment opportunities and healthy multiplier effects in commodity production chains.

Of course, high prices alone will not guarantee sustainable livelihoods for the world's poorest farmers. A range of national and international policies, from credit, land, technology and transportation to tariff protection and access to markets, is essential if agricultural production is to bring a better future for farmers.

<u>Balance-of-payments provisions</u> Trade liberalization is part of a bigger macroeconomic policy package. There is a strong relation between trade and monetary and fiscal policies. The relation goes beyond the simple references to exchange rate over- or undervaluation, and involves the wider issues surrounding finance, capital flows and the policy space in the context of capital account deregulation. From this perspective, greater recognition must be given to balance-of-payments provisions (BOPs) as a tool for adjustment: in today's world of flexible exchange rates these BOPs are not redundant (Nadal 1996).

Recognizing the need for exceptional measures to meet balance-of-payments crises, the original GATT provided contracting parties with temporary exceptions from GATT obligations. Article II established the central principle that in case of balance-of-payments difficulties countries could restrict the quantity or value of imports. The Uruguay Round ratified the possibility of resorting to tariff surcharges and import deposits. The Understanding on Balance of Payments Provisions established several disciplines for this. The important point here is that imposing restrictions on trade flows may be less damaging to an economy than resorting to a macro-devaluation and then imposing draconian fiscal adjustment measures. Responsible use of BOPs, with due respect for their disciplines, does not imply a return to protectionist measures. Employed with restraint, they reduce financial vulnerability. The use of these instruments entails inferior social and environmental costs in case of balance-of-payments difficulties (ibid.).

Reinforcing coherence among trade and monetary policies is important, but must go hand in hand with changes in the role and operations of the IMF. The role, nature and mission of the IMF need to be clearly redefined: the world has changed, so the IMF has to adapt. For one thing, it must stop imposing conditionality and seeking deeper and faster financial liberalization. It should learn from the nature of financial crises today and prevent bailouts that promote moral hazard. The IMF must also transform its decision-making process and prepare to play a responsible lender-of-last-resort role.

e) Financing global environmental stewardship A new credit facility must be established for the purpose of providing enough resources for programmes related to social and environmental sustainability. Resources currently available for what could be described as global sustainability are simply not enough. The current crisis will worsen this picture. In particular, developing countries should have access to additional sources of finance in order to ensure that environmental stewardship is not pushed to the back burner while recovery programmes are given high priority.

The relentless downward trend of ODA resources in the past twenty years needs to be reversed. The resources available through the World Bank (including the GEF) have been insufficient. The growing needs arising from climate policies and the global impacts of deforestation, biodiversity loss and the deterioration of oceanic ecosystems have led to various proposals to guarantee a stable and trustworthy flow of resources to meet this challange. The world requires a new funding facility oriented towards long-term social and environmental sustainability projects. The operational details of this new facility (selection of projects, elegibility, regional coverage, etc.) would be worked out through multilateral negotiations.

There are at least three sources of finance that could be tapped for this new entity. The first is related to the mechanism described above for the international reserve currency and for the destiny of the 'excessive credit balances' of creditor/surplus countries. The new fund could use resources from countries that have accumulated large international non-borrowed reserves.

The second source is a tax on the currency transactions market. The volume of trade in the currency markets of the world has expanded from about US$4 trillion in 1973 (when the Bretton Woods system collapsed) to more than US$450 trillion in 2007 (Hillman et al. 2006). The Stamp Out Poverty initiative proposes a Currency Transaction Development Levy (CTDL) at a very low level (0.005 per cent) and shows that this can generate a significant and stable amount of resources. The difference with the original Tobin tax is that the new CTDL proposal has a different purpose, namely to raise enough funds for sustainable development projects on a global scale. Projects would have to be selected carefully. The absorption capacity of individual countries would have to be taken into account.

The third source of finance is a tax on transactions in the stock exchanges of the world's most important financial centres. World equity markets have registered a very rapid increase in turnover during the past two decades. A tax on currency transactions markets and financial operations such as share trading, bond trading and operations with derivatives could generate significant revenues. In addition, as over-the-counter operations become the object of new regulations, they too can offer a new source of revenues. As Pollin (2005) says, this small tax would create a negligible burden on owners who intend to hold their asset for the long term (although it would constitute a significant charge for agents engaging in multiple and speculative short-term transactions). The costs of collecting these taxes are very low, as is the evasion potential.

The technical feasibility of these taxes has been demonstrated and is not an obstacle (Hillman et al. 2006). The objection that if these taxes are enforced markets will be distorted or capital flight will ensue has been disproved. In fact, London is one of the most important financial capitals in the world and it already has a stamp duty on share transactions that generates US$7 billion per year.

The conservative calculations offered in the Stamp Out Poverty initiative help support the feasibility of these schemes. A modest increment in the tax levies, as well as the expansion of coverage (for example, to equity markets and over-the-counter operations with derivatives), would result in higher fiscal revenues. The original list of recipients of these resources (ibid.) has three important headings: provision of clean drinking water and basic sanitation, human health, and a special Central Emergency Response Fund. These are critical priorities, but with expanded resources we could also envisage other dimensions of sustainable development programmes in housing, education and support for small-scale agriculture. In fact, schemes like the Yasuní proposal advanced by Ecuador could very well be financed through this system of international environmental stewardship.

Concluding remarks

This chapter has covered many proposals for reform. But two of these entail a truly radical change in the way in which the world's economy is managed, the monetary system and the need to harness capital flows.

In this we have ventured into a landscape where debates rage. There are those who think that radical reform will not work (Eichengreen 1999). To them, the risk of creating moral hazard is smaller than the danger of a global financial meltdown. The problem with Eichengreen's analysis is the original question it tries to address. Because he believed in 'the manifest benefits of financial liberalization' and all that it involves, his problem was how to keep this sick economic system called neoliberalism churning along.

By now, the global crisis of 2008 has shown beyond doubt that the time has come for fundamental changes in the way the world economy is being handled. It is now clear that we need to modify its trajectory and set it on a course of social and moral responsibility, on one hand, and of healthy environmental stewardship on the other. The reforms discussed in this and the previous chapter constitute a set of urgent measures that are needed to start moving in the right direction. They should be seen as a list of examples instead of a closed catalogue of reforms. We have not itemized the innumerable details that are required to implement these changes. But the changes that we have proposed here touch upon the main problems that affect the world economy today: its asymmetries, the unfairness of indebtedness and the power of mega-corporations that act above the law. This list of reforms is a minimum threshold of actions that need to be taken to start harnessing the economic forces that have been acting unbridled over the past forty years and which threaten us with global destruction.

One of the policy dimensions we have omitted in this chapter relates to the regulatory regime for various aspects of global environmental change. Climate change and biodiversity come to mind immediately, but are not the only theme for debate. For example, the oil spill after the sinking of BP's Deepwater Horizon in the Gulf of Mexico signals the need for adequate supervision and monitoring of deep-sea drilling and mining. The International Seabed Authority established by the United Nations Conference of the Law of the Sea needs to be revitalized before prospecting, exploration and mining for the polymetallic nodules beneath the seabed degenerate into another race towards more environmental damage. Reforming the world's macroeconomic regime should dovetail with a series of just and and sustainable regulatory regimes for the global commons.

Conclusion

In the final chapter of his *General Theory of Employment, Interest and Money*, John Maynard Keynes wrote about a subject he had left untouched. The chapter's title is revealing: 'Concluding notes on the social philosophy towards which the General Theory might lead'. The text concentrates on the two main problems which Keynes thought affected capitalism – unemployment and inequality. But the sentence that stands out is the following (Keynes 1973: 378): 'I conceive, therefore, that a somewhat comprehensive socialisation of investment will prove the only means of securing approximation to full employment.'[1]

One can only wonder what Keynes would be writing today, as the first decade of the twenty-first century draws to an end. He had concentrated on the problem of why capitalist economies can remain operating at activity levels below what is required for full employment and paid less attention to their chronic disposition to generate and endure financial and economic crashes. But the present global crisis and the prospect of a repetition of the Great Depression would certainly have been at the centre of his analysis.

Something else would have caught his attention. The circumstances that surround this crisis include the most intense and dangerous process of environmental destruction the world has ever seen. Keynes would have been aware of the fact that this level of environmental degradation imperils humankind's ability to survive. And as with full employment, there is no automatic adjustment mechanism capable of maintaining an economy in a state of 'environmental equilibrium'.

Of course, the policy interventions that Keynes would have recommended for environmental sustainability are a matter for speculation. But if he thought that comprehensive socialization of investment was needed to approach full employment, at the very least he would have recommended radical changes to the existing macroeconomic framework. For it is this same policy framework which today constitutes a formidable obstacle to environmental sustainability. It not only distorts the allocation of resources at a macroeconomic level (among other things, by shifting resources to the financial sector under the mantra of a primary surplus). It destroys people's livelihoods and the social fabric of communities that have been the custodians of the environment for centuries, impairing their ability to conserve soils, aquifers and genetic diversity. Finally, it prevents economies from generating the required resources to invest in environmental stewardship and conservation, undermining the capacity for future improvements in living standards and social welfare.

Macroeconomic policy has been subdued by financial capital in that monetary and fiscal priorities closely correspond to the interests and needs of finance.[2] In this sense, macroeconomic policies are the link between financial capital and environmental destruction. This is why speculation, volatility and instability have accompanied slow growth, inequality and environmental decline. Our analysis has shown that in order to transcend this difficult stage in history, a serious redefinition of macroeconomic policy priorities is required. The neoliberal claim to stability and efficiency is not only without foundations, it is also incompatible with social justice and environmental sustainability.

The deep economic and financial crisis in which the world is immersed today has led to certain reforms in policy-making. Some of them are tepid changes in the financial system. Others (such as the fiscal stimulus) have a decidedly Keynesian flavour. But there is and will continue to be an obstinate resistance to deep change. A good indicator of this was the recent (June 2010) meeting of the G20 in Toronto, where the final declaration was a call to continue the neoliberal experience and to halve deficits by 2013. This will have a devastating impact on the recovery and sustainability because the weapons of choice for deficit reduction and fiscal austerity are the retrenchment of social spending and the shrinking of resources for environmental stewardship. Taxes on the wealthy and on financial transactions, or the closing of tax loopholes and the elimination of subsidies for mega-corporations, are not an option for those with decision-making powers.

Thus, preventing the return to neoliberalism is critical for sustainability at this juncture. To overcome resistance to change, a new balance of political forces is needed. According to Keynes, 'the necessary measures of socialisation can be introduced gradually and without a break in the general traditions of society' (ibid.: 378). Perhaps, but it is important to understand that maybe economic democracy is incompatible with the essence of capital. In any event, if there is one lesson from recent historical experience, it is that only a new political correlation will allow us to drive this much-needed transformation in macroeconomic policy. In rekindling the discussion on the alternatives to neoliberalism, we must blend together the questions of environmental stewardship with the top macroeconomic priorities of social justice. Our analysis urges progressive movements, social activists and environmentalists to reclaim the right to define the general trajectory of macroeconomic policy.

Notes

Introduction

1 The background documents used in the update meeting of heads of state in September 2010 at the UN in New York failed to mention macroeconomic policies.

2 From this perspective, the Global Green New Deal initiative is a step back from previous analyses in which the effects of macroeconomic policies were analysed in the context of structural adjustment programmes (SAPs). These were imposed on many developing countries as a condition for debt rescheduling and new loans. The SAPs were used to improve the balance in fiscal budgets and balance-of-payments accounts through draconian austerity programmes based on cuts in allocations for healthcare, education and environmental protection. They had severe negative social and environmental effects. From this perspective, they are the antithesis of anything that ressembles sustainable development. Reed (1992) carried out a study of the effects of these SAPs on people's livelihoods and the environment. The conclusion of this pioneering work was that SAPs had detrimental effects on the environment and on long-term development.

3 Sustainable development was defined by the Brundtland Report (1987) as 'development that meets the needs of the present without compromising the ability of future generations to meet their own needs'.

4 In fiscal policy this terminology is usually associated with the need to generate a primary surplus. The primary balance of the fiscal accounts compares fiscal revenues (tax and non-tax) with expenditures net of financial charges. This means that expenditures *before* payments of debt service (principal and interest payments) are taken into consideration. A surplus in the primary balance can be attained by augmenting fiscal revenues, or by cutting spending on things such as healthcare, education, the environment or infrastructure. The surplus is then used to cover debt service (this is why it is associated with 'responsible debt management'). When fiscal policies are acclaimed as a success because there is a primary surplus it is important to examine the structure of the primary balance.

5 The US$2.50-per-day level is of course a convenient poverty indicator for the World Bank. According to this institution the proportion of people making US$10 per day is 80 per cent, a level of income that could qualify as dangerously close to the poverty line.

6 In 1996 the International Monetary Fund convened a seminar to analyse the relationship between macroeconomics and the environment (Gandhi 1996). The main conclusions were not surprising, coming from an institution that has played a prominent role in extending

(and imposing) neoliberal macroeconomic policies worldwide. The first is that macroeconomic stability is a minimum and necessary condition for the preservation of the environment. Second, macroeconomic policies can bring about environmental degradation only in the presence of market or policy failures related to the use of natural resources. In this manner, the neoliberal macroeconomic policy package was enshrined as the precondition for environmental sustainability. And as long as there are no frictions, markets will continue to play their role in the efficient allocation of resources.

7 A defence of this world of irrelevant modelling was recently presented by Nobel laureate Robert Lucas (2009), when he stated that mainstream models do not suggest that a crisis could not erupt; rather, they make a forecast of what the world would be like if there was no crisis. Talk about irrelevance!

8 This perception of things was epitomized by Nobel laureate Robert Lucas's presidential address at the American Economic Association annual meeting in 2003, when he asserted that macroeconomics had succeeded and 'the central problem of depression-prevention had been solved, for all practical purposes'. The long string of financial crises in the 1990s was not enough to shake out of complacency those who believed in the Great Moderation hypothesis. At last central bankers and treasury departments had mastered the art of conducting macroeconomic policy. Clearly, crises in the developing world and so-called emerging markets didn't count. The world had to wait for the 2008 crisis to see that everything was up in the air and open for discussion once more.

1 Macroeconomics and the environment

1 We return to these insights and their implications in Chapter 2.

2 In fact, the postulate that changes in factor prices induce factor-saving (or factor-augmenting) innovations has been subjected to severe criticism, both at the theoretical level and by empirical analyses. See the classic work of Salter (1960), Fellner (1962) and Nelson and Winter (1982). Technology historians are also sceptical about the role of relative prices in inducing technical change: Rosenberg (1982), Habakkuk (1962) and David (1974).

3 The school of ecological economics (SEE) looks at the economy as a subsystem of the ecosystem. One of its main areas of interest is the preservation of natural capital. Typically, ecological economics rejects the idea that natural capital can be replaced by man-made capital. It is normal to find that ecological economics operates within the logic of a 'limits to growth' approach. In opposition, environmental economics applies mainstream concepts to environmental problems. Its most important concepts are market failures and externalities. Market failure causes markets to misallocate resources, while externalities refer to choices that affect other people and are not accounted for by market prices. Both schools of thought fail in making a comprehensive critique of mainstream economic theory.

4 The failure to provide a rational demonstration of how equilibrium prices are formed (by the free play of market forces) is perhaps the greatest fiasco in economic theory. But this is now a well-known fact among serious professional economists: economic theory has never provided

a model demonstrating that market forces, if left to act freely, will lead to a set of equilibrium prices (i.e. one in which at those prices supply equals demand, while all agents maximize their objective functions). This question touches upon a very important set of issues with serious implications for our analysis.

5 This involves an unsolved problem affecting all models using an aggregate measure of capital, including new endogenous growth models and several models from the school of ecological economics. On the other hand, this critique does not apply to general equilibrium theory because it lacks an aggregate measure of capital. General equilibrium theory has its own fatal flaws (Ackerman and Nadal 2004).

6 The introduction of money in these growth models poses deep problems that need to be addressed. These are related to the way in which economic theory has dealt with money ever since it was born as an autonomous discipline. Scientific analysis was considered to be on the side of 'real value': in the absence of money, prices were expressed in terms of rates of exchange between physical quantities of goods (i.e. as 'relative prices'). Of course, the underlying idea was that the analysis of price determination would not be affected by the introduction of money. We now know this is not the case (Hahn 1965; Benetti 2004). And this has to be taken into account when analysing the relations between economics and the environment.

7 The interdependencies of the model showed how its various components would interact. For the agricultural system, for example, the LG model assumed that it could expand output by using chemical inputs, but the industrial production of these inputs would not be able to keep pace with increased demand. The collapse in the system of food production would be a question of time. This type of bleak message led to accusations of neo-Malthusianism and a fierce debate concerning the role of technology. The Stiglitz model discussed above was part of this debate.

8 The critique addressed at the LG model concerning the assumptions on technology is correct, but technological optimists should bear in mind too that, frequently, technology is part of the problem and not necessarily a 'solution'.

9 The central critique of the MIT model was that its neo-Malthusian structure translated into the non-sustainability of the world economy. The main constraint to reducing global poverty came from the exhaustion of natural resources (and high pollution levels). The LG model presented these constraints as inevitable, so avoiding catastrophe would have to come about *not* from the passage to a more equitable society, but by reducing consumption levels in rich countries, and population in poor countries.

10 The only resource with relevant limitations in the context of the model was arable land in Asia (which would pose a problem around 2050). But the model concluded that even in this case, the deficiency could be compensated by land availability and productivity in other regions.

11 Barnett and Morse (1963) examined the inflation-adjusted prices and costs of production of natural resources traded in the USA between 1870 and 1957. They found that although population in the USA had quadrupled and economic

output had increased by a factor of twenty, most costs and prices had declined. The two cases where production costs had increased were commercial fisheries and forestry.

12 Ecological economics also places some emphasis on distribution and equity, as well as on the distinction between quantitative growth and (qualitative) development. According to SEE, mainstream economics confuses these two notions. However, the distributional and equity problems in ecological economics are examined (as, for example, in Daly and Cobb 1994) without any reference to macroeconomic policies, as if these had no relation whatsoever with distributional issues.

13 This notion ignores the measurement problems that affect the notion of aggregate capital, K, which we have examined above.

14 The studies that went this far were, in a way, establishing an implicit relation between neoliberal macroeconomic policies and the environment.

15 The statistical analysis of the EKC leaves much to be desired. For a detailed critique, see Stern (2004) and Perman and Stern (2003).

16 This assumption is similar to the notion of weak sustainability in which the environment and manufactured capital can coexist.

17 Information in this paragraph provided by the Reverend Awala Longkummer, a social and environmental activist in Assam (personal communication).

18 The set of accompanying policy recommendations can be found in the Declaration of Barcelona 2010, www.degrowthpedia.org.

2 The macroeconomic policy connection

1 Today we include under this label all neoclassical economists.

2 A corollary of all this was social harmony as every social group, or for that matter every individual, received as income the equivalent of its contribution to social product. This is without a doubt one of the most important ideological messages of this worldview.

3 The model appeared to involve a certain circularity of reasoning because in order to determine the equilibrium level of income in the goods market, the interest rate must first be known (as it determines investment, a crucial component of aggregate demand), and in order to determine the interest rate in the money market, the level of income must first be known (as it determines the demand of money for transactions). This apparent circularity is resolved when both equations (goods and money market) are solved simultaneously.

4 Another case is when speculators are unanimous in the belief that the interest rate is already below its normal level and think that bond prices will fall in the future. This is the so-called liquidity trap, a case in which monetary policy is helpless.

5 In the IS–LM model the decisions of all economic agents are made compatible in the product and money markets. The product market balances supply and demand for products, while the money market balances the demand for money with the supply of money provided by the government and banks. At the intersection of the IS–LM curves, all economic aggregates, including national income and the rate of interest, adjust, so that the demand

for product equals national income, and the demand for money equals the supply of money.

6 Keynes himself was partly responsible for this recovery by mainstream academics for a number of reasons. One is that he failed to distance himself from the orthodox ideas he was trying to criticize. Second, he had also provided room for this alternative explanation in his own writings. For example, his analysis (in Chapter 19 of his *General Theory*) of how falling wages could bring about a change in prices and cause a drop in the interest rate supported the idea that the economy could move on to full employment in the long run.

7 Monetarists rely on the related concept of the non-accelerating inflation rate of unemployment or NAIRU. This is the unemployment rate that corresponds to a constant inflation rate. When unemployment is at the level of the NAIRU, there is no risk of wages chasing higher prices. Monetarists insisted that attempting to reduce unemployment below the NAIRU would only lead to higher inflation rates. Together, the NRU and the NAIRU became critical for neoliberalism.

8 This rebirth of interest in 'Keynesian' themes was preceded by work on real economic cycles, especially by Edward Prescott. In his work, fluctuations are brought about by the random variations in the rate of technical progress and the diffusion of their effects through the inter-temporal decision-making process of agents.

9 According to Solow (2008: 243–4) this is the Ramsey model transformed from a normative account of socially optimal growth into a positive story that is supposed to describe day-to-day behaviour in a modern industrial capitalist economy. The abstractions that accompany it result from the 'arbitrary suppression of clues [...] because they are inconvenient for cherished preconceptions'. This not only does not solve the aggregation problem, it also eliminates the issue of coordination in transactions.

10 The name 'Post-Keynesians' was assigned to these authors following their attempts to rebuild economic theory by taking as a starting point some of Keynes's ideas, and in some cases adopting a more progressive standpoint. The work of Joan Robinson, Nicholas Kaldor, Hyman Minsky and Paul Davidson must be recognized in this respect.

11 The works examined here completely ignore the issue of unemployment in using the IS–LM model. This is a serious omission. On the other hand, Daly and Farley (2004: 304) even use the new classical conception of the labour market in their analysis.

12 In that case one would have to contend with the objections raised in Box 1.1.

13 Heyes (2000) and Lawn (2003) use a modified IS–LM model in which rational expectations are introduced. Under this assumption, the effectiveness of both fiscal and monetary policies is seriously called into question, but this is not examined in their analyses.

14 The IS–LM model has had a long history. It has come under attack from all quarters. The reason for this is that it appears to be loosely consistent with different (and even opposing) visions and strands of macroeconomic theory. In a way, its chameleon-like nature has

allowed it to survive as a device for rough-and-ready discussions on the role of fiscal and monetary policies, more than for its theoretical qualities. On this point see Collander (2006) on the strange persistence of the IS–LM model.

15 The general equilibrium model created by Léon Walras is made up of equations depicting the behaviour of consumers and producers and their reactions to changes in prices. At any given moment in time, and with a given price system, consumers maximize satisfaction subject to their budget constraints, while producers maximize profits. The price system is an array of 'relative prices' (which are in fact rates of substitution between goods) in a non-monetary economy. All agents are passive price-takers (perfect competition is assumed). The existence of a price-adjusting entity (the fictitious auctioneer) is assumed. For every commodity this entity announces a price and determines whether demand is greater (or less) than supply. The price-adjusting rule corresponds to the law of supply and demand: for any given commodity, if demand is greater than supply, the price is increased. If it is smaller, the price is lowered. If there is equilibrium (supply equals demand) the price remains unchanged. With this rule the price-adjusting entity then recalculates prices until equilibrium is reached. Even with these and many other assumptions general equilibrium theory has been unable to demonstrate that in the general case market forces lead to the formation of equilibrium prices.

16 Mäler and Munasinghe (2002: 92) make a reference to Arrow and Hahn, but simply assume that there is no problem with the introduction of money in a general equilibrium setting. This is unacceptable.

17 In addition, the view that it is necessary to lower wages in order to attain a balance in the 'labour market' comes out of this analysis as a completely discredited notion. In fact, in an economy driven by effective demand, this will lead to greater unemployment.

18 Financial liberalization was supposed to promote productive investment. However, real gross domestic capital formation rates actually decreased during the period in which financial liberalization was fully implemented. Financial liberalization was also meant to lead to a decrease in real interest rates. Once again, this did not happen: in the G7 countries, average long-term interest rates were 2.6 per cent in 1959–70, 0.4 per cent in 1971–82, 5.6 per cent in 1982–89, and 4 per cent in 1990–97. Finally, as a result of this poor performance, unemployment rates increased under the regime of deep financial liberalization. For the OECD countries, during the period 1960–73 the average unemployment rate was 3.2 per cent. This rate increased to 5 per cent for 1973–79 and to 7.4 per cent for 1979–2000. At the same time, the rate of labour productivity fell from 4.6 per cent during 1960–73 to 1.7 per cent between 1973 and 1997.

19 For a detailed analysis of these contradictions, see Nadal (2004a).

20 In his *General Theory* Keynes made a deliberate decision not to try to explain why depressions and slumps occur in favour of discussing why they continue and are difficult to stamp out.

3 Macroeconomic policies and climate change

1 Nordhaus and Dasgupta rely on mainstream models that have as many problems as the tools used in the *Stern Review*. Nordhaus assumes that in a perfectly competitive market the discount rate would equal market interest rates, but the process by which this comes to take place is unclear. Dasgupta believes that per capita incomes in the world will continue to grow for the foreseeable future, a conjecture that remains problematic in a world marked by deep asymmetries and a global economic and financial crisis. For a detailed account of this debate, see Ackerman (2009).

2 Macroeconomic considerations have always been part and parcel of the discussions and analysis of climate-change dynamics. The reason is that this feeds into scenarios of growth and emissions of GHG. But, once again, the discussion of macroeconomic *policies* is nowhere to be seen. In the Fourth Assessment Report, Chapter 11, on 'Mitigation from a cross-sectoral perspective', has a section on macroeconomic effects devoted basically to a discussion of the macroeconomic costs of mitigation. This relies heavily on the policy studies for the Third Assessment Report, but most of those studies at the macro level focused on ways to reduce mitigation costs, comparing an economy-wide tax with a tradable permit system. There is no analysis of monetary and fiscal policies. Chapter 13, on 'Policies, instruments and co-operative arrangements', makes a reference to subsidies and taxes but manages to ignore macroeconomic policies.

3 These are the costs from damage that cannot be avoided at a reasonable cost and must be accepted today as unavoidable given current projections of temperature rises. The disappearance of islands is typically included as part of the residual cost, but for their inhabitants it is clear that the word residual adds insult to injury.

4 The AR4 A1 scenario family describes a future world of very rapid economic growth, global population that peaks in mid-century and declines thereafter, and the rapid introduction of new and more efficient technologies. The scenarios include per capita income convergence among regions, as well as strong capacity-building. The A1B scenario includes a balance between fossil-intensive and non-fossil-intensive energy sources.

5 One important consideration is the degree of 'protection' against the damage of climate change. The UNFCCC report is unclear about this important issue.

6 This study assumes that these levels of adaptation may lead to avoiding 80 per cent of damage (thus, 20 per cent of damage will not be avoided).

7 A major problem is the absence of case studies to test the top-down form of UNFCCC analysis. The few national figures available tend to suggest costs in excess of the UNFCCC estimates. For example, agencies responsible for flood management in England and Wales have estimated a need to spend (owing to climate change) an additional US$30 million annually in 2011, growing to US$720 million by 2035 (Parry et al. 2009: 11).

8 Using World Bank data, Crotty (2000) shows the rate of growth of global real gross domestic investment was 7.0 per cent from 1966 to

1973, at the end of the Golden Age. It then fell to 2.2 per cent from 1974 to 1979, rose modestly to 2.8 per cent from 1980 to 1989, then fell slightly to 2.7 per cent from 1990 through 1996, the last year for which data are available. Investment growth was especially sluggish in the developed world. OECD countries had an average annual growth of real gross capital formation of 6.3 per cent in 1960–73, 1.5 per cent in 1973–79, 2.4 per cent in 1979–89, and 1.5 per cent in 1989–95.

9 Carbon offsets are not adequate instruments for emissions reductions. The reason is that when a project in the South is implemented to offset emissions in the North, pollution can continue to pump GHG into the atmosphere. This is a gimmick that can help in pretending that compliance with reduction targets is taking place while generating some resources for developing countries. However, these resources will in many cases accrue to the same enterprises that are the main actors in these 'offsets'.

10 The linkages between macroeconomic policies and sector-level policies are critical. The combination of the passive posture of macroeconomic policies, together with restrictions imposed in trade and investment agreements, will have extremely negative consequences. The linkages between credit policies and investments in energy-intensive industries (aluminium, cement, glass, pulp and paper, steel, energy, etc.) require greater attention. This is an area in which the relation between interest rates, rates of return and discount rates needs to be examined, especially given the long amortization periods of heavy investments in capital goods.

11 If financial crises may explode in patterns that closely resemble a so-called 'Minsky moment', this is exacerbated in the case of capital flows in the context of a deregulated capital account. See Kregel (2004).

12 This theme is related to the question of debt management, a point discussed in Chapter 7.

13 The IMF (2008) study on *The Fiscal Implications of Climate Change* makes no reference to this important aspect of fiscal policy. A critical item pending in macroeconomic policy in much of the developing world is that of progressive fiscal reform. In recent years, the tax reform schemes that have been promoted concentrate more fiscal pressure on value-added taxes and relax the impact of income taxes. The rationale has been that a VAT is easier to implement, but the fact is that this is a regressive tax. In any event, tax revenues have been clearly insufficient in most developing countries, bringing about greater pressure to cut badly needed public expenditures.

14 A carbon tax is considered an alternative path for 'getting carbon prices right'. This would be a direct (at the source) tax that would increase the prices of all fossil fuels and would have a cross-sector impact. It is hoped that this would generate the economic forces leading to systemic technical change. This has its own problems because there is not a continuum of readily available technologies and therefore it is not obvious that the economy would shift rapidly and smoothly from a fossil-fuel energy profile to a renewable profile as technologies are replaced. There is an adjustment process that can be more or less long and filled with shocks. On the other hand, a carbon tax could have very

important distributional impacts, especially in developing countries, and this would have to be redressed through other mechanisms.

4 Green Economy Initiative

1 Even today, the reforms to the banking sector in the USA announced by President Obama on 29 January 2010 leave some of these problems unchanged. The so-called 'Volcker rule' in these reforms will not close the swaps-dealer loophole which allows greater involvement of financial investors in commodity futures trading and increases significantly the positions that swap dealers hold in commodity futures markets.

2 This explains why the reforms suggested by the GGND report are relatively superficial. The reference to the alignment of incentives carries the same overtones used to impose financial liberalization and fiscal 'competitiveness' on developing countries.

3 Minsky's financial instability hypothesis relates to a model of a capitalist economy that does not rely upon exogenous shocks to generate business cycles. The hypothesis holds that, historically, business cycles are compounded of (i) the internal dynamics of capitalist economies and (ii) the system of interventions and regulations that are designed to keep the economy operating within reasonable bounds. There are three distinct income–debt relations for economic units, labelled hedge, speculative and Ponzi finance. Hedge financing units are those which can fulfil all of their contractual payment obligations through their cash flows. For Ponzi units, the cash flows from operations are not sufficient to fulfil either the repayment of principal or the interest due on outstanding debts through their cash flows from operations. Speculative finance units are units that can meet their payment commitments on 'income account' on their liabilities, even as they cannot repay the principal out of income cash flows. Such units need to 'roll over' their liabilities. In particular, over a protracted period of good times, capitalist economies tend to move from a financial structure dominated by hedge finance units to a structure in which there is large proportion of units engaged in speculative and Ponzi finance (Minsky 1992).

4 The GGND devotes considerable attention to climate change. In order to reduce carbon dependency it proposes to get rid of subsidies currently benefiting fossil fuels, to implement 'carbon pricing policies' and to increase support for renewable energies. Here one important question is whether or not the subsidies that will be withdrawn from fossil fuels will make much of a difference. In fact, the GGND recognizes that these subsidies amount to about US$7 billion in the United States. The report recommends for the USA a cap-and-trade mechanism in which the revenues from permit sales would be allocated to renewable energies. Although this is better than simply giving away the emissions quotas for free, the GGND does not engage in a more serious discussion of the problems that surround cap-and-trade schemes.

5 On the other hand, the GGND ignores other large-scale, capital-intensive activities of primary production in highly concentrated industries, such as mining and oil drilling. Extractive industries in the world are behind some of the worst

cases of environmental destruction, for example through open pit mining. Other manufacturing industries that are close to the natural resource base and which have very important effects upon the environment and on people's livelihoods should also be included in any examination of primary production. Industries such as cement, metallurgy, pulp and paper, aluminium and glass, for example, are in the interface between primary production and downstream manufacturing industries. They are energy intensive and frequently leave environmental ravages in their wake.

6 The IAASTD process was initiated by the World Bank in open partnership with a multi-stakeholder group of organizations, including FAO, GEF, UNDP, UNEP, WHO and UNESCO, and representatives of governments, civil society, the private sector and scientific institutions from around the world.

7 The role played by agriculture in providing food, animal feed, fibre and fuel plays a key role in efforts to achieve global sustainable development. It is a major occupational sector in developing countries, with the poorest countries being those with predominantly agricultural economies and societies (FAO 2000). Approximately 2.6 billion people – men, women and children – rely on agricultural production systems, be it farming, livestock production, forestry or fishery. Food security for a growing world population is positioned to remain a challenge in the next few decades.

8 The IAASTD (2009) recognizes that trade liberalization can lead to long-term negative effects on poverty alleviation, food security and the environment without basic national institutions and infrastructure being in place. The priorities of the neoliberal fiscal policy stance based on generating a primary surplus are a powerful obstacle here. The case of Mexico is a very good example of how the combination of fiscal policy constraints and trade liberalization has wrought havoc on small-scale agricultural producers. The prices of the products of these small-scale farmers have collapsed, while the prices of inputs have increased significantly. At the same time, the economic support measures that were promised to local farmers, such as the income deficiency payments which are delinked from output mix and technology decisions and are WTO compatible, have been losing value in real terms. In addition, investments in R&D, extensionism and infrastructure (irrigation and storage facilities, as well as roads) have fallen substantially. Thus, the notion of improving primary production in the case of the agricultural systems of developing countries is something that requires a serious revision of trade liberalization and of fiscal policy priorities.

9 Recently the UN Special Rapporteur on the Right to Food recognized that small producers are at a disadvantage by virtue of the limited number of buyers they have access to. This puts them in a deeply unequal bargaining position for their crops. The outcome is a structure of prices that benefits commodity buyers. Ironically, this situation helps explain why over half of the billion who are hungry in the world today are part of the food system: small independent food producers or waged agricultural workers toiling on farms in the formal or informal sector. The full report is available at www.srfood.org.

10 Of course, not all PES schemes have to rely on what amounts to a public subsidy. If payments for environmental services are going to come from the general public or the direct users of those services, there may be some interesting distributional questions that need to be answered (for example, when landless peasants are excluded from the benefits of a particular PES scheme).

11 The faith in 'market-based instruments' is a common theme in the GGND. In its discussion concerning water scarcity, the GGND report endorses the UNDP recommendation that developing countries invest 1 per cent of GDP in clean water and sanitation investments, but without any discussion as to the fiscal policy implications of this policy advice. Instead, the GGND goes on to recommend the removal of 'subsidies and other incentive distortions, adopting market-based instruments and implementing other measures to increase the efficiency of water allocation' (UNEP 2009b: 59). The GGND appears to be unaware of the intense debate surrounding the issues of market-based mechanisms in water distribution in developing countries. The privatization schemes that have accompanied the *commodification* of water in Latin America, just to mention one example, should be carefully examined in the GGND. Together with the environmental implications, their negative distributional effects also need to be taken into account.

12 The project is supported by the European Community, the German Ministry of the Environment and the United Kingdom Ministry of the Environment.

13 The ILO report *Green Jobs:* *Towards Decent Work in a Sustainable, Low Carbon World* is available at www.unep.org/labour_environment/features/greenjobs.asp.

14 For example, falling wages can accelerate the rate of a recession and bring about greater levels of unemployment.

15 The TEEB report seems to rely on discount rates and cost–benefit analysis as valuation methodologies. Baumol's analysis of reswitching of discount rates is highly relevant in this context as it clearly reveals the limitations of this methodology (Baumol 1997).

16 This is a similar starting point to that of the law and economics school of thought. For a critique of this see Nadal (2007).

5 Latin American focus

1 One word of caution is required at this stage. To speak of the 'Latin American economy' is a risky venture. After all, this is a set of highly heterogeneous economies in a vast continent. The differences between the countries in the region have intensified in the past fifteen years. Today, discrepancies in economic policy (at almost all levels) are quite visible. Clearly, the aggregation of the Latin American countries in one unit really lacks analytical value (Urquídi 2005: 49).

2 In some cases, especially in the smallest countries, the development strategy relied on the old model based on exports of primary products.

3 For a rigorous and insightful analysis of the experience in South Korea, see Amsden (1989).

4 Monetary policy in Latin America during the same period had the overarching objective of full employment. This did not mean that

price and exchange-rate stability was unimportant. Most countries in the region did not rely on a free market for credit and established strong regulatory regimes for credit allocation. However, these credit regulations lacked priorities and did not incorporate industrial policy criteria. The vast majority of loans went to consumption and some working capital in industry. Productive investments in industry were the object of self-finance by corporations.

5 In this discussion we use the standard representation of the Mundell-Fleming open economy model.

6 Within a flexible exchange-rate framework, the adjustment through variations in the exchange rate should follow automatically. The General Agreement on Tariffs and Trade (GATT) prevented signatory parties from systematically resorting to controls on trade flows in order to tackle external deficits. But GATT's Article XII established the possibility of *exceptionally* resorting to measures such as quantitative restrictions and tariff surcharges to re-establish equilibrium in the balance of payments, while imposing disciplinary measures to avoid abuses. Interestingly, the North American Free Trade Agreement (NAFTA) cancelled the possibility of resorting to exceptional measures. Under these conditions, if there is a deficit in the balance of trade, the adjustment must be made exclusively using the relative price system (i.e. the exchange rate). For a detailed account of these provisions in the context of the Mexican 1994 crisis, see Nadal (1996).

7 In the case of Mexico, intervention with sterilization has been taking place since the crisis in 1994. This has allowed authorities to maintain an overvalued exchange rate, bringing inflation under control but further reducing competitiveness and damaging the trade balance. As international reserves have increased to historic levels, the central bank has continued to pursue a restrictive monetary policy, maintaining interest rates at even higher levels. This limits the economy's capacity to attain adequate growth rates, while, at the same time, maintaining high rewards for foreign capital. The capital flows that result from this further contribute to the appreciation of the exchange rate and the deterioration of the country's external accounts.

8 Capital inflows do not necessarily reflect a healthy state of the economy. In fact, they turn the capacity to import into an exogenous variable. The liberalization of the financial sector and of the capital account opens the possibility of increased private sector indebtedness. As a result, a country's capacity to import becomes disconnected from its ability to generate foreign currency through exports. In this context, higher levels of investment and capital flow make aggregate demand and income grow. But this expansion in aggregate demand translates into greater imports, which have a contractionary effect on domestic production. As Bhaduri points out (1998: 155), this perverse effect will appear even when a higher level of capital flow leads to greater investment and exports, as long as the marginal propensity to import associated with capital flows is larger than the corresponding marginal propensity to invest and export.

9 A formal treatment of this is presented in Nadal (2005).

10 This section summarizes five

case studies in Latin America. It is based on the results of a project carried out as part of the activities of the Theme on the Environment, Macroeconomics, Trade and Investment (TEMTI) of the Commission on Environmental, Economic and Social Policy (CEESP) of the International Union for Conservation of Nature (IUCN).

11 This section is based on the country-level study carried out by Alan Cibils for the TEMTI–3I-C Study.

12 The forced disappearance of 30,000 social movement activists, a tight control over the media and a generalized climate of terror effectively reduced the ability of the opposition to fight against such reforms.

13 The first crisis was in 1982 when Argentina, together with Mexico and Brazil, defaulted on its debt. In 1989/90 there were repeated episodes of hyperinflation and in 2001/02 Argentina's spectacular crash attracted world attention and resulted in a world-record-setting default (Cibils et al. 2002).

14 Roughly 24 per cent of those affected by defaulted debt did not accept the Argentine swap conditions and are still awaiting a settlement at the time of writing.

15 This is a reference to Rachel Carson's 1962 *Silent Spring*, one of the first books warning of the effects of widespread use of pesticides.

16 In Chaco province, 118,000 hectares were deforested for soybean production between 1998 and 2002. In Santiago del Estero, 223,000 hectares were deforested for the same reason and in the same period; Pengue (2006: 15).

17 See, for example, Nadal (2005) on how small-scale corn growers in Mexico rely more heavily on genetic diversity as a risk-management tool.

18 This section is based on the country-level study carried out by Sergio Schlesinger for the TEMTI–3I-C project.

19 Trade liberalization in itself was seen as subordinate to the macroeconomic objectives of price stabilization, rather than responding to the notion of comparative advantages and efficient resource allocation. This is another interesting example of how macroeconomic policy priorities dominate trade liberalization. The same can be said of Mexico's decision to proceed with trade liberalization. In 1987, when authorities decided the country should become a member of the GATT, the main objective was the need to control inflation through cheaper imports.

20 The *real*'s value was set using a predetermined rate against the dollar. The system included a scheme for daily mini-fluctuations around the target value. This did not prevent the appreciation of the currency.

21 This has been more or less constant in Brazil's fiscal stance. In 2009, as a result of the international financial crisis, Brazil's economy weakened and fiscal revenues dropped. Also, the implementation of counter-cyclical measures will prevent Brazil from reaching the goal of a primary surplus of 2.5 per cent of GDP in 2010.

22 This process left behind a series of deep changes in the rural sector and the environment. Family farms, which are less capital intensive and provide up to 70 per cent of rural jobs, have been one of the first casualties. Between 1985 and 2005, the number of family farms dropped significantly and, with this, rural

employment also suffered a severe fall. Most soybean production takes place in large-scale commercial operations that are capital intensive and employment generation is low: roughly ten full-time jobs for every thousand hectares, with six of them temporary jobs. Land concentration is also well documented, with the consequent generation of landless labourers.

23 See *Mongabay News* at news.mongabay.com/2008/0428-brazil.html.

24 Livestock production in Brazil is undertaken through extensive methods (it is estimated that one head of cattle requires one hectare); cattle production occupies first place in terms of land usage.

25 This section is based on the country-level study carried out by Carlos Murillo for the TEMTI−3I-C project.

26 The programme was also strengthened in 2001–05 by a special non-recoverable loan from the Global Environmental Facility. A new phase of this is currently being implemented with another special non-recoverable loan of US$30 million and a special contribution from the World Bank of US$10 million. This loan imposed conditions related to the participation of the private sector in order to ensure the financial sustainability of the programme. As of today, revenues from the private sector represent no more than 1 per cent of total revenues.

27 This section is based on the country-level study carried out by Pablo Samaniego for the TEMTI−3I-C project.

28 Between 1984 and 1987 shrimp farms grew at an average rate of 9.6 per cent and mangrove forests declined rapidly. In 1969 Ecuador had 203,000 hectares of mangrove forests. By 1987 this had dropped to 175,000 hectares.

29 The flows of foreign direct investment have followed and strengthened this pattern. More than one third of FDI flows go to the primary sector, without counting investments in agribusiness.

30 This word means 'true humans'.

31 See Oilwatch (2007), *Project ITT*, at www.amazoniaporlavida.org/es/La-propuesta/ Original document: 'Scientists concerned for Yasuní National Park. 2004. Technical advisory report on: the biodiversity of Yasuní National Park, its conservation significance, the impacts of roads and our position statement'.

32 On 3 August 2010, Ecuador and the UNDP signed the Memorandum of Agreement for the Yasuni-ITT Initiative to leave this oil underground in exchange for an international contribution equivalent to at least half of the resources that would be received if Ecuador exploited its oil in this area.

33 This section is based on the country-level study carried out by Marcos Chávez for the TEMTI−3I-C project.

34 Minimum wages, a key reference for contractual wages, have been indexed with the expected inflation rates established by the central bank. Throughout the period, real inflation rates have exceeded expected inflation, leading to a systematic drop in real wages and greater inequality and poverty.

35 Agricultural policy in Mexico has been shaped by this macro-economic policy framework with important long-term environmental implications (Nadal 2000).

36 Venezuela has the natural

resources required to support a process of change that will take years to come to fruition. But using these resources (for example, the huge reserves of very heavy crude oil in the Orinoco river basin) will depend on a number of factors (oil prices, a future agreement on greenhouse gas emissions, etc.). On the other hand, Bolivia has a weaker resource endowment, but it has significant natural gas reserves, and may be sitting on the world's largest lithium reserves. Bolivia, like other Andean countries, will be severely affected by climate change as its glaciers melt away and fresh water supplies decline.

6 Guidelines for macroeconomic policy

1 The evolution of monetary thinking in Keynes is a good example of this. His first views on monetary theory were marked by the Victorian years of stability. His first theoretical expressions were those of a staunch Cambridge quantity theorist, with a preference for price stability (Moggridge and Howson 1974).

2 This is why the structural features of developed (industrialized) economies are part and parcel of these macroeconomic models. This does not mean that *all* the relevant features of developed capitalist economies were taken into account by macroeconomic reasoning: as we have already seen in Chapter 2, that monetary and fiscal policy measures have distributional implications should have been obvious right from the beginning, but that was assumed away. But what should also be taken into account when using some of these models in developing countries is that there is a question of applicability and lack of realism. For example, in some of Keynes's analyses, the role of the capital goods sector is important, but in the vast majority of developing economies there is simply no capital goods sector.

3 The market is not a 'social mechanism' capable of providing guidance as we move to an equilibrium position, as if on automatic pilot, for the economy. Economic theory attempted to build a model that would prove this but failed: there is no economic theory demonstrating that markets converge to equilibrium. And this is not because neoclassical theoretical models are unrealistic or because their assumptions do not apply to developing countries, etc. It is because these models, regardless of the assumptions that they embody, have been incapable of reproducing in theoretical terms the dynamics of a market system that converges to equilibrium. These theoretical models are inconsistent and do not fulfil their claimed objectives. The irony about the modern educational system is that although there is a consensus on the failings of microeconomic market theory, this theme has been exiled from the syllabus of most economics departments.

4 In addition, the conceptual apparatus that is built to understand these functional relations is not (to use an old expression) 'neutral'. It discriminates between facts that it chooses to consider as pertinent and those that are discarded because they are irrelevant. For example, why is it that certain obviously relevant phenomena find no place within macroeconomic models? What explains the fact that the traditional IS–LM model assumes that monetary and fiscal policies do not have any effects upon income distribution?

What defines the choice of which facts should be taken into account? It cannot be scientific necessity because science is still in its infancy here. It is the Schumpeterian 'vision' that translates into political choices.

5 Macroeconomists do focus on certain structures, such as the maturity structure of debt, but this is not enough and mainstream macro theory is quite indifferent to the issues we raise here.

6 One extreme example of the rigidities that are imposed by monetary and exchange-rate policies is provided by the crisis of the Greek economy in 2009/10. The exchange rate of the euro may be right for Germany or France, but not for Greece or Spain. This rigidity is difficult to overcome.

7 This debate has ignored the fact that discount rates can be the object of a reswitching phenomenon, much like the one described in the controversy over capital theory (Baumol 1997).

8 This figure is in real 2005 dollars and comes from the World Bank's Human Development Indicators for 2008.

9 The so-called Laffer curve (named after economist Arthur Laffer) is a thought experiment showing that as tax rates increase, so does fiscal revenue. But this holds only up to a certain level because at very high taxation rates agents have no incentive to earn any income. In addition, when tax rates are cut, economic activity will increase and government revenues will also rise. This is a theoretical construct that was used in the days of the Reagan administration as part of so-called supply-side economics. This was used to justify reducing taxes in the belief that this would bring about increased investment. In fact, this did not happen, and the Reagan and Bush tax reductions did not pay for themselves.

10 For a general overview see Jha (2006).

11 Using World Bank data, the Committee for the Abolition of Third World Debt (CADTM) reveals that the internal public debt of all developing countries rose from US$1,300 to US$3,500 billion between 1997 and 2005. See www.cadtm.org.

12 The nominal value of commodities derivatives reported to the Bank of International Settlements was US$13 trillion in June 2008 (Suppan 2009).

13 This is the description of Warren Buffett after he purchased General Reinsurance and found that one of its subsidiaries was a derivatives dealer.

7 International macroeconomic reform

1 Wallerstein's and Arrighi's analyses show that the history of capitalism involves five long-term systemic cycles of capital accumulation. The first one takes place around the northern Italian cities of Venice and Genoa in the fifteenth to sixteenth centuries. The second cycle is organized around Amsterdam as the centre of world capital accumulation was displaced from Italy to the Netherlands in the seventeenth to eighteenth centuries. The third cycle revolves around England during the late eighteenth and nineteenth centuries as the British Empire was consolidated. Finally, the last long-term world cycle of accumulation takes place under the hegemony of the United States during the late nineteenth century and then the twentieth century.

2 The promotion of financial market liberalization by developing countries was justified with the claim that foreign banks had greater know-how in risk management and credit assessment than domestic banks. It was also argued that entry of developed countries' banks into these markets would increase the competencies of domestic banks. The massive failures of US banks have cast doubt on the validity of that presumption (UN Financial Reform Commission 2009).

3 Through sterilization the domestic money supply remains constant. It is performed through open market operations that withdraw from circulation an amount that is equivalent to the converted incoming capital flows.

4 Commodities have properties that make them attractive as assets in an investment portfolio: their returns are negatively correlated with those of other assets over the business cycle and they are less volatile. Besides, because many commodities are an important component of the basket of goods that is used to measure price changes, these commodities are a good protection against inflation (their returns are positively correlated with price increases). Investment returns become the objective function and replace hedging against price fluctuations.

5 The CFTC controls potential market manipulation and excessive speculation through the Commitment of Traders (COT) report. But this was severely downgraded and rendered useless by the Commodity Futures Modernization Act enacted in 2000. In addition, the regulatory and monitoring capacity of the CFTC was further eroded when it allowed the Intercontinental Exchange (ICE) to use its trading terminals in the United States for trading in US commodity futures contracts on the ICE futures exchange in London. Later, ICE Futures allowed traders in the United States to use ICE terminals in the United States to trade its synthetic futures contracts on the ICE Futures London exchange. This not only allowed unregistered funds to effectively bypass registration, it also contributed to distributing the effects of these operations worldwide.

6 Futures markets involve contracts in which traders pledge to buy or sell a commodity in the future at a preset price. The contract can be traded so that the agent does not have to actually take delivery of the commodity when the date expires. In the case of options, traders have the right but not the obligation to purchase or sell a commodity at a preset price at a future date and they pay a premium to the agents who make the opposite pledge.

7 See also Andrew Batson, 'China takes aim at dollar', *Wall Street Journal*, 24 March 2009.

8 In a fourteen-page letter to BP's CEO, Representatives Henry Waxman (California) and Bart Stupak (Michigan) identify five questionable decisions made by BP management in the days leading up to the explosion. They note that a common feature of these decisions is that they posed a trade-off between cost and well safety. The letter, supplemented by sixty-one footnotes and dozens of documents, states that 'time after time, it appears that BP made decisions that increased the risk of a blowout to save the company time or expense' (*Huffington Post*, 14 June 2010).

9 The relation between trade and

macroeconomic policy can be fully appreciated in the following passage from Keynes's *General Theory*, which is highly relevant to our discussion on sustainability: 'If nations can learn to provide themselves with full employment by their domestic policy [...] there need be no important economic forces calculated to set the interest of one country against that of its neighbours. There would still be room for the international division of labour and for international lending in appropriate conditions. But there would no longer be a pressing motive why one country need force its wares on another [...] with the express object of upsetting the equilibrium of payments so as to develop a balance of trade in its own favour. International trade would cease to be what it is, namely, a desperate expedient to maintain employment at home by forcing sales on foreign markets and restricting purchases, which, if successful, will merely shift the problem of unemployment to the neighbour [...]' (Keynes 1973: 383–4).

10 The IMF already issues an international reserve unit (the Special Drawing Right, SDR), but under rules that have to be revised and changed to allow for anti-cyclical policies.

11 The Basle III accord (approved on 12 September 2010, see www.bis.org) strengthened capital requirements, raising the minimum common equity requirement from 2 per cent to 4.5 per cent, plus another 2.5 per cent to be phased in by 2019. This is a step in the right direction, but the accord has several weak spots. The first is that much of the shadow banking system and its operations are ignored, leaving the volatile and risky business of this sub-sector without regulation. The second is that capital ratio can be meaningless if assets are overvalued and the Basle III accord does not include binding guidelines for valuation. Finally, Basle III does not have a strong chapter on enforcement.

12 Another possibility is to have the Joint Forum of the Basle Committee on Banking Supervision address projects where social responsibility and environmental sustainability are critically compromised. The Joint Forum is concerned with issues that are common to the banking, securities and insurance sectors, and from this standpoint it can provide a starting point for the design of meaningful supervisory standards in this field. The specific issue of how to incorporate triple-bottom-line accounting (economic, social and environmental) into Generally Accepted Accounting Practices should be the core mission of a new working group within the Joint Forum.

13 The international economic system should recognize the *rebus sic stantibus* clause (Latin for 'things thus standing'). Article 62 of the 1969 Vienna Convention on the Law of Treaties states that a fundamental change of circumstances can be invoked to terminate treaty obligations when the change radically transforms the extent of obligations still to be performed. Unfortunately, the Vienna Convention does not cover treaties between states and international organizations.

14 The system the URAA helped enshrine must be redesigned. Developing countries must have the right to use quantitative restrictions (QRs) to protect themselves from dumping practices and to delink their key strategic sectors from the paradigm of the URAA. These QRs are compatible with the WTO and

are recognized by Article XVIII of the original GATT. Safeguards should also be made available for developing countries to protect their producers from the effects of dumping.

Conclusion

1 This is one of the clearest statements by which Keynes puts to rest the established and narrow interpretation according to which he believed that, in the long term, capitalism would converge to full employment. That view minimizes the deep differences between the General Theory and mainstream economics.

2 There is another aspect of Keynes's remarks about socialization of the investment process highly relevant in today's world economy. Keynes understood that following his policy schemes 'would mean the euthanasia of the rentier, and, consequently, the euthanasia of the cumulative oppressive powers of the capitalist to exploit the scarcity-value of capital' (Keynes 1973: 376).

Bibliography

Abaza, H. (1995) 'UNEP/World Bank workshop on the environmental impacts of structural adjustment programmes – New York, 20–21 March 1995', *Ecological Economics*, 14(1): 1–5.

Ackerman, F. (2009) *Can We Afford the Future? The Economics of a Warming World*, London and New York: Zed Books.

Ackerman, F. and A. Nadal (2004) *The Flawed Foundations of General Equilibrium. Critical Essays on Economic Theory*, London: Routledge.

Amsden, A. (1989) *Asia's Next Giant. South Korea and Late Industrialization*, Oxford: Oxford University Press.

Arrighi, G. (1994) *The Long Twentieth Century. Money, Power and the Origins of Our Times*, London: Verso.

Arrow, K., H. D. Block and L. Hurwicz (1959) 'On the stability of the Competitive Equilibrium II', *Econometrica*, 27: 82–109.

Arrow, K. and F. Hahn (1971) *General Competitive Analysis*, San Francisco, CA: Holden Day.

Banco Central de Costa Rica (2007) *Deuda y los efectos de la política fiscal. Evaluación de vulnerabilidades para la economía costarricense*, Departamento de Investigaciones Económicas, Documento de Investigación DIE-01-2007-DI.

Barker, T., I. Bashmakov, A. Alharthi, M. Amann, L. Cifuentes, J. Drexhage, M. Duan, O. Edenhofer, B. Flannery, M. Grubb, M. Hoogwijk, F. I. Ibitoye, C. J. Jepma, W. A. Pizer, K. Yamaji (2007) 'Mitigation from a cross-sectoral perspective', in B. Metz, O. R. Davidson, P. R. Bosch, R. Dave, L. A. Meyer (eds), *Climate Change 2007: Mitigation*, Contribution of Working Group III to the Fourth Assessment Report of the Intergovernmental Panel on Climate Change, Cambridge: Cambridge University Press.

Barnett, H. J. and C. Morse (1963) *Scarcity and Growth. The Economics of Natural Resource Availability*, Baltimore, MD: Johns Hopkins University Press.

Barnett, W. (2006) 'Is macroeconomics a science?', MPRA Paper Series, available online at mpra.ub.uni-muenchen.de/415/MPRA Paper No. 415, posted 7 November 2007.

Baumol, W. J. (1997) 'Reswitching, social discount rate and environmentalism', in P. Arestis, G. Palma and M. Sawyer (eds), *Capital Controversy, Post-Keynesian Economics and the History of Economics. Essays in Honour of Geoff Harcourt*, vol. I, London: Routledge, pp. 45–51.

Becker, R. A. (2008) 'Tranversality condition', in S. N. Durlauf and L. E. Blume (eds), *The New Palgrave Dictionary of Economics*, London: Palgrave Macmillan.

Benetti, C. (2004) 'Money and prices:

the limits of the General Equilibrium Theory', in F. Ackerman and A. Nadal, *The Flawed Foundations of General Equilibrium. Critical Essays on Economic Theory*, London: Routledge.

Bhaduri, A. (1998) 'Implications of globalization for macroeconomic theory and policy in developing countries', in D. Baker, G. Epstein and R. Pollin (eds), *Globalization and Progressive Economic Policy*, Cambridge: Cambridge University Press.

— (2009) *The Face You Were Afraid to See. Essays on the Indian Economy*, New Delhi: Penguin Books India.

Bhaduri, A. and R. Skarstein (1996) 'Short-period macroeconomic aspects of foreign aid', *Cambridge Journal of Economics*, 20(2): 195–206.

Blanchard, O. and S. Fischer (1989) *Lectures on Macroeconomics*, Cambridge, MA: MIT Press.

Brack, D. and K. Gray (2003) *Multilateral Environmental Agreements and the WTO*, Royal Institute of International Affairs and the International Institute for Sustainable Development (IISD).

Braudel, F. (1982) *The Wheels of Commerce*, New York: Harper and Row.

— (1984) *The Perspective of the World*, New York: Harper and Row.

Brundtland Report (1987) *Our Common Future*, United Nations World Commission on Environment and Development, Oxford: Oxford University Press.

Butler, R. A. (2007) 'Reducing tropical deforestation rates will help fight global warming', www.rainforests.mongabay.com, posted 10 May.

Butler, T. (2005) 'Deforestation in Borneo. Kalimantan at the crossroads: dipterocarp forests and the future of Indonesian Borneo', rainforests.mongabay.com.

Chang, H.-J. (2002) *Kicking Away the Ladder – Development Strategy in Historical Perspective*, London: Anthem Press.

— (2003) *Foreign Investment Regulation in Historical Perspective*, Global Policy Forum, www.globalpolicy.org.

Chichilniski, G. and G. Gallopín (2001) 'The environmental impact of globalization on Latin America', in *Managing Human-Dominated Ecosystems*, pp. 271–303.

Chick, V. (1983) *Macroeconomics after Keynes*, Cambridge, MA: MIT Press.

Chinn, M. and J. Frankel (2008) 'The euro may over the next 15 years surpass the dollar as leading international currency', National Bureau of Economic Research, NBER Working Paper no. 13909, April, available at www.nber.org.

Cibils, A., M. Weisbrot and D. Kar (2002) 'Argentina since default: the IMF and the depression', Centre for Economic and Policy Research (CEPR), September, available at www.cepr.net.

Cloquell, S. (ed.) (2007) *Familias rurales: el fin de una historia en el inicio de una nueva agricultura*, Buenos Aires: Homo Sapiens.

Collander, D. (ed.) (2006) *Post-Walrasian Macroeconomics. Beyond the Dynamic Stochastic General Equilibrium Theory*, Cambridge: Cambridge University Press.

CONABIO (2007) *Sistema Nacional sobre la Biodiversidad en México*, www.conabio.gob.mx/institucion/snib/doctos/acerca.html.

Cornia, G. A. (ed.) (2006) *Pro-Poor Macroeconomics: Potential and

Limitations, London: Palgrave Macmillan.

Croce, E. and V. Hugo Juan-Ramón (2003) 'Assessing fiscal sustainability: a crosscountry comparison', Working Paper WP/03/145, International Monetary Fund.

Crotty, J. (2000) 'Structural contradictions of current capitalism', Presented at the Conference on Globalization, Structural Change and Income Distribution, Chennai, December.

Daly, H. (2002) 'Elements of environmental macroeconomics', in M. Munasinghe, *Macroeconomics and the Environment*, Cheltenham: Edward Elgar, pp. 63–77. Also published in R. Costanza (ed.), *Ecological Economics: The Science and Management of Sustainability*, New York: Columbia University Press, pp. 32–46. Originally published in *Land Economics* in 1991.

Daly, H. and J. Cobb (1994) *For the Common Good. Redirecting the Economy toward Community, the Environment and a Sustainable Future*, Boston, MA: Beacon Press.

Daly, H. and J. Farley (2004) *Ecological Economics. Principles and Applications*, Washington, DC: Island Press.

Daly, N. (1994) 'Ravaging the redwood: Charles Hurwitz, Michael Milken and the costs of greed', available at multinationalmonitor. org/hyper/issues/1994/09/mm0994_07.html.

Dasgupta, P. (2007) 'Comments on the Stern Review on the Economics of Climate Change', *National Institute Economic Review*, 199(1): 4–7.

David, P. (1974) *Technical Change, Innovation and Economic Growth*, Cambridge: Cambridge University Press.

Davidson, P. (1999) 'Global employment in open economy macroeconomics', in J. Deprez and J. T. Harvey (eds), *Foundations of International Economics. Post-Keynesian Perspectives*, London and New York: Routledge.

Debabrata Patra, M. and P. Ray (2010) 'Inflation expectations and monetary policy in India: an empirical exploration', IMF Working Paper 10/84, Washington, DC: International Monetary Fund.

Debreu, G. (1974) 'Excess demand function', *Journal of Mathematical Economics*, 1: 15–21.

Delli Gatti, D., M. Gallegati and A. Kirman (2000) *Interaction and Market Structure: Essays on Heterogeneity in Economics*, Berlin and Heidelberg: Springer Verlag.

Domar, E. (1946) 'Capital expansion, rate of growth and employment', *Econometrica*, 14: 137–47.

Dumenil, G. and D. Lévy (2004) *Capital Resurgent: Roots of the Neoliberal Revolution*, Cambridge, MA: Harvard University Press.

Eatwell, J. and L. Taylor (2000) *Global Finance at Risk. The Case for International Regulation*, New York: New Press.

Eichengreen, B. (1996) *Globalizing Capital. A History of the International Monetary System*, Princeton, NJ: Princeton University Press.

— (1999) *Toward a New International Financial Architecture. A Practical Post-Asia Agenda*, Washington, DC: Institute for International Economics.

Engel, S., T. Wünscher and S. Wunder (2009) 'Increasing the efficiency of forest conservation. The case of payments for environmental services in Costa Rica', in C. Palmer and S. Engel (eds),

Avoided Deforestation. Prospects for Mitigating Climate Change, London: Routledge.

England, R. W. (2000) 'Natural capital and the theory of economic growth', *Ecological Economics*, 34: 425–31.

Fajnzylber, F. (1983) *La industrialización trunca de América Latina*, Mexico: Editorial Nueva Imagen.

Falconi Benítez, F. (2005) 'La construcción de una economía con cimientos ecológicos', in A. Acosta and F. Falconi (eds), *Asedios a lo imposible: propuestas económicas en construcción*, Ecuador: ILDIS y Flacso.

Fankhauser, S. (2009) 'The range of global estimates', in M. Parry et al., *Assessing the Costs of Adaptation to Climate Change: A Review of the UNFCCC and Other Recent Estimates*, London: International Institute for Environment and Development and Grantham Institute for Climate Change.

FAO (2000) *The State of Food and Agriculture 2000. Lessons from the Past Fifty Years*, Rome: Food and Agriculture Organization, available at www.fao.org.

Fearnside, P. (2006) 'Fragile soils and deforestation impacts: the rationale for environmental services of standing forest as a development paradigm in Amazonia', in D. Posey and M. Balick (eds), *Human Impacts on Amazonia: The Role of Traditional Ecological Knowledge in Conservation and Development*, New York: Columbia University Press.

Felix, D. (2006) 'The past as future? The contribution of financial globalization to the current crisis of neo-liberalism as a development strategy', available at econpapers.repec.org.

Fellner, W. (1962) 'Does the market direct the relative factor-saving effects of technological progress?', in H. M. Groves (ed.), *The Rate and Direction of Inventive Activity*, Cambridge, MA: National Bureau Committee for Economic Research.

Ferreres, O. (2005) *Dos siglos de economía argentina*, Buenos Aires: Fundación Norte y Sur.

Ffrench-Davis, R. (2000) *Reforming the Reforms in Latin America: Macroeconomics, Trade, Finance*, London: Macmillan.

Ffrench-Davis, R. and H. Tapia (2004) 'The Chilean style of capital controls: an empirical assessment', Document prepared under the ECLAC project 'Management of volatility, financial liberalization and growth', presented at the Latin American Studies Association meeting, Las Vegas, October.

Fisher, F. (1983) *Disequilibrium Foundations of Equilibrium Economics*, Cambridge: Cambridge University Press.

Frankfurter, M. M. and D. Accomazzo (2007) 'Is managed futures an asset class? The search for the beta of commodity futures', *Social Science Research Network*, 31 December, available at ssrn.com/abstract=1029243.

Friedman, M. (1968) 'The role of monetary policy', *American Economic Review*, 58: 1–17.

Furman, J. and J. Stiglitz (1998) 'Economic crises: evidence and insights from East Asia', Brookings Papers on Economic Activity no. 2, Washington, DC: Brookings Institution.

Galbraith, J. K. (2000) *Created Unequal. The Crisis in American Pay*, Chicago, IL: University of Chicago Press.

Gallagher, K. (ed.) (2005) *Putting Development First. The Importance of Policy Space in the WTO and International Financial Institutions*, London and New York: Zed Books.

Gandhi, V. (ed.) (1996) *Macroeconomics and the Environment*, Washington, DC: International Monetary Fund.

Georgescu Roegen, N. (1967) *Analytical Economics. Issues and Problems*, Cambridge, MA: Harvard University Press.

Giarracca, N. and M. Teubal (2006) 'Democracia y neoliberalismo en el campo argentino: una convivencia difícil', in G. Hubert (ed.), *La construcción de la democracia en el campo latinoamericano*, Buenos Aires: CLACSO.

Gilbertson, T. and O. Reyes (2009) *Carbon Trading: How It Works and Why It Fails*, Critical Currents no. 7, Uppsala: Dag Hammarskjöld Foundation.

Goodfriend, M. and R. G. King (1997) 'The new neoclassical synthesis and the role of monetary policy', Working Paper Series WP 98-05, Federal Reserve Bank of Richmond.

Grossman, G. M. and A. B. Krueger (1994) 'Environmental impacts of a North American Free Trade Agreement', in P. Garber (ed.), *The US–Mexico Free Trade Agreement*, Cambridge, MA: MIT Press.

— (1995) 'Economic growth and the environment', *Quarterly Journal of Economics* (CX-2), May, pp. 353–77.

Guissé, E. H. (2004) 'Effects of debt on human rights', Working paper, United Nations Sub-Commission on Human Rights (E/CN.4/Sub.2/2004/27).

Habakkuk, J. (1962) *American and British Technology in the Nineteenth Century*, Cambridge: Cambridge University Press.

Hahn, F. (1965) 'On some problems of proving the existence of an equilibrium in a monetary economy', in F. Hahn and F. P. R. Brechling (eds), *Theory of Interest Rates*, London: Macmillan.

— (1984) 'On money and growth', in *Equilibrium and Macroeconomics*, Oxford: Basil Blackwell, pp. 194–213. Originally published in *Journal of Money, Credit and Banking*, May 1969.

Hahn, F. and R. Solow (1997) *A Critical Essay on Modern Macroeconomic Theory*, Cambridge, MA: MIT Press.

Halsnæs, K., P. Shukla, D. Ahuja, G. Akumu, R. Beale, J. Edmonds, C. Gollier, A. Grübler, M. Ha Duong, A. Markandya, M. McFarland, E. Nikitina, T. Sugiyama, A. Villavicencio and J. Zou (2007) 'Framing issues', in B. Metz, O. R. Davidson, P. R. Bosch, R. Dave and L. A. Meyer (eds), *Climate Change 2007: Mitigation*, Contribution of Working Group III to the Fourth Assessment Report of the Intergovernmental Panel on Climate Change, Cambridge: Cambridge University Press.

Hansen, A. (1963 [1949]) *Monetary Theory and Fiscal Policy*, Hightstown, NJ: McGraw-Hill Education.

Harrod, R. F. (1939) 'An essay in dynamic theory', *Economic Journal*, 49: 14–33.

Hartley, J. E. (1997) *The Representative Agent in Macroeconomics*, London: Routledge.

Harvey, J. T. (1999) 'Volatility and misalignment in the post-Bretton Woods era', in J. Deprez and J. T. Harvey (eds), *Foundations of International Economics. Post-*

Keynesian Perspectives, London: Routledge.

HDR (2007/08) *Human Development Report 2007-2008. Fighting Climate Change: Human Solidarity in a Divided World*, United Nations Development Programme.

Herrera, A. (1977) *Catastrophe or New Society?*, Ottawa: International Development Research Centre (IDRC).

Heyes, A. (2000) 'A proposal for the greening of textbook macro: "IS-LM-EE"', *Ecological Economics*, 32(1): 1-7.

Hicks, J. R. (1937) 'Mr Keynes and the "Classics"; a suggested interpretation', *Econometrica*, 5(2): 147-59.

— (1981) 'IS-LM: an explanation', *Journal of Post Keynesian Economics*, 3(2): 139-54.

Hillman, D., S. Kapoor and S. Spratt (2006) *Taking the Next Step. Implementing a Currency Transactions Development Levy*, Report commissioned by the Norwegian Ministry of Foreign Affairs, available at www.stampoutpoverty.org.

Howse, R. (2007) *The Concept of Odious Debt in Public International Law*, UNCTAD/OSG/dp/2007/4 no. 185, available at www.unctad.org.

Howson, S. (1973) 'A dear money man? Keynes on monetary policy 1920', *Economic Journal*, 83(330): 456-64.

IAASTD (2009) *International Assessment of Agricultural Knowledge, Science and Technology for Development, Global Report*, ed. B. McIntyre, H. Herren, J. Wakhungu and R. Watson, Washington, DC: Island Press.

Ibenholt, K. (2002) 'Materials flow analysis and economic modelling', in R. Ayres and L. Ayres (eds), *A Handbook of Industrial Ecology*, Cheltenham: Edward Elgar.

— (2003) 'Material accounting in a macroeconomic framework', *Environmental and Resource Economics*, 26(2).

ILO (2008) *Global Wage Report, 2008/09. Minimum Wages and Collective Bargaining: Towards Policy Coherence*, Geneva: International Labour Organization.

IMF (2008) *The Fiscal Implications of Climate Change*, Fiscal Affairs Department, International Monetary Fund.

IPCC (2007) *Climate Change 2007: Synthesis Report. Contribution of Working Groups I, II and III to the Fourth Assessment Report of the Intergovernmental Panel on Climate Change*, Geneva: IPCC.

ITUC (2009) *A Recipe for Hunger: How the World is Failing on Food*, Brussels: International Trade Union Confederation.

Jha, R. (2006) 'Pro-poor fiscal policy in the globalized economy', in G. A. Cornia (ed.), *Pro-Poor Macroeconomics. Potential and Limitations*, London: Palgrave Macmillan and UNRISD.

Jubilee Australia (2007) *A Debt-for-Development Swap with Indonesia*, Policy paper by Jubilee Australia, April.

Kallis, G. (2010) 'The degrowth propositions and research questions', Panel, 2nd International Conference on Economic Degrowth for Ecological Sustainability and Social Equity, 26-29 March, Barcelona.

Kaminsky, G. L., C. M. Reinhart and C. A. Vegh (2004) 'When it rains, it pours: procyclical capital flows and macroeconomic policies', *NBER Macroeconomics Annual*, vol. 19, National Bureau of Economic Research (NBER).

Kandelaars, P. (1999) *Economic Models of Material-Product Chains for Environmental Policy Analysis*, Kluwer Academic Publishers.

Kandelaars, P. and J. van den Bergh (2001) 'A survey of material flows in economic models', *International Journal of Sustainable Development*, 4(3).

Keynes, J. M. (1973) *The General Theory of Employment, Interest and Money*, Cambridge: Macmillan/Cambridge University Press for the Royal Economic Society (first published 1936).

— (1980) *The Collected Writings of John Maynard Keynes*, vol. 25, ed. D. Moggridge, London: Macmillan.

Kregel, J. (2004) 'Can we create a stable international financial environment that ensures net resource transfers to developing countries?', *Journal of Post Keynesian Economics*, 26(4): 573–90.

Lall, S. (2004) 'Reinventing industrial strategy: the role of government policy in building industrial competitiveness', G24 Discussion Papers no. 28, Geneva: United Nations Conference on Trade and Development (UNCTAD).

Lavoie, M. (2006) *Introduction to Post-Keynesian Economics*, Basingstoke and New York: Palgrave Macmillan.

Lawn, P. (2003) 'On Heyes' IS–LM–EE proposal to establish an environmental macroeconomics', *Environment and Development Economics*, 8(1): 31–56.

Leijonhufvud, A. (2008) 'Keynes and the crisis', *Policy Insight*, 23, Center for Economic Policy Research.

— (2009) 'Macroeconomics and the crisis: a personal appraisal', *Policy Insight*, 41, Center for Economic Policy Research.

Leontief, W. in collaboration with A. Carter and P. Petri (1977) *The Future of the World Economy*, New York: Oxford University Press.

Lohmann, L. (2006) *Carbon Trading. A Critical Conversation on Climate Change, Privatisation and Power*, Development Dialogue, Uppsala: Dag Hammarskjöld Centre.

Lopez, R. (2003) 'The policy roots of socioeconomic stagnation and environmental implosion: Latin America 1950–2000', *World Development*, 31(2): 259–80.

Lucas, R. (2009) 'In defence of the dismal science', *The Economist*, 6 August.

Maddison, A. (2001) *The World Economy, A Millennial Perspective*, Paris: OECD.

Mäler, K.-G. and M. Munasinghe (1996) 'Macroeconomic policies, second-best theory and the environment', *Environment and Development Economics*, 1: 149–63.

— (2002) 'Macroeconomic policies, second-best theory and the environment', in M. Munasinghe (ed.), *Macroeconomics and the Environment*, Cheltenham: Edward Elgar.

Mantel, R. (1976) 'Homothetic preferences and community excess demand functions', *Journal of Economic Theory*, 12: 197–201.

Martínez-Alier, J., U. Pascual, F.-D. Vivienc and E. Zaccaid (2010) 'Sustainable de-growth: mapping the context, criticisms and future prospects of an emergent paradigm', *Ecological Economics*, 69: 1741–7.

Marx, K. (1973) *Grundrisse*, online edn transcribed for MEIA from the Penguin edn, trans. M. Nicolaus, 1973, used by permission of the translator, available at www.marxists.org/archive/marx/works/1857/grundrisse/.

MEA (Millennium Ecosystem Assessment) (2005) *Ecosystems and Human Well-being: Current State and Trends*, vol. 1, Millennium Ecosystem Assessment, Washington, DC: Island Press, available at www.millenniumassessment.org.

Meadows, D. H., D. L. Meadows, J. Randers and W. H. Behrens (1972) *The Limits to Growth*, New York: University Books.

Meiksins Wood, E. (2002) *The Origin of Capitalism. A Longer View*, London and New York: Verso.

Mesarovic, M. and E. Pestel (1974) *Mankind at the Turning Point*, New York: Dutton/Reader's Digest.

Millet, D. and E. Toussaint (2009) *The Debt in Figures 2009*, Committee for the Abolition of Third World Debt, available at www.cadtm.org.

Minsky, H. P. (1957) *John Maynard Keynes*, London: Macmillan Press.

— (1986) *Stabilizing an Unstable Economy*, New Haven, CT: Yale University Press.

— (1992) *The Financial Instability Hypothesis*, Working Paper 74, Jerome Levy Economics Institute of Bard College.

Mkandawire, T. (2005) 'Foreword', in G. A. Cornia (ed.), *Pro-Poor Macroeconomics. Potential and Limitations*, London: Palgrave Macmillan.

Modigliani, F. (1944) 'Liquidity preference and the theory of interest and money', *Econometrica*, 12(1): 45–88.

Moggridge, D. E. and S. Howson (1974) 'Keynes on monetary policy, 1910–1946', *Oxford Economic Papers* (New Series), 26(2): 226–47.

Montiel, P. and L. Servén (2004) *Macroeconomic Stability in Developing Countries: How Much is Enough?*, Policy Research Working Paper Series no. 3456, World Bank.

Moore, B. (2007) 'Does inflation targeting increase the deflationary bias in the world economy?', in P. Arestis, E. Hein and E. Le Heron (eds), *Aspects of Modern Monetary and Macroeconomic Policies*, New York: Palgrave Macmillan.

Moreno-Brid, J. C. and C. Rozo (2000) 'Dolarización: conveniencias y disconveniencias para México', in G. Mantey and N. Levy (eds), *De la desregulación financiera a la crisis cambiaria: experiencias en América Latina y el Sudeste Asiático*, Mexico: UNAM, ENEP Acatlán.

Munasinghe, M. (2002) *Macroeconomics and the Environment*, Cheltenham: Edward Elgar.

Munasinghe, M. and W. Cruz (1994) *Economywide Policies and the Environment*, Washington, DC: World Bank.

Muradian, R. and J. Martínez Alier (2001) 'Trade and the environment: from a "Southern" perspective', *Ecological Economics*, 36: 281–97.

Muradian, R., M. O'Connor and J. Martínez Alier (2001) *Embodied Pollution in Trade: Estimating the 'Environmental Load Displacement' of Industrialised Countries*, Fondazione Eni Enrico Mattei, Nota di lavoro 57-2001, available at www.feem.it/web/activ/_activ.html.

Nadal, A. (1996) 'Balance of payments provisions in the GATT and NAFTA', *Journal of World Trade*, 30(4): 5–24.

— (2000) *The Environmental and Social Impacts of Economic Liberalization on Corn Production in Mexico*, WWF and Oxfam.

— (2003) 'Natural Protected Areas and social marginalization in Mexico', Occasional Papers Series CEESP, I(1), Geneva: International Union for Conservation of Nature (IUCN), pp. 1–28.

— (2004a) 'Contradictions of the open economy model as applied in Mexico', in F. Ackerman and A. Nadal (eds), *The Flawed Foundations of General Equilibrium. Critical Essays on Economic Theory*, London: Routledge.

— (2004b) 'Freedom and submission: individuals and the invisible hand', in F. Ackerman and A. Nadal (eds), *The Flawed Foundations of General Equilibrium. Critical Essays on Economic Theory*, London: Routledge.

— (2005) 'Estabilidad y flujos de capital en el modelo de economía abierta', in A. Nadal and F. Aguayo (eds), *Experiencias de crisis y estrategias de desarrollo. Autonomía y globalización*, Mexico: El Colegio de México.

— (2007) 'Coasean fictions: law and economics revisited', *Seattle Journal of Social Justice*, 5(2): 569–601.

Nelson, R. and S. Winter (1982) *An Evolutionary Theory of Economic Change*, Cambridge, MA: Belknap Press of Harvard University Press.

Nicholls, R. (2007) *Adaptation Options for Coastal Zones and Infrastructure*, Report to the UNFCCC Financial and Technical Support Division.

Nordhaus, W. D. (2007) 'A review of the Stern Review on the Economics of Climate Change', *Journal of Economic Literature*, 45(3).

Ocampo, J. A. (2003) 'Capital account and counter cyclical prudential regulations in developing countries', *Serie Informes y Estudios Especiales*, CEPAL, 6 February.

— (2004/05) 'Beyond the Washington Consensus. What do we mean?', *Journal of Post Keynesian Economics*, 27(2): 293–314.

Ocampo, J. A. and M. Á. Parra (2003) 'Los términos de intercambio de los productos básicos en el siglo XX', *Revista de la CEPAL*, 79: 7–35.

Ocampo, J. A. and C. E. Tovar (2003) 'La experiencia colombiana con los encajes a los flujos de capital', *Revista de la CEPAL*, 81: 7–32.

Oilwatch (2007) 'Conservar el crudo en el subsuelo, por el país, por el Yasuní, por su gente', available at www.amazoniaporlavida.org/es/files/guardar_el_crudo_en_el_subsuelo.pdf/.

Oxfam (2007) *Adapting to Climate Change. What's needed in poor countries and who should pay*, OXFAM Briefing Paper 104, available at www.oxfam.org/files.

Palley, T. I. (2009) 'The limits of Minsky's financial instability hypothesis as an explanation of the Crisis', IMK Working Paper 11/2009, available at www.boeckler.de.

Palmer, C. and S. Engel (eds) (2009) *Avoided Deforestation. Prospects for Mitigating Climate Change*, London: Routledge.

Parry, M., N. Arnell, P. Berry, D. Dodman, S. Fankhauser, C. Hope, S. Kovats, R. Nicholls, D. Satterthwaite, R. Tiffin and T. Wheeler (2009) *Assessing the Costs of Adaptation to Climate Change: A Review of the UNFCCC and Other Recent Estimates*, London: International Institute for Environment and Development and Grantham Institute for Climate Change.

Pengue, W. (2004a) 'La ingeniería genética y la intensificación de la agricultura argentina: algunos comentarios críticos', in A. Bárcena et al., *Los transgénicos en América Latina y el Caribe: un debate abierto*, Santiago: CEPAL.
— (2004b) 'Transgenic crops in Argentina and their hidden costs', in E. Ortega and S. Ugliati (eds), *Proceedings from the Biennial International Workshop on Advances in Energy Studies*, Unicamp, Campinas, São Paulo, 16–19 June.
— (2005) 'Transgenic crops in Argentina: the ecological and social debt', *Bulletin of Science, Technology and Society*, 25(4).
— (2006) 'La soja transgénica en América Latina', *Biodiversidad*, 47.
Perman, R. and D. I. Stern (2003) 'Evidence from panel unit root and cointegration tests that the environmental Kuznets curve does not exist', *Australian Journal of Agricultural and Resource Economics*, 47: 325–47.
Petri, F. (2004) *General Equilibrium, Capital and Macroeconomics*, Cheltenham: Edward Elgar.
Phelps, E. S. (1967) 'Phillips curves, expectations of inflation and optimal employment over time', *Economica*, 34(3): 254–81.
Pollin, R. (2005) 'Applying a Securities Transactions Tax to the U.S.: design issues, market impact, revenues estimates', in G. Epstein (ed.), *Financialization and the World Economy*, Cheltenham: Edward Elgar.
Ray, D. E., D. de la Torre Ugarte and K. J. Tiller (2003) *Rethinking US Agricultural Policy: Changing Course to Secure Farmer Livelihoods Worldwide*, Agricultural Policy Analysis Center, University of Tennessee, available at ag-policy.org.
Reed, D. (1992) *Structural Adjustment and the Environment*, Boulder, CO: Westview Press.
Robinson, J. (1956) *The Accumulation of Capital*, New York: Macmillan.
Rogner, H.-H., D. Zhou, R. Bradley, P. Crabbé, O. Edenhofer, B. Hare (Australia), L. Kuijpers and M. Yamaguchi (2007) 'Introduction', in B. Metz, O. R. Davidson, P. R. Bosch, R. Dave and L. A. Meyer (eds), *Climate Change 2007: Mitigation. Contribution of Working Group III to the Fourth Assessment Report of the Intergovernmental Panel on Climate Change*, Cambridge and New York: Cambridge University Press.
Rosenberg, N. (1982) 'Technological expectations', in *Inside the Black Box. Technology and Economics*, Cambridge: Cambridge University Press.
Sachs, J. D. and J. W. McArthur (2005) 'The Millenium Project: a plan for meeting the Millennium Development Goals', *Lancet*, 365: 347–53.
Salter, W. (1960) *Productivity and Technical Change*, Cambridge: Cambridge University Press.
Samuelson, P. (1966) 'A summing up', *Quarterly Journal of Economics*, 80: 568–83.
Sathaye, J., A. Najam, C. Cocklin, T. Heller, F. Lecocq, J. Llanes-Regueiro, J. Pan, G. Petschel-Held, S. Rayner, J. Robinson, R. Schaeffer, Y. Sokona, R. Swart and H. Winkler (2007) 'Sustainable development and mitigation', in B. Metz, O. R. Davidson, P. R. Bosch, R. Dave and L. A. Meyer (eds), *Climate Change 2007: Mitigation. Contribution of*

Working Group III to the Fourth Assessment Report of the Intergovernmental Panel on Climate Change, Cambridge: Cambridge University Press.

Scarf, H. (1960) 'Some examples of global instability of the competitive equilibrium', *International Economic Review*, 1: 157–72.

Selden, T. and D. Song (1994) 'Environmental quality and development: is there a Kuznets for air pollution emissions?', *Journal of Environmental Economics and Management*, 27: 147–62.

Sen, A. K. (ed.) (1971) *Growth Economics*, Harmondsworth: Penguin.

Shafik, N. and S. Bandyopadhyay (1992) 'Economic growth and environmental quality: time series and cross country evidence', Background paper for the *World Development Report 1992*, Washington, DC: World Bank.

Shah, A. (2005) *The Scale of the Debt Crisis. Global Issues*, 2 June, available at www.globalissues.org.

Shrivastava, A. (2007) *Globalised World. Who Gains, Who Loses?*, Pune: Centre for Communication and Development Studies.

Sigl-Grüb, C. and D. Schiereck (2008) 'Returns to speculators in commodity futures markets: a comprehensive revisit', 9 April, available at ssrn.com/abstract=1115802.

Sim, N. (2006) 'Environmental Keynesian macroeconomics: some further discussion', *Ecological Economics*, 59(4): 401–5.

Smith, R. (2010) 'Beyond growth or beyond capitalism?', *real-world economics review*, 53: 28–42, www.paecon.net/PAEReview/issue53/Smith53.pdf.

Solomon, S., D. Qin, M. Manning, Z. Chen, M. Marquis, K. B. Averyt, M. Tignor and H. L. Miller (eds) (2007) *Technical Summary. Climate Change 2007: The Physical Science Basis. Contribution of Working Group I to the Fourth Assessment Report of the Intergovernmental Panel on Climate Change*, Cambridge: Cambridge University Press.

Solow, R. (1956) 'A contribution to the theory of economic growth', *Quarterly Journal of Economics*, 70: 65–94.

— (2008) 'Comment on the state of macroeconomics', *Journal of Economic Perspectives*, 23(2).

— (2009) 'Dumb and dumber in macroeconomics', Remarks at Joe Stiglitz 60th birthday conference, 25 October 2003, available at economistsview.typepad.com/economistsview/2009/08/solow-dumb-and-dumber-in-macroeconomics.html.

Sonnenschein, H. (1973) 'Do Walras' identity and continuity characterize the class of community excess demand functions?', *Journal of Economic Theory*, 6: 345–54.

Stern, D. I. (2004) 'The rise and fall of the environmental Kuznets curve', *World Development*, 32(8): 1419–39.

Stern, N. (2006) *The Stern Review: The Economics of Climate Change*, London: HM Treasury.

Stiglitz, J. (1974) 'Growth with exhaustible natural resources: efficient and optimal growth paths', *Review of Economic Studies*, 41: 123–37.

Suppan, S. (2009) 'Regulating commodities speculation: normative and fiscal means', UNCTAD Public Symposium Paper, May, available at www.tradeobservatory.org.

Swan, T. W. (1960) 'Golden ages

and production functions', in A. K. Sen (1971), *Growth Economics*, Harmondsworth: Penguin.

Taylor, J. and M. Woodford (1999) *Handbook of Macroeconomics*, Amsterdam: North Holland.

Taylor, L. (2004) *Reconstructing Macroeconomics. Structuralist Proposals and Critiques of the Mainstream*, Cambridge, MA: Harvard University Press.

TEEB (2008) *The Economics of Ecosystems and Biodiversity. An Interim Report*, European Communities and UNEP, Cambridge: Banson Production.

Teubal, M. (2008) 'Expansión de la soja transgénica en la Argentina', Global Development and the Environment Institute, Working Group on Development and the Environment in the Americas Discussion Paper no. 22.

Teubal, M. and J. Rodríguez (2002) *Agro y alimentos en la globalización: una perspectiva crítica*, Buenos Aires: Editorial La Colmena.

Teubal, M., D. Domínguez and P. Sabatino (2005) 'Transformaciones agrarias en la Argentina: agricultura industrial y sistema agroalimentario', in N. Giarracca and M. Teubal (eds), *El campo argentino en la encrucijada: estrategías y resistencias sociales, ecos en la ciudad*, Buenos Aires: Alianza Editorial.

Thampapillai, D. J. (1995) 'Environmental economics: towards filling an empty box', *Indian Economic Journal*, 42(4): 43–58.

Tily, G. (2007) *Keynes's General Theory, the Rate of Interest and Keynesian Economics*, Basingstoke and New York: Palgrave Macmillan.

Tirole, J. (1992) *Financial Crises, Liquidity, and the International Monetary System*, Princeton, NJ. Princeton University Press.

UN Financial Reform Commission (2009) *Report of the Commission of Experts of the President of the United Nations General Assembly on Reforms of the International Monetary and Financial System*, United Nations General Assembly, June.

UN Millennium Project (2005) *Investing in Development: A Practical Plan to Achieve the Millennium Development Goals*, New York: United Nations, available at www.unmillenniumproject.org.

UNCTAD (2003) *Trade and Development Report 2003*, United Nations Conference on Trade and Development, New York and Geneva: United Nations, available at www.unctad.org.

— (2008) *Trade and Development Report*, Geneva: United Nations Conference on Trade and Development.

— (2009) *The Global Economic Crisis: Systemic Failures and Multilateral Remedies*, Report by the UNCTAD Secretariat Task Force on Systemic Issues and Economic Cooperation, UNCTAD/GDS/2009/1, available at www.unctad.org.

UNDESA (2007) *World Urbanization Prospects. The 2007 Revision Population Database*, United Nations Department of Economic and Social Affairs, available at esa.un.org/unup.

UNDP (2005) *Human Development Report 2005*, United Nations Development Programme, Oxford: Oxford University Press.

— (2007) *Human Development Report 2007/2008. Fighting Climate Change: Human Solidarity in a Divided World*, New York:

United Nations Development Programme.

UNEP (2007) *Global Environmental Outlook 4*, United Nations Environment Programme, Valletta: Progress Press Ltd.

— (2009a) *An Introduction to the Green Economy Report*, Electronic version available at www.unep.org/greeneconomy.

— (2009b) *Rethinking the Economic Recovery. A Global Green New Deal*, Report prepared for the Economics and Trade Branch, Division of Technology, Industry and Economics, United Nations Environment Programme, April.

UNFCCC (2008) 'Investment and financial flows to address climate change: an update', Technical Paper FCCC/TP/2008/7.

UNIDO (2002) *Industrial Development Report 2002/2003 – Competing through Innovation and Learning*, United Nations Industrial Development Organization, available at www.unido.org.

Urquídi, V. L. (2005) *Otro siglo perdido. Las políticas de desarrollo en América Latina (1930–2005)*, Mexico: Fondo de Cultura Económica.

Wallerstein, I. (1974) *The Modern World System. Capitalist Agriculture and the Origins of the European World Economy in the Sixteenth Century*, New York: Academic Press.

Wertz-Kanounnikoff, S. and M. Kongphan-Apirak (2008) 'Reducing forest emissions in Southeast Asia. A review of drivers of land-use change and how payments for environmental services (PES) schemes can affect them', CIFOR, Working Paper 41, Centre for International Forestry Research.

Whalley, J. and Y. Yuan (2009) 'Global financial structure and climate change', NBER Working Paper no. w14888, available at www.nber.org/papers/w14888.

Williamson, J. (1990) 'What Washington means by policy reform', in J. Williamson (ed.), *Latin American Adjustment: How Much Has Happened?*, Washington, DC: Peterson Institute for International Economics.

World Bank (2006) *Investment Framework for Clean Energy and Development*, Washington, DC: World Bank.

— (2008) *Development Indicators*, Washington, DC: World Bank.

Zalasiewicz, J., M. Williams, W. Stefen and P. Crutzen (2010) 'The new world of the anthropocene', *Environmental Science and Technology*, 25 February, available at pubs.acs.org.

Zhou Xiaochuan (2009) *Reforming the International Monetary System*, People's Bank of China, 23 March, available at www.pbc.gov.cn.

Index

A1B scenario, 68
Abaza, H., 53
Accademia dei Lincei, 16
Agenda 21, 22
aggregate biophysical equilibrium, 50
aggregate demand, 39, 45, 60, 173, 175, 179; as economic driver, 36
aggregates, homogeneous, 56-7
aggregation, 56-7
agricultural frontier, expansion of, 105
agriculture, 70; as instrument for environmental stewardship, 97; contribution to sustainability, 95; dumping in, 96; industrial, 115, 116; labour-intensive, 97; large-scale, 116, 119, 169; productivity of, 184-5; small-scale, 95, 96, 97, 122, 156, 169, 185; sustainability of, 94 (technologies for, 95)
Amazon rainforest, deforestation of, 121-2, 160
animal spirits, 46
arbitraging, 20, 159
Archer Daniels Midland company, 119, 120
Argentina, 111-17, 138; default on debt, 113-14; soybean cultivation in, 114-17
Arrow, K., 52
Arunachal Pradesh, 29

balance of payments provisions, 188-9
balance of trade, 151, 152, 172
balanced budgets, 29
Bank for International Settlements (BIS), 167, 181
banks, expansion of liabilities of, 166
Bariloche model, 18-19

Barnett, William, 140
Basle accords, 181
Basle Committee on Banking Supervision, 181
Bhaduri, Amit, 28
biodiversity, 121, 127, 130, 131, 185, 189, 191; destruction of, 101, 102; in Latin America, 104; islands of, 126; loss of, 116, 120, 178; of Costa Rica, 122; of Mexico, 133
biomass resources, 130
biosphere reserves, 182
Blanchard, Olivier, 43
Bolivia, 139
Borges, Jorge Luis, 13
Brazil, 117-22, 138; Plano Real, 117-18; soybean production in, 119-22, 160
Bretton Woods system, 10, 19, 20, 100; demise of, 165, 189
British Petroleum, 58; Deepwater Horizon rig disaster, 51, 173, 191
Bunge company, 119, 120

capital: accumulation of, centres of, 164; aggregate measure of, 14; concept of, controversial, 15; conception and measurement of, 26; control over, 81, 152; flight of, 113, 155, 190; natural, 26, 57; purpose of, 31
capital flows, 166; control of, 157; destabilizing nature of, 80; freedom of, 110, 140; regulation of, 180-2; weight of, 163
capitalism: as historically determined system, 54; long-term evolution of, 164
carbon dependency, reduction of, 88, 93

227

carbon dioxide emissions of, 74, 76–7; reduction of, 131, 132; stabilization of, 82
carbon market, 76–7, 79, 81, 82
carbon pricing, through taxes, 78, 82
Cargill Bank, 119
Cargill company, 120
cattle ranching: as driver of deforestation, 121–2; displacement of, in Brazil, 121
cerrado (Brazil), destruction of, 120–1
Chávez, Hugo, 138
child labour, 29
Chile, reserve requirements in, 180
China: dependence on US policies, 170; export performance of, 173
circulation, types of, 145
class, issue of, 54–5
climate change, 6, 191; and macroeconomic policy, 65–85; costs of, 66–74 (adaptation costs of, 66–70); financial liberalization problem of, 80–1; importance of technology development for, 75; increasing risks of, 81; mitigation of, 75, 80 (costs of, 70–4); narrowness of debate about, 78; problem of fiscal policies, 79, 81–3; problem of poverty and vulnerability, 84; problem of trade liberalization, 83–4; vulnerability to, 84–5 (of poor countries, 67, 68)
Club of Rome, creation of, 16; *The Limits to Growth*, 9
Commission for Reform of the International Financial and Monetary System, 183
commodities, primary, as class of assets, 167
Commodity Futures Modernization Act (2000) (USA), 91, 168
Commodity Futures Trading Commission (CFTC) (USA), 91, 168
commodity markets, financialization of, 167–9

competition, 31, 54
conditionality, 189
Convention on Biological Diversity (CBD), 22
Copenhagen Accord, 73
Correa, Rafael, 138
corruption, 111, 142
Costa Rica, 122–7; fiscal policy in, 125; forest conservation in, 98; monetary policy in, 124–5; payment for environmental services in, 126–7
Costanza, Robert, 23
counter-cyclical monetary policy, 151–3, 181
credit, 188; access to, 96, 98, 147
credit balance, excessive, 179
crisis, economic: global, 9, 43, 86, 105, 140, 161, 171, 191, 192, 193 (origins of, 2, 91, 158); in Mexico, 108, 113, 135; localized, 92, 109, 164; of banking, 129; triple, 87
crops, restriction on trading in, 168
currency, international reserve: 179; creation of, 169–71; dollar as, 180; new, 178–9
currency speculation, 92, 110
Currency Transaction Development Levy, 189–90
currency transactions, taxation of, 189

Daly, Herman, 23, 24, 25, 35, 40, 47, 48–9, 64
dams, building of, in India, 29
debt, 92, 98, 118, 122, 124, 127, 128, 136, 175, 176; Argentinian default on, 113–14; cancellation of, 177, 183; crisis, 104, 108; management of, 155; Mexican default on, 133; multiplication of, 177; odious, 177; predicament, solving of, 182–4; proposal of International Court, 184; relief of, 72, 182–4; servicing of, 21, 113, 117, 122, 137, 176–7; threat of, 176–8
deficits, halving of, 193
deforestation, 22, 53, 73, 105, 107,

115, 116, 122, 127, 153, 178, 189; driven by cattle ranching, 121–2; in Amazon, 121–2, 160
deindustrialization, 111, 149
democracy, 142; founding of democratic states, 89
Depression, Great, 11, 36
deregulation, 78, 83, 84, 89, 143, 147, 172; of financial system, 20, 80, 91, 92, 108, 110, 111, 119, 134, 165; of banks, 169
derivatives, 165
development banks, dismantling of, 80
development theory, 141
discount rates, 150; choice of, 65
dollar: as reserve currency, 180; leading role of, 169
dollarization, 133; in Ecuador, 129–30
Dreyfus company, 120
dumping of agricultural goods, 185
Dutch disease syndrome, 128
Dynamic Stochastic General Equilibrium (DSGE), 44

ecological capacity, 49
ecological economics, 23–6, 55
ecological footprint, reduction of, 31
ecological scarcity, reduction of, 93–9
Economic Commission for Latin America and the Caribbean (ECLAC), 105
economics: neoclassical, 14, 15; steady-state, 30–2 *see also* environmental economics and neoclassical economics
eco-tourism, 122
Ecuador, 127–33
education, primary, 77
effective demand, 37, 45
El Niño event, 129
employment, 100–2
energy prices, rise of, 87
England, R. W., 25–6
entropy of economic processes, 23
environment: and macroeconomic policy, 47–53; as a normal good, 27
environmental degradation, 3, 9, 27–8, 32, 51, 53, 77, 86, 87, 88, 99, 105, 130, 138, 143, 152, 163, 192; in Mexico, 137–8; linkage to financial transactions, 159; monitoring of, 121
environmental economics, 35, 53–8
environmental irreversibility, 57
environmental issues, 4–5, 52
environmental Kuznets curve (EKC), 27–8
environmental policy, as macroeconomic policy, 143
environmental stewardship, 99–100, 154, 177, 178, 189–90, 193–4
Equator Principles, 182
equilibrium: economic, 33, 36, 37, 40, 44, 45, 51, 52, 60, 63; environmental, 47, 48, 50, 64; in money market, 60; Keynesian, 41; unemployment equilibrium, 40–1
ethical norms for environment, 102
euro, erosion of, 170
European Union Emissions Trading Scheme, 76–7
exchange rates, 29, 56–7, 69, 110, 113, 124, 128, 134, 142, 144, 145, 152, 162, 166; as anchor of price system, 109; fixed, abandoned, 19–20; flexible, 59, 165, 188; floating, 20, 166; volatility of, 72, 106
export crops, growing of, 53
export-led growth, 171–3
exports, promotion of, 172

Farley, J., 48–9, 64
financial crisis, global *see* crisis, global
financial operations, banning of, 160
Financial Requirements of the Public Sector (FRPS), 136
financial sector, expansion of, 163–9
financialization of commodity markets, 167–9
fiscal deficit, 107–8

fiscal policy, 44, 47, 63, 154, 155, 175, 177; and environmental considerations, 115; for agricultural development, 150; heterogeneity of, 146; hijacking of, 156; in Costa Rica, 125; regressive, 169
Fondo Nacional de Financiamiento Forestal (FONAFIFO) (Costa Rica), 126
foreign direct investment (FDI), 186
forests: conservation of, in Costa Rica, 98; in Indonesia, 22; recuperation of, 150; redwood, destruction of, 159 *see also* deforestation and reforestation
fossil fuel usage, reduction of, 132
free trade zones, 123, 124
Friedman, M., 42-3
full employment, 24, 40, 45, 143, 157, 171, 192
Fundación Bariloche, 18
futures markets, 168-9

G20 meeting (Toronto), 193
Galbraith, J. K., 55, 100, 146
General Agreement on Tariffs and Trade (GATT), 10, 185, 188
General Agreement on Trade in Services (GATS), 165, 181
general equilibrium theory (GET), 24
Generally Accepted Accounting Principles, 159
genetically modified crops, 115, 120
Georgescu Roegen, Nicholai, 24, 55; *The Entropy Law* ..., 23
Glass-Steagall Act (1933), 91
Global Environment Facility (GEF), 73
Global Green New Deal (GGND), 2, 6, 87-95
global warming, 65
glyphosate herbicide, 115-16
gold, 20; as exchange standard, 10
goods market, 59-60
Gramm-Leach-Bliley Financial Services Modernization Act (USA), 91

Gran-St Germain Act (USA) (1982), 91
Great Moderation, 5
Green Economy Initiative *see* UN Environment Programme (UNEP), Green Economy Initiative (GEI)
green national accounts, 161
greenhouse gas emissions, 3, 66, 138; increase of, 87; reduction of, 70, 71, 73, 74, 75, 79
Greenspan, Alan, 93
growth, 11-13, 54; after Second World War, 10-26; and steady-state economics, 30-2; as friend or foe, 26-32; equilibrium determinants of, 13; growth mania, 31; Latin American model of, 18; limits to, 13, 16-19, 27, 30, 50, 53; models of, 25-6 (critique of, 13-16); optimal, 16; organic, 18; predatory, in India, 28-30; sustained, 11; zero, 9, 31, 54

Hahn, F., 52
Hansen, Alvin, 38
Harrod-Domar model, 12
Heavily Indebted Poor Countries (HIPC) initiative, 177, 183
herbicides, use of, 115, 116
heterogeneity, in macroeconomic policy, 145-9
Heyes, A., 48, 64
Hicks, John, 38, 40
High Level Panel on Financing for Development, 73
'history matters', 57
Hurwitz, Charles, 159

import substitution industrialization strategy, 104, 105-8, 111, 117, 133, 172
income distribution, 46, 50, 54-5, 82, 154; asymmetries of, 145; inequality of, 26 (international, 175-6)
incomes policies, 154
India: banking reserves in, 29; predatory growth in, 28-30
Indonesia, forests in, 22

industrial agriculture model *see* agriculture, industrial
inequality, 36, 146, 175, 176; as enemy of sustainability, 153–4; in Costa Rica, 125–6
inflation, 12, 20–1, 92, 108, 110, 117, 124–5, 129, 134, 135, 140, 143, 144, 152, 154, 166, 172; control of, 84; targeting of, 44, 156–7
instability of economy, 54, 57
insurance markets, and climate change, 81
interest rates, 20, 37, 39, 40, 46, 48, 50, 60–1, 62, 72, 79, 80, 81, 108, 109, 110, 117–18, 119, 129, 134, 142, 145, 147, 157, 162, 172
Intergovernmental Panel on Climate Change (IPCC), 6, 72, 75, 82; AR4, 83, 176 (macroeconomic policies in, 74–7); reports of, 80, 86
International Assessment of Agricultural Science and Technology for Development (IAASTD), 95
International Bank for Reconstruction and Development (IBRD), 10
International Clearing Union (ICU), 179
international commodity agreements (ICAs), 187–8
International Debt Court, proposal for, 184
International Energy Agency (IEA), 74
International Labour Organization (ILO), Green Jobs initiative, 87, 100–2
International Monetary Fund (IMF), 10, 21, 22, 108, 117, 122, 165, 170, 172, 178, 179, 182, 183; changing role of, 189; special drawing rights, 170
International Seabed Authority, 191
International Union for Conservation of Nature (IUCN), 32
investment, 37; geographical targeting of, 98; in green economy, 87, 89; short-termism in, 151
'invisible hand', 24
IS-LM model, 39–40, 47, 48, 49, 50, 59–64
Ishpingo-Tambococha-Tiputini (ITT) project (Ecuador), 130–3

Kalecki, Michael, 141
Keynes, John Maynard, 141, 145, 172–3, 179, 193; *General Theory ...*, 35–8, 192
Keynesianism, 40, 41, 42, 45, 46 *see also* post-Keynesianism
King, Alexander, 16
Kirchner government (Argentina), 138
Kuznets, Simon, 26
Kuznets curve, 51, 58 *see also* environmental Kuznets curve
Kyoto Protocol, 78, 85

labour market, 55
Laffer curve, 154
land acquisition policy, in India, 29
land tenure rights, overriding of, 22
land-use, concentration of, 116
Latin America: as research focus, 6, 104–39
laundering of money, measures against, 181
Lawn, P., 48, 50, 64
Lehman Brothers Holdings Inc., 158
liberalization: financial, 3, 29, 100, 111, 117, 119, 122, 152, 165, 166, 189, 191; of trade, 70, 78, 80, 96, 128, 171
liquidity preference, 37, 60–1
logging, illegal, 138
Lucas, Robert, 42

macroeconomic policy, 33–64, 86; absent from debates, 1; and climate change, 65–85; and the environment, 47–53; constraints on, 93–102; control over, 161–2; guidelines for reform of, 153–61; in IPCC AR4, 74–7;

in Mexico, 133–7; objectives of, 78 (redefinition, 4, 140–62); reform of, 163–91; related to sustainability, 140–62; role of, 2–3; time horizons of, 58
macroeconomics: and the environment, 9–32; as science or politics, 140; crisis of, 144–53; environmental, 53–8; evolution in theory of, 34, 35–46; New Keynesian, 43, 44, 51–3; objective of, 5; reformed for sustainability, 178–9
Maggi, Blairo, 121
Mäler, K.-G., 51–2
Mankiw, Gregory, 43
manufacture, decline of, 109
maquiladora sector, 134
market: as allocator of resources, 51, 103, 108; assumptions regarding, 14; not same as capitalism, 54
market-friendly instruments for environmental development, 99
market power, and transnational corporations, 173–5
markets: distortion of, 174; role of, 24–5
Marquette v. First Omaha case (1978), 91
Marshall Plan, 10, 11
Marx, Karl, 31, 54; *Capital*, 145
Massachusetts Institute of Technology, 16
material flows analysis, 56
MAXXAM company, 159
Menem, Carlos, 111, 113
mergers and acquisitions, 174, 186
Mesarovic and Pestel (MP) model, 17–18, 19
Mexico, 133–8; biodiversity of, 133; crisis in, 108, 113, 135; environmental degradation in, 137–8; financial crisis in, 181; National Protected Areas (NPAs), 133; trade balance with USA, 135
microeconomics, realistic, 57–8
Millennium Development Goals (MDG), 1, 69, 77–8, 84, 88, 95, 155

Millennium Ecosystem Assessment (MEA), 32, 86, 93
mining industry in US, production costs in, 19
Minsky, Hyman, 46, 92
Mkandawire, Thandika, 78
Modigliani, Franco, 38, 40, 63
monetary policy, 42, 47–8, 52, 152, 166; heterogeneity of, 80, 147; in Costa Rica, 124–5; objectives of, 156–8
monetary system: international, changing of, 178–8; disarray of, 169–71
money: as problem, 16; creation of, by banks, 148; endogenous, 148; fiat money, 30–1; role of, 55–6
money market, 60–1
monoculture, 53; expansion of, 120, 121
Monsanto Corporation, 115
Morales, Evo, 138
Multilateral Debt Relief Initiative, 183
Multilateral Investment Agreement, 186
multinationals *see* transnational corporations
Munasinghe, M., 51–2

national environmental accounts, 151
natural resources, seen as capital asset, 161
neoclassical economics, 40–1, 55; new, 44
neoliberalism, 5, 58–9, 70, 72, 75, 78, 89, 92–3, 103, 127, 140, 142, 149, 152, 171, 178, 191; decline of, 138; in Argentina, 111; in Latin America, 108–11
New Deal, 2, 88–9; rhetoric of, 89–93
North American Free Trade Agreement (NAFTA), 134, 152, 187

Obama administration, 158
off-balance-sheet transactions, 158, 165

official development assistance (ODA), 18, 72–3; downward trend of, 189
oil: dependence on, 134; prices of, 76
oil crisis (1973), 20, 105
oil reserves, left underground, in Ecuador, 131
opacity, of financial sector, 165
open economy model, 7, 108–11, 117, 152, 157
optimal scale of economy, 23–4
Organization of the Petroleum Exporting Countries (OPEC), 20
over-the-counter operations, banning of, 159, 160

Pacific Lumber company, 159
Palley, T. I., 92
Paris Club, 183
payments for environmental services (PES), 97–8, 126–7, 156
pension systems, reform of, 137
Phillips, Alban, 41
Phillips curve, 25, 41–2
policy space for development strategies, 83
pollution, 17, 27, 52; taxes on, 48 *see also* water, pollution of
population growth, 4, 18
post-Keynesianism, 45–6, 53, 141, 148, 179, 199
poverty, 2, 4, 21, 22, 86, 113, 152, 176, 178; and ecological scarcity, 93–9; in Costa Rica, 125–6; in relation to climate change, 84–5; linked to biodiversity loss, 101; reduction of, 1, 77, 82, 88, 94, 97, 126, 142 (targeted programmes, 98–9, 153); rural, 126; urban, 98
price: adjustment of, 24; flexibility of, 37, 45; of crops, 185; of food and energy, 176; of primary resources, 187; setting of, 14; stability of, 143, 152, 156; stickiness of, 42, 51; volatility of, 168
pricing of environmental resources, 102
primary products, prices of, 187

primary surplus, generation of, 150
private investment, in climate change mitigation, 71
privatization, 21, 78, 80, 84, 89, 111, 113, 128, 134, 143; of money creation, 148; of risk, 20
Programme for Payment of Environmental Services, 126–7
proprietary operations of banks, 158
protectionism, 106
public sector, role of, 161

R&D spending, in developing countries, 84
rational expectations hypothesis, 42–3
raw materials, prices of, 21
reconstruction, post-war, 11
reforestation, 107, 132
regulation: financial, 90, 91, 100, 107, 113, 143, 147–8, 158–61, 180–2; of foreign direct investment, 161 *see also* deregulation and re-regulation
relocating populations, costs of, 70
remittances of migrant workers, in Mexico, 135
renewable energy, subsidies for, 82
renewable resources, harvesting rates of, 25
representative agent, concept of, 43, 52, 56
reprimarization of economies, 109, 115, 128, 129
re-regulation: financial, 80, 152, 156, 158, 160; of banking sector, 148, 157
resource scarcity, 13; definition of, 18
Riegle-Neal Act (USA) (1994), 91
Robinson, Joan, 13, 38
Roosevelt, Franklin D., 2, 88

Samuelson, P., 40
Sargent, Thomas, 42
Say's Law, 36
school of ecological economics (SEE), 23, 47, 55, 56
Second Law of Thermodynamics, 55

sector-level policies, 149–50
Securities and Exchange Commission (SEC), 91
short and long run, as heterogeneity, 150–1
shrimp aquaculture, effect on mangrove forests, 128
Silva, Inacio 'Lula' da, 138
Smith, Adam, 24
social justice, 30, 89, 194
soil: conservation of, 107; degradation of, 115–16, 122, 178
Sonnenschein, H., 24
South Africa, apartheid period debts of, 177
soybean: cultivation of (in Argentina, 114–17; in Brazil, 119–22, 160); transgenic, 115
special and different treatment (SDT), 185–6
special economic zones, 29
Sraffa, Piero, 14
stagflation, 25; in USA, 20
Stamp Out Poverty initiative, 189–90
state, role of, 38, 46, 142
sterilization of capital, 109, 166
Stern Review, 1, 76, 65–6, 67–8
Stiglitz, Joseph, 13, 15, 43
structural adjustment programmes (SAPs), 21, 22, 50, 53, 125, 172, 182
subsidies, role of, 155–6
sustainability, 86, 87, 90, 103, 169, 182, 185, 192; and counter-cyclical policies, 151–3; and macroeconomic policy, 140–62; as key priority for macroeconomic policy, 141–2; crisis of, 144–53; ecological, 48, 50, 53, 54, 57, 59; environmental, 131; macroeconomics reformed for, 163–91, 178–9; of primary production, 94; policies for, 150–1; related to inequality, 153–4; resources for, 154–6; social and environmental (SES), 154; weak, 25
sustainable development, 2, 4, 75, 77, 190; definition of, 3

taxation, 193; income tax, 146; of currency transactions, 189; of financial transactions, 147; of stock exchange transactions, 190; principles of, 146–7; progressive, 154; regressive, 146–7, 166
technical change, concept of, 15
technology, determination of, 15
Thampapillai, D. J., 47, 63–4
The Economics of Ecosystems and Biodiversity (TEEB), 87, 100–2
time, historical and logical, 45
Tobin tax, 190
total primary energy supply (TPES), 74
tradable resource permits, 48, 78
trade regime, international, reform of, 184–9
Trade-Related Aspects of Intellectual Property Rights (TRIPS), 83
Trade-Related Investment Measures (TRIMs), 174, 186–7
trade unions, attack on, 175
transnational corporations, 174; and market power, 173–5
transparency, 111, 142, 174; in trade, 188; lack of, in financial sector, 160; of markets, 187
Treaty for the Functioning of the European Union, 170–1
trickle-down effect, 153
Triffin dilemma, 19–20, 169
tuna fishing, 51

uncertainty, 46, 57
Understanding on Balance of Payments Provisions, 188
unemployment, 2, 12, 21, 36, 40, 45, 51, 52, 87, 101, 117, 134, 178; natural rate of, 42–3
unit of account, new, 179
United Nations (UN), 9
UN Conference on Trade and Development (UNCTAD), 174, 187
UN Conference on the Environment and Development (UNCED), 21–2
UN Environment Programme (UNEP), 73, 103, 104; Global

Environmental Outlook, 32, 99;
Green Economy Initiative (GEI),
  1–2, 6, 86–103
UN Framework Convention on
  Climate Change (UNFCCC),
  1, 21–2, 65, 67–9, 71, 72, 76;
  Conference of the Parties
  (COP15), 65; objective of, 66
UN General Assembly, 77
UN Millennium Project, 69
UN Programme on Reducing
  Emissions from Deforestation and
  Forest Degradation in Developing
  Countries (REDD), 126
United States of America (USA): trade
  balances of, 180 (with Mexico, 135)
urbanization, 105

Venezuela, 139
volatility, economic, 58–9, 166
vulnerability: economic and social,
  116–17; to climate change, 84–5

wages, 94, 100–2; compression of, 4,
  93, 100–1, 123, 125, 129, 136, 144,
  158, 173, 175
Washington Consensus, 21, 22, 78,
  104, 108, 151
water: access to, 190; management
  of, 107; pollution of, 138, 184;
  right to, 29; scarcity of, 87, 88
Wolfsberg Group, 181
World Bank, 21, 67, 70, 98, 108, 122,
  175; Development Indicators, 99
World Resources Institute, 32
World Social Forum, 5
World Trade Organization (WTO),
  22, 83, 149, 165, 171, 174–5,
  181, 185, 186; Doha Round, 97;
  Uruguay Round Agreement on
  Agriculture (URAA), 96, 185, 188

Yasuní National Park (Ecuador),
  biosphere reserve, 131–3, 190
Yasuní project *see* Ishpingo-
  Tambococha-Tiputini project

Zhou Xiaochuan, 169

HB 172.5 .N33 2011
Nadal Egea, Alejandro.
Rethinking macroeconomics
 for sustainability